James Leaton

History of Methodism in Illinois

From 1793 to 1832

James Leaton

History of Methodism in Illinois
From 1793 to 1832

ISBN/EAN: 9783337326067

Printed in Europe, USA, Canada, Australia, Japan

Cover: Foto ©ninafisch / pixelio.de

More available books at **www.hansebooks.com**

HISTORY

OF

METHODISM IN ILLINOIS,

From 1793 to 1832.

BY REV. JAMES LEATON, D. D.,

OF THE ILLINOIS CONFERENCE.

*

CINCINNATI:

PRINTED BY WALDEN AND STOWE,

FOR THE AUTHOR.

1883.

Members of the Illinois Annual Conference:

DEAR BRETHREN,—

Five years ago you honored me by the appointment of Conference Historian. I have during these years been engaged in collecting matter bearing upon the history of Methodism in Illinois. But the care of heavy pastoral charges, and the necessity of establishing the truth of the matter obtained, have prevented me from making that progress with the work that I had expected when commencing it. The first installment is now published with the hope that it will meet your expectations, and prove available to the future historian. Should you approve this volume, if the life of the compiler be spared, it will be followed by a second, and possibly a third, for which a large amount of matter has already been gathered, and some progress made in the arrangement of it.

Your fellow-laborer,

JAMES LEATON.

RUSHVILLE, ILLINOIS, *June* 18, 1883.

CONTENTS.

Part I.

WESTERN CONFERENCE,

1793—1811.

CHAPTER I.

Introductory—First Settlers—Joseph Ogle—Joseph Lillard—John Clarke—Hosea Rigg—William Scott, . . Page 27

CHAPTER II.

Conference at Mt. Gerizim, Kentucky, 1803 — Illinois Mission formed—Benjamin Young—Thomas Harrison—John Kirkpatrick—Lewis Garrett, ... 34

CHAPTER III.

Conference of 1804—Joseph Oglesby—Locates—Practices Medicine—Usefulness and Labors—Visits Missouri, . . . 41

CHAPTER IV.

Appointments for 1805—Charles R. Matheny—William McKendree—Entrance upon the ministry, ... 45

CHAPTER V.

Western Conference, 1806—Jesse Walker—Camp-meetings—Church at Shiloh, St. Clair County—First Sermon in Chicago—St. Louis—Cape Girardeau—Pioneering—Enoch Moore, ... 48

CHAPTER VI.

Western Conference, 1807 — John Clingan — James Ward, ... Page 66

CHAPTER VII.

Conference, 1808—Samuel Parker—Personal Appearance—Labors—Incident, ... 70

CHAPTER VIII.

Conference, 1809 — Abraham Amos — Marriage — Location, ... 74

CHAPTER IX.

Conference, 1810—Daniel Fraley—First Society at Union Grove—Thomas Kirkman—Learner Blackman—Josias Randle—Incident, ... 76

CHAPTER X.

Conference, 1811—Appointments—George A. Colbert—Baker Wrather—James Axley—Characteristics—His Preaching—Death—Description of Axley by Peter Cartwright, . 85

———•———

Part II.

TENNESEE CONFERENCE,

1812—1815.

———

CHAPTER I.

Division of Western Conference—First Session of Tennessee Conference, 1812—Arrangement of the Work—James Dixon—John Smith—David Gardner—Peter Cartwright, . 95

CHAPTER II.

Conference of 1813—Ivy Walke—James Porter—Josiah Patterson—IIis Appointments—Personal Appearance and Peculiarities—Labors and Exposure, ... Page 101

CHAPTER III.

Conference, 1814—Appointments—James Noland—John C. Harbison; 104

CHAPTER IV.

Conference, 1815—Work Arranged—First Churches—Presbyterianism Introduced—Itinerant Labors—Large Circuits—Hardships—A Winter Trip—At a Tavern—John Scripps—Superannuation—Characteristics—Church relations—Death, ... 107

Part III.

MISSOURI CONFERENCE,

1816—1823.

CHAPTER I.

First Session of Missouri Conference, 1816—Samuel H. Thompson—Appearance and Character—"Beggar-General"—Superannuation—Jesse Haile—Characteristics—Jacob Whitesides—William R. Jones—John Harris,—Camp-meeting, . 131

CHAPTER II.

Conference, 1817—Samuel Mitchell—Zadoc Casey—Anecdote—Joseph Pownal—William Sterrett—Conversion—Incidents of his life, ... 146

CHAPTER III.

Illinois Admitted as a State—Conference Session, 1818—Appointments—Thomas Hellums—Thomas Davis—Charles Slocumb—Style and Characteristics, ... Page 151

CHAPTER IV.

Conference, 1819—Mt. Carmel founded—William Beauchamp—Character—Mt. Carmel Circuit—Nathaniel Pinckard—Bennett Maxey—John D. Gilham—A Missionary Society Founded—David Sharp—James Lowry, ... 157

CHAPTER V.

Conference, 1820—Joseph Dixon—Sangamon County—John Cooper—Nathan Scarritt—New Settlements—The Corrie Family—Parham Randle—Jacob Lurton—Alexander McAllister—Hackaliah Vredenburg—Francis Moore—John Stewart—James Simms, ... 167

CHAPTER VI.

Conference, 1821—Joseph Basey—William Padon—Robert Delap—Thomas Rice—James Scott—Parham Randle—John Glanville, ... 178

CHAPTER VII.

Conference, 1822—Reuben Harrison—Samuel Hull—William H. Smith—Anthony W. Casad—Cornelius Ruddle—John Blaisdell—William Townsend—Isaac N. Piggott—His Career, ... 183

CHAPTER VIII.

Conference, 1823—New Settlements—Beginnings of Methodism in Paris and Elsewhere—William McReynolds—Frederick B. Leach—John Dew—Orceneth Fisher—Jesse Green—John Miller, ... 190

Part IV.

ILLINOIS CONFERENCE,

1824—1831.

***

CHAPTER I.

Illinois Conference Organized — Proceedings of Conference—Preachers in Illinois—Changes in the Work—Circuits—Peoria—James Armstrong—Samuel Bassett—William Moore—Thomas Randle—James E. Johnson—William Medford—Ebenezer T. Webster—Peter Cartwright—Mrs. Cartwright—Controversies—Characteristics, ... Page 205

CHAPTER II.

Illinois Conference, Second Session, 1825—Mission Work—Conference Action—Leven Green—Charles Holliday—James Hadley—John W. McReynolds—Philip Cole—Asa D. West—Joseph Foulks—William Chambers—William See, . . . 228

CHAPTER III.

Conference, 1826—Correspondence—Changes Made—Revivals—Dr. John Logan—Isaac Landis—Richard Gaines—Eli P. Farmer—Thomas H. Files—William Evans—Richard Hargrave—Effects of his Preaching—Traits of Character—Joseph Tarkington—Isaac S. House—Characteristics, ... 244

CHAPTER IV.

Conference, 1827—Business Transacted—Course of Study Recommended — Conference Seminary — Indian Mission — Heresy Investigation — Camp-meetings — New Societies formed — Abel L. Williams — Educational Interests — Miles Hart—John Fox—Style of Preaching—Aaron Wood—Samuel C. Cooper—John Hogan—William Echols—John Kerns—

Smith L. Robinson — Isaac Scarritt — Circumstances of his Conversion and Call to Preach—Labors—John T. Johnson—Samuel Bogart, ... Page 257

CHAPTER V.

Conference, 1828 — Proceedings — Lebanon Seminary — Methodist Protestant Controversy — Jacob Baker — George Locke—Style and Habits—Asahel L. Risley—Wm. Mavity—Miles Huffaker—Asahel E. Phelps—Debate with Mormons—William L. Deneen — James McKean — John H. Benson — Hardin A. Tarkington—John E. French, ... 278

CHAPTER VI.

Conference, 1829 — Business of Conference — Seminary Established — Articles of Agreement — Conference Action — Indian Mission Closed—Papers Presented—Changes Made—John A. Decker—Alfred W. Arrington—His Career—Anthony F. Thompson—Wilson Pitner—Call to the Ministry—Ludicrous Incident—Anecdote—Characteristics—Eccentricities—Style of Preaching — Lorenzo Edwards — James Bankson — David B. Carter—Benjamin C. Stephenson, ... 300

CHAPTER VII.

Illinois Conference, 1830—Proceedings—Sunday-school Union — McKendree College — Missions Constituted — Revivals — Benjamin Hypes — Dr. George H. Harrison — New Places Occupied—Samuel Sackett—William Peter—Thomas Kersey — Hiram M. Tremble — Edward R. Ames — As a Preacher—As a Presiding Officer—His Benevolence—William H. Askins—Philip T. Cordier—James P. Crawford—Spencer W. Hunter—Amos Prentice—John Sinclair—In Snow and Ice—His Characteristics—Simeon Walker—William D. R. Trotter — His Career — Summary of Character — John Van Cleve—Boyd Phelps—S. M. Otwell—Stephen R. Beggs, . 335

CHAPTER VIII.

Conference Session, 1831 — Proceedings — Sunday-school Union—Temperance—A Draft Withheld—Resolutions—New

Arrangements—New Places Occupied—Church built—James Plasters—James M. Massey—William McHenry—James Walker—Barton Randle—Superannuation—Levi Springer—John T. Mitchell—Outline of his Life—As a Pastor—In Church Work—William S. Crissey—His Faithfulness—William Royal—Removal to Oregon—Incidents on the Way—Concluding Note, ... Page 378

PRELIMINARY ESSAY.

THIS is not so much a history as a collection of material for the use of the future historian. Webster defines history as "a statement of the progress of a nation or an institution, with philosophical inquiries respecting effects and causes, in distinction from *annals*, which relate simply the facts and events of each year in strict chronological order, without any observations of the annalist; and from biography, which is the record of an individual's life."

The larger the field of the historian, and the longer the period embraced in his work, the more fully can he carry out this definition of the great lexicographer, and make the philosophical element the more prominent. But as his field becomes less, and his time shorter, the more will the annalistic and biographical elements predominate over the philosophical.

The stately, but unreadable, histories of Gibbon and Hume, the former covering a period of more than fourteen hundred years, and embracing the whole civilized world, and the latter covering the whole period of English history, afford examples of the one; whilst that most interesting and readable of modern historical·works, Macaulay's England, confined as it is to the events of a brief period, well illustrates the other. So in ecclesiastical history, whilst the magnificent volumes of Neander, with their grand thoughts, well rounded periods, and philosophic generalizations, will find a place on the shelves of the library and be occasionally referred to by the student, the sketchy volumes of that model denominational historian, Abel Stevens, will find their place on the study or centre table, to be read and re-read with continually increasing delight.

In the very limited field assigned the writer, the preparation of a history of Methodism in a single State, annals and biography must necessarily be made more prominent features than history in the proper or Websterian sense of the term. The field is too limited, the period too brief, and the actors too few, for philosophic generalizations. A simple narration of facts and events in their chronological order, biographical sketches of the principal actors, with such occasional reflections as may be suggested by the circumstances narrated, must constitute the leading features of a history of Methodism in Illinois.

And yet in the preparation of such a work, simple and easy as it may appear to one who had not paid special attention to the subject, serious difficulties are encountered. As Dr. Stevens says in the preface to his History of the Methodist Episcopal Church, "Such are the paucity, the carelessness even, and consequent inac.curacy of our early documents, that my task has had extreme embarrassments." "The private correspondence, the collection and combination of fugitive and fragmentary accounts, the collation of documents, the harmonization of conflicting statements, the grouping of events lacking often their most essential connecting links, the portraiture of characters, historically important but almost totally obscured in undeserved oblivion, present embarrassments which may well constrain the writer to throw down his pen in despair."

Let us look at the authorities to be consulted by the historian of Methodism in Illinois, the sources whence he is to draw facts and events, often obscure, sometimes apparently contradictory, and combine them in one continuous, harmonious, and truthful whole.

And first in order, though not in importance, are the Journals of the General Conference. From them we learn the changes that have been made in the boundaries of the annual conferences, and the names of the brethren who occupied seats in the General Conference as delegates. It is true that the boundaries of the annual conferences are set forth in the Book of Discipline; but the earlier editions of the Discipline are now very scarce, and virtually inaccessible to most of us. And it is also true that the journals of the annual conferences show who were elected as delegates to the General Conference, but they do not show who of those elected as delegates actually served. Until 1856 no list of reserve delegates was published in the General Conference journals, so that the lists of delegates as published in them often vary from the statements of elections in the annual conference journals.

For instance, in 1831 the Illinois Conference elected as its delegates to the General Conference of 1832 John Strange, Allen Wiley, George Locke, James Armstrong, S. H. Thompson, John Dew, William Shanks, P. Cartwright, and C. W. Ruter; and as its reserves Thos. S. Hitt, James Scott, Joseph Oglesby, and Jesse Haile. But in the Journal of the General Conference the names of Strange, Dew, and Cartwright do not appear, and Hitt is named as one of the delegates. So that, although nine delegates and four reserves were elected by the Illinois Conference, the actual representation in the General Conference was only six of the delegates and one of the reserves. A comparison of the General and Annual Conference journals thus becomes necessary in order to ascertain the facts.

The second authority, and in some respects the most important, to be consulted by the historian of Methodism in Illinois, is the General Minutes. From them we learn the conference history and standing of all the preachers from the time they are received on trial until they cease to be itinerant Methodist preachers by death, location, withdrawal, or expulsion. There should be no difficulty in tracing the career of every one who has ever belonged to an annual conference. And yet he who attempts it will soon discover that there are many errors and omissions in the General Minutes, causing him great present perplexity, and often requiring hours of labor for their correction. There are many errors in names. The bishops who furnish the manuscript for the Minutes are not always the most legible or careful of writers, and sometimes their mistakes are as ludicrous as they are embarrassing. Who could imagine, for instance, as he looks over the Minutes of the Illinois Conference for 1843 that Scollin meant Leollin, that Halton was intended for Hatton, that Melburn was Milburn, or that Joseph Seaton meant James Leaton? It is sometimes the case, too, that a preacher, though appointed to a certain charge by the bishop, is afterwards changed to another by the presiding elder, and the General Minutes fail to show the change. For example, the Minutes show that Bradley Hungerford was appointed to the Shelbyville Circuit in 1856 as junior preacher. Yet after traveling there a few months he was transferred to the newly formed Pana Circuit. In 1875 D. H. Stubblefield was appointed by the bishop to Irving and Butler, as the Minutes show, but before commencing his labors there for the year he was removed by the presiding elder to Tower Hill. And such changes occur almost every year. There are, too, many omissions of names in the General Minutes. By the carelessness of some one a name is dropped out of the list, and in some cases remains out two or three years before the omission is discovered and rectified. Previous to the year 1869 the writer discovered that there had been omissions of the names of preachers connected with the Illinois Conference amounting in all to one hundred and thirty-two years. Again there are perplexing omissions of the manner in which preachers cease to travel. There are seventeen preachers, once connected with the Illinois Conference, whose names simply disappear from the Minutes; and the only way in which we can ascertain what became of them—whether they were located, expelled, withdrew, or died—is by an examination of the journals of the conferences of which they were members at the time of their disappearance.

The General Minutes purport to give memoirs of those who have died in the work; though in many cases, when looking for the memoir of a deceased preacher, we are met with the disappointing notice, "Memoir not received." Some of these memoirs are of great value to the historian, as well as highly edifying to the Christian; but as a whole they are too monotonously laudatory. Some of them are defective in very important matters, giving no account of the nativity or conversion of the deceased; whilst others furnish a bare statement of the appointments of the departed without any estimate of his character or account of his labors. And but few present to us a faithful portrait of the real man, as Tyerman does in his Life of Wesley.

We learn, too, from the General Minutes the changes

that have taken place in the plan of the work, the new charges formed, and the changes in the districts. To understand these changes, however, a very thorough knowledge of the topography of the country is indis- pensable, as well as a very careful examination of the quarterly conference records. And even then the exact territory embraced in the charges must often remain in doubt. It is only since the circuits have been named after the chief towns in them that we can determine their location with certainty. So long as they were called by the name of some stream upon which they might touch, as Wabash, or Muddy River, or Okaw, we have to look to other authorities than their names, to de- termine their whereabouts. The General Minutes of 1824 tell us that Wm. Medford was assigned to the Mississippi Circuit. We have to go to other sources than the Minutes to learn that it embraced what are now the counties of Jersey, Greene, Scott, Morgan, and Macoupin. So the General Minutes of 1828 tell us that S. H. Thompson and W. L. Deneen were appointed to the Shoal Creek Circuit. And yet, but for a letter from the latter, we should not have known that that circuit embraced all the territory from Trenton, in St. Clair County, to the head-waters of the Okaw, in what is now Champaign County. And so with most of the earlier charges in the conference.

The General Minutes also furnish us with the statis- tics of the Church, from which we learn its growth in numbers, wealth, and benevolence. Previous to 1838 the only reports published were of numbers, the distinction between white and colored members being kept up until 1856. In 1839 the number of local preachers was first reported; and in 1848 the probationers were reported, as distinct from the members in full connection. And since then the reports have become more and more extensive with each successive quadrennium, until now almost every thing connected with the numbers, property, work, or benevolence of the Church is made a matter of record, and published in the General Minutes.

There is one peculiarity in the dates of the early Minutes that has been overlooked by some writers. Previous to the year 1836 the Minutes of the Western and most of the Southern conferences are dated one year in advance of the true time. For instance, the Minutes of the Illinois Conference for 1824 are found in the General Minutes for 1825. The reason of this is that the Minute year began with the first of the Fall conferences, and closed with the last of the Spring conferences, and the volume received the date of the latter. Since 1836, however, the dates have conformed to the actual time. Dr. Cartwright and others have, in some instances, overlooked this peculiarity, and have thus given the wrong dates in their works.

The journals of the annual conferences furnish our third source of information. In them we have accounts of the proceedings of the conferences at their annual sessions, the changes that occur in the relations of the preachers, accounts of elections to orders, and the various resolutions adopted and action taken on the matters before the body. But though the journals of the conferences in Illinois have been usually well kept, and the old journal from 1824 to 1835 especially is a mine of curious and valuable information, in two respects the journals fail to meet the wants of the writer of Methodist history. First, they cover only a part of the existence of Methodism in Illinois. For the first ten years of the life of Methodism in this region, from 1793 to 1803, it was not connected with any conference, and had no ministerial oversight, save that of local preachers. From 1803 to 1812 it was connected with the Western Conference, which then embraced all the territory west of the Alleghany Mountains; and whether the journals of its sessions are in existence the writer can not learn. From 1812 to 1816 it was a part of the Tennessee Conference, the journals of which probably still exist, as they are often referred to in the works of Drs. McFerrin and Redford. From 1816 to 1824 it constituted a part of the Missouri Conference. Whether its journals for that period are in being the writer has been unable to ascertain. And, secondly, there are in the old conference journals numerous references to documents placed on file, many of which can not now be found. Sometimes reports of committees of inquiry in cases affecting the character of some of the preachers are merely referred to in the conference journal, and the reference is so obscure that, without the report itself, we can not learn the nature of the complaint made, and, consequently, must remain ignorant of some of the facts needed to enable us to form a correct estimate of the individual. An instance of this is found in the journal for 1827, an account of which is given in the body of this work.

The journals of the quarterly conferences, which ought to be among the most satisfactory and reliable sources of information to the Methodist historian, are, unfortunately, amongst the most uncertain and unsatisfactory. Most of the early quarterly conference records are lost or destroyed. The oldest that the writer has yet discovered reaches back only to 1834. Some of those now existing have been shamefully mutilated. An old record fell into the hands of the writer some years ago that had been used by somebody as a scrap-book, clippings from newspapers having been pasted over all the quarterly conference proceedings. It took a day's labor of two persons, with damp cloths and paper knives, to remove this extraneous matter. Fortunately the paper upon which and the ink with which the record had been kept were so good that the writing was still legible. Some of the old quarterly conference journals are in the hands of private individuals, who refuse to surrender them to the authorities of the Church; and some even refuse to allow them to be copied. In some cases the penmanship in these journals is such as to be almost illegible ; and as to the orthography in some of them, that of Josh Billings is perfection in comparison. Most of these records are so brief as to be valueless. In many cases, as in the annual conference journals, references are made to documents placed on file that can not now be found; and in but few instances are the "Pastors' Reports," which ought to supply to the historian his most valuable material, placed on record at all; and even when they are, many of them are so meagre as to be of but little value. There are a few quarterly conference journals, however, in which the " Pastors' Reports" are not only copied in the record, but present, in addition to the statistics called for by the Discipline, a full history of the charge for the quarter. And such should they all be.

From published histories and biographies much valuable matter may be obtained. Stevens's " History of the Methodist Episcopal Church" supplies a few items of interest. But to Redford's " History of Methodism in Kentucky," McFerrin's " Methodism in Tennessee," and McAnally's " Methodism in Missouri," the historian of Methodism in Illinois will find himself compelled to refer most frequently for information in regard to the early preachers in Illinois, most of whom came to us from Tennessee and Kentucky. The " History of the West and North-west," by Rev. S. R. Beggs, contains much valuable information in regard to early Methodism in Illinois as well as in Indiana. The writings of Dr. J. M. Peck, the noted Baptist divine, contain much of interest in regard to the early settlement of the country and the pioneers of Methodism in it. The autobiography of Peter Cartwright is also valuable so far as it relates to his own personal history. From "Morris's Miscellany," "Recollections of John Johnson," J. C. Smith's "Early Methodism in Indiana," and W. C. Smith's "Indiana Miscellany," some information may be obtained in regard to some of the early Illinois preachers. The secular histories of the State, particularly Reynolds's and Ford's, must also be consulted. The eccentric U. S. Linder, in his "Recollections," gives sketches of a few prominent Methodists. And from the county histories, now becoming so common, some valuable matter may be obtained. It is true that many errors, particularly in dates, are to be found in these histories, yet many items of interest may be gathered from them, and in most cases their errors can readily be corrected by comparison with other and more reliable authorities. Some valuable local sketches have also been published, of which the historian of Methodism will gladly avail himself. Such are the pamphlets of Dr. Stevenson on Methodism in Rushville, the Semi-centennial of the Presbyterian Church at Hillsboro, the Annual Compendium of Methodism in Chicago, etc.

The periodicals of the Church constitute another valuable source of supply to the Methodist historian. The obituaries, the revival notices, the accounts of church building and dedications, the controversies on doctrine and Church polity, and the occasional historical sketches constitute an invaluable treasure to the compiler of Methodist history. And, fortunately, full files of the leading papers have been preserved, and are accessible. The old volumes of the *Methodist Magazine* contain many interesting revival notices and sketches from Theophilus Arminius and others. And in the files of the *Western, Northwestern,* and *Central Christian Advocates* may be found numerous articles of great interest and value.

Another source of information, of which the writer has largely availed himself, is correspondence with the ministers and laymen of the Church. Whilst a few of those to whom he has written have paid no attention to his requests, from some of them he has received sketches that are invaluable, and items of history that could have been gathered from no other sources. And he would here especially acknowledge his obligations to Dr. Aaron Wood and Rev. Joseph Tarkington, of the Indiana Conferences; Revs. Ephraim Joy and James B. Woolard, of the Southern Illinois Conference; Rev. S. R. Beggs, of the Rock River Conference; and the late J. H. Dickens and Rev. W. T. Bennett, of the Illinois Conference. From many others he has received very valuable information; but the communications of these brethren have been so copious, and in the case of Brothers Wood and Dickens so frequent, as to deserve especial mention.

The last means of obtaining information to be referred to is the interviewing of the living; and this the writer has done as far as his duty as a pastor would permit him. This is, in some respects, the most productive field for the cultivation of the Methodist item-gatherer. Many of those who have accumulated large stores of information in regard to Methodist history have never been accustomed to put their thoughts on paper—writing is an irksome task to them—so that the only way to draw from them their stores of knowledge and transmit them to future generations is by interviewing. And these pioneers, these men who can say of our Illinois Methodism, " Omnia quæ vidi, et magna pars quorum fui," are fast passing away, and as they disappear their knowledge disappears with them. The writer can only regret that more frequent opportunities of drawing from this source have not been afforded him. And he would suggest to the conferences in Illinois that no better investment could be made than the employment of a competent person for a few years to travel over the State, and gather from the pioneers who are so rapidly leaving us those items in regard to our early history which will otherwise be lost to the Church forever.

PART I.

IN THE WESTERN CONFERENCE.

1793 to 1811.

Part I.

IN THE WESTERN CONFERENCE.

1793 to 1811.

CHAPTER I.

INTRODUCTORY.

IN most of the Western States the first settlement of the country and the introduction of Methodism were contemporaneous. Scarcely had the pioneer erected his cabin, before the itinerant was there with his saddle-bags containing his Bible, hymn-book, and Discipline, to proclaim to him and his household the glad tidings of a free salvation, and to gather them into the fold of Christ. But this was not the case in Illinois. The State had been settled more than a century before the first Methodist sermon was preached in it, and it was more than thirty years after that before a Methodist conference was organized in its territory.

The first settlers of Illinois were French Canadians, who, under the leadership of LaSalle, established themselves first at Peoria, in 1680, where a fort was built, and in 1682 at Cahokia, Kaskaskia, and one or two other points on the Mississippi. They were strict Roman Catholics, bringing with them their priests and all the appliances for their peculiar worship. The towns continued for more than a century to be mere trading-posts and mission stations. It was only in their immediate neighborhood that the soil was cultivated; and no attempt was made to extend the settlements into the interior of the country. About thirty years after the settlements on the Mississippi had been made by the French, Fort Massacre was built by them on the Ohio River, and occupied, as was their custom, both as a fortress and a mission station for the conversion of the Indians.

In 1763 the territory east of the Mississippi that had been claimed by the French came into possession of the English; but it was not until after the War of the Revolution that Americans began to settle in the country; and they came so slowly that at the beginning of the present century there were not more than two or three thousand inhabitants; and the census of 1810 reported only between twelve and thirteen thousand in what is now the fourth State in the Union.

In 1809 the country, which, after its transfer to the United States, had formed a part, first of the North-west Territory, and then of the Indiana Territory, was organized as the Illinois Territory, with its seat of government at Kaskaskia; and nine years afterward it was admitted into the Union as a State.

The exact year in which Methodism was introduced is not positively known. But it seems probable that the first Methodist was Captain Joseph Ogle, who was converted through the instrumentality of James Smith, a Separate Baptist preacher of Kentucky, who visited and preached in Illinois in 1787, and who was undoubtedly the first Protestant preacher who visited the Territory.

CAPTAIN OGLE was a native of Virginia, born in 1741. He removed from the south branch of the Potomac to Wheeling in 1769, and in the Summer of 1785 came to Illinois, settling first in the American Bottom, in the present county of Monroe, and afterwards removed to St. Clair County, about eight miles north of Belleville, where he died, in February, 1821, aged eighty. Having seen service as a soldier during his residence in Virginia, Mr. Ogle was selected by his neighbors as their captain to lead them in their skirmishes with the Indians. He was a man scrupulously honest, punctual and strict in the performance of all his engagements, and demanding from others the same promptness that he observed himself. With uncommon firmness and energy he united great kindness and gentleness, and ruled the people by a happy blending of fear and love. He was always a moral man, but after his conversion he became a devout Christian.[1]

The first Methodist preacher who visited the country was JOSEPH LILLARD, then a local preacher of Kentucky, who, during his visit, gathered the few scattered Methodists into a class, and appointed Captain Ogle as their leader. This was in 1793; and this was the first Methodist class in a State in which the membership now numbers more than a hundred and twenty-five thousand.

[1] Dr. J. M. Peck.

Mr. Lillard had been for a short time a traveling preacher. He was born near Harrodsburg, Kentucky; was received on trial in the traveling connection in 1789 (there were no conferences then), and appointed to Limestone Circuit as junior preacher with Samuel Tucker. The next year he traveled the Salt River Circuit, with Wilson Lee as his colleague, and at the close of the year was discontinued. He settled in Kentucky near his birthplace, and labored as a local preacher until his death. During his visit to Illinois he became temporarily deranged, made his escape from his friends, and took the trail to Kaskaskia. On the way he came across the body of a man named Sipp, whom the Indians had killed and scalped. The sight so startled him that his mind was restored, and he returned to his friends at New Design.[2] He was a very ordinary preacher, but was regarded as a good man and truly pious, though somewhat eccentric. He was liberal in the support of the Church and her institutions. About nine miles from Harrodsburg is a large brick church, built principally by him, and named after him Joseph's Chapel. At his house the itinerant was always welcome; and though of such moderate ability as a preacher, yet by his deep piety and liberality he was very useful. He died in a good old age whilst on his return from a visit to Missouri.[3]

Four or five years after Mr. Lillard's visit, JOHN CLARKE, who had been a traveling preacher in South Carolina, visited the settlements in Illinois,

---

[2] Dr. J. M. Peck.   [3] Dr. Redford.

and then crossed into Missouri in 1798, being, it is believed, the first Protestant minister who preached the Gospel west of the Mississippi. Mr. Clarke was a Scotchman, born near Inverness, November 29, 1758. His mother was a strict Presbyterian, and taught him from childhood to fear God. He received a good education. When about twenty he went to sea. Whilst in the British navy he was taken prisoner and sent to Havana, where he remained in prison nineteen months. Being exchanged, he some time afterward left the sea, and wandered into South Carolina and Georgia during the Revolutionary War. In 1786 he was converted whilst reading Russell's "Discourse on the Sin against the Holy Ghost," and united with the Methodists. He subsequently visited England, and had several conversations with Mr. Wesley, and often heard him preach. In 1791, two years after his return, he was received on trial in the traveling connection. He traveled for five years in South Carolina, and in 1796 withdrew from "our order and connection," and removed to the West, to be free from the embarrassments of slavery. He was an ardent lover of liberty. Injustice in every form was abhorrent to his nature. He would not even receive money that had been earned by the labor of slaves. He was a very conscientious and a very devout man, habitually referring every thing to God, and making it the subject of prayer. He had a gift of prayer that was quite uncommon, seeming to hold converse with the Lord of heaven as with a familiar friend. He was accustomed to travel his circuits on foot, and, when asked for his reason, said, "The Savior walked on his preaching excursions in Judea." After his withdrawal from the Church, he traveled on foot to Kentucky, and then, meeting with James Gilham, who was about moving to Illinois, accompanied him and his family in their boat. Mr. Gilham landed at Kaskaskia, and settled on the American Bottom, twenty-five or thirty miles above the town. For some time Mr. Clarke labored as an independent Methodist preacher, but about 1811 he joined an organization of Baptists, calling themselves "Friends of Humanity," formed a circuit in Illinois and Missouri, and continued traveling it until his death in 1833, in his seventy-fifth year. His change of views and of Church relation did not alienate him from his former associates. He still retained the confidence and love of the Methodists, and when he died funeral services were held for him all over the country.[4]

In the same year that Mr. Clarke came, HOSEA RIGG, the first local preacher in Illinois, settled in the American Bottom, in St. Clair County. He was a native of Western Pennsylvania, born in 1760. He was a soldier in the War of the Revolution. When twenty-two years old he was converted, and soon afterwards was licensed to exhort. Finding the class, of which Captain Ogle had been appointed leader a few years before, disorganized, he gathered the old members together—Joseph Ogle and family, Peter Casterline and family, and Wm. Murray, an Irishman—and placed them again under Mr. Ogle's

---

[4] Dr. Peck.

charge. Some time afterwards he organized another class in what is now Madison County, in the Goshen settlement, between Edwardsville and the American Bottom. In appearance Mr. Rigg was tall and quite thin. He had a voice of wonderful power. He was a man of deep and active piety, abundant in labors, very tenacious for Methodist doctrine and usage, and very useful in the Church. "He was a good man, a faithful preacher, lived a Christian life, and died a Christian death " in 1841, at his residence, near Belleville, at the age of eighty-one.[5]

Another of the early settlers who aided in the establishment of Methodism was WILLIAM SCOTT, who was born in Botetourt County, Virginia, May 17, 1745. In 1797 he moved from Kentucky to Illinois, and settled at Turkey Hill. He died in 1828.

---

[5] Dr. Peck.

CHAPTER II.

1803.

Cumberland District—Lewis Garrett, P. E.
Illinois—Benjamin Young, Missionary.

IN 1803 Mr. Rigg visited Kentucky to consult the authorities of the Church, and secure from the Western Conference, which then embraced all the country west of the Alleghany Mountains, a regular preacher for Illinois. As a result of his visit, at the session of the conference held at Mt. Gerizim, Kentucky, the Illinois mission was formed, and Benjamin Young appointed its first missionary. It was connected with the Cumberland District, of which Lewis Garrett was presiding elder.

Benjamin Young, a brother of Dr. Jacob Young, was born on Back Creek, Berkeley County, Virginia, before the Revolutionary War. In childhood he moved with his parents to Pennsylvania, and thence in 1796 to Kentucky. He was converted through the instrumentality of his brother Jacob; united with the Church, and soon after commenced preaching. Under his labors a gracious revival commenced at the mouth of the Kentucky River, that spread up and down the Ohio till many were happily converted to God. He was received on trial in the Western Conference, held at Bethel Academy,

Kentucky, in 1800, and was appointed to Cumberland Circuit. The next year he was on the Scioto and Miami Circuit; the next year on Powell's Valley; and in 1803 was sent, as stated above, to the Illinois mission. At the conference of 1804, at the close of his year in Illinois, he was expelled from the Church.

Dr. Jacob Young, in his autobiography, thus speaks of his expulsion: "My brother Benjamin, who was then a missionary in Illinois, had fallen into some improprieties, though nothing worthy of expulsion, or even of great censure, was brought against him. IIis convictions being deep and piercing, he deeply repented of his follies. McKendree (who presided at the conference), not having a favorable opinion of him, took a very strong view of his imprudences, and thought he had been guilty of immoral conduct. He was accordingly expelled from the Church, as I thought then and think now, most cruelly. I was strengthened in my opinion the next year. Bishop Asbury, being then present, gave it as his opinion that Benjamin had been wrongfully expelled, and made an attempt to have the case reconsidered, but was overruled by the conference. Brother McKendree afterward went to Illinois, where my brother then lived in a backslidden state. He was reclaimed under McKendree's preaching, who took him into the Church, and, I believe, had his parchments restored." His end was very sad. He remained in Illinois and engaged in schoolteaching. But he gradually became deranged, and avowed infidel principles. He died in 1815 in the old fort in the Goshen settlement.[1] A letter from him, in possession of Rev. Dr. De Hass, gives us some insight into his labors and sufferings during his year on the Illinois mission. It is dated " Indiana Territory, Randolph County, June 1, 1804." In it he says, " I am and have been very sickly since I have been here, but I hope I 'm on the mend. As for the state of religion, it is bad. I have formed a circuit and five classes of fifty members. In some places there is a revival. About twenty have professed to be converted since I came, but the bulk of the people are given up to wickedness of every kind. Of all places, it is the worst for stealing, fighting, and lying. My soul, come not into their secret places! I met with great difficulties in coming to this country. I lost my horse in the wilderness, fifty miles from any settlement, and had to walk in and hire a horse to go and find mine. The Kickapoo Indians had stolen him and Mr. Reed's, who was with me, but we got them with cost and trouble. When I got to Kaskaskia I preached there, but they made me pay two dollars for the room, and twenty shillings for two days' board. I am out of money and had to sell my books. At last the people began to help me, but I thank God I can make out, though I have suffered with cold. Last Winter my clothes were thin and worn out, and I had no money to buy new. But I trust I am in the way to heaven, and I know my heart is engaged in the work of God. As I do not expect to come to conference, I may not see you again in

---

[1] Rev. R. Randle.

this life, but I hope to meet you in a better world."
Mr. Young, despite his discouragements, reported
to conference a membership of sixty-seven. His
mission embraced all the settlements from the mouth
of the Kaskaskia River to Wood River in Madison
County. One of his preaching places was the house
of Esquire Reynolds, father of Governor John Reynolds, a short distance east of Kaskaskia. Another
was in the New Design settlement, a few miles
south of where Waterloo now stands. The Turkey
Hill settlement, in St. Clair County, three miles
south-east of Belleville, which had been established
by William Scott in 1787, contained a number of
Methodists, but the preaching place for some years
was at Shiloh, six miles north of it. The Goshen
settlement, a few miles south of Edwardsville,
founded by the Gilhams and Whitesides in 1802,
was most likely another of his appointments; and it
is not improbable that during the Summer of 1804
he preached in the Wood River settlement, which
was formed that season by Cummins, Waddle, and
others, whose names were afterwards well known in
Methodism. Amongst the valuable accessions to
the mission this year was REV. THOMAS HARRISON,
a local preacher, who settled in St. Clair County,
and whose family afterwards became leading members of the Church in Belleville.

Mr. Harrison was a faithful Christian, careful in
his dealings, and of strict integrity. He had a fine
voice and was an excellent singer. He was a fair
preacher, quite animated and energetic. He settled
first a few miles south of where Belleville now

stands, and established a cotton gin. He afterwards moved to the town, and died there, highly respected.

Among the principal members of the Church this year was JOHN KIRKPATRICK, who had removed from Georgia in 1802, and settled in the neighborhood of Edwardsville. He was probably the first local preacher who received license in Illinois, but whether he received authority to preach this year or later is not known. He moved to Springfield at an early day, where he built a horse mill, the first and only mill there at that time. In 1829 he moved to Adams County, and afterwards to the neighborhood of Ottumwa, Iowa, where he died in 1845. He was an active and earnest preacher, and was occasionally employed as a supply under the presiding elder. In one of his charges two members of the Church, neighbors, got into a quarrel, and preferred charges against each other and demanded a trial. A committee was accordingly called, and the accused and accuser brought face to face. But before entering upon the trial, Mr. Kirkpatrick asked both of them to go alone with him to the woods. Then, after praying earnestly himself for them, he called on each of them in succession to pray, and the result was they were then and there reconciled, and returned to the house in love and friendship with each other. About the time he moved to Adams County he inherited three slaves in Georgia, a woman and two little boys. Bringing them to Illinois, he gave them all their freedom; but that the boys might be prepared to make a better living than as mere day laborers, he apprenticed them to a man in Quincy to learn a trade. The boys were afterwards kidnaped, probably run into a slave State, and it is supposed that the man to whom they were bound was not altogether clear of the crime. His wife testified that she had seen them in bed the night before, and that was the last she or Mr. Kirkpatrick ever saw of them.[2]

LEWIS GARRETT, the presiding elder, was a native of Pennsylvania, born in 1772, but removed with his parents, whilst he was a child, to Virginia, and afterwards to Kentucky. In 1790 he was converted, and four years afterwards entered the traveling connection. He died in Mississippi in 1837. Dr. McFerrin says of him, " He was an extraordinary man and accomplished much for the Church. His voice was full and mellow, his accent and articulation superior, his manner very deliberate, and his sermons at times overpowering." The connection of Mr. Garrett with the work in Illinois was probably only nominal. Peter Cartwright gives it as his opinion that he never visited the distant Illinois mission during the two years that he was its presiding elder. He made an effort to reach it once, and failed. In his " Recollections of the West," Mr. Garrett says : " In the Spring of the year 1804 the writer of these sketches and that laborious, useful pioneer, Jesse Walker, designed visiting Illinois, to which place a missionary had been sent the preceding Fall, but the season being wet, the Ohio had

---

[2] Rev. J. S. Kirkpatrick.

overflowed its banks and obstructed our passage so that we could not proceed." Failing in this they turned up the Ohio, swam the Tradewater, and, searching out the new settlements, formed a number of societies, and organized them into a circuit.

CHAPTER III.

1804.

CUMBERLAND DISTRICT—Lewis Garrett, P. E.
Illinois—Joseph Oglesby.

FROM the conference of 1804, which was also held at Mt. Gerizim, Kentucky, and which was under the presidency of William McKendree, Bishop Asbury being kept from it by sickness, JOSEPH OGLESBY was appointed to Illinois. He was a man of great energy and power, and was very successful in his efforts to extend vital godliness in the fields in which he labored. Of the time or place of his birth we are not informed. He· united with the Western Conference in 1803, and, after traveling in succession the Miami Circuit in Ohio, the Illinois in what was then the Indiana Territory, the Little Kanawha in Virginia, the Shelby in Kentucky, the Nashville in Tennessee, and the Maramee in Missouri, six charges in six different States and Territories, he located in 1809. In 1831 he was readmitted in the Illinois Conference, but the next year fell into the newly formed Indiana Conference, traveling the Lawrenceville Circuit two years, the Lexington, one, and the Bloomington District, two, when he again located in 1836. Ten years afterwards he was readmitted in the Indiana Conference, and placed on the superannuated list, in which he continued, with the exception of one year, till his death, which occurred in the city of Louisville, Kentucky, September 9, 1852. His memoir in the General Minutes says: "He was a pioneer Methodist minister. Nearly fifty years ago he began his arduous. toils. Ohio, Indiana, Kentucky, Illinois, and Missouri he traversed, preaching everywhere 'the Gospel of the kingdom,' 'the Word of this salvation.' No history of Methodism in the Mississippi Valley can be complete which does not speak largely of the labors of Joseph Oglesby. Much of it he was. In the days of his strength he stood among the strong men of Methodism. 'He was an able minister of the New Testament.' As old age pressed upon him his zeal did not abate. He continued in his superannuated days to preach Jesus almost every Sabbath, and often through the week. The last Sabbath before his short and fatal illness he preached with great power from 'O that thou hadst hearkened to my commandments; then had thy peace been as a river, and thy righteousness as the waves of the sea.' He died with his armor on, and fell in sight of glory. Many shall rise up and call him blessed." Rev. S. R. Beggs, in his Early History of the West and North-west, describes him as being fully six feet in height, very straight, with dark hair, a penetrating eye beneath a prominent forehead, and a thin, tapering face. His manner was dignified, his gestures correct, and his whole appearance impressive. At a camp-meeting on the Vincennes Circuit, during Mr. Beggs's administration, he preached from the text, "The Master is come and calleth for thee." "No words of mine," says Mr. Beggs, "could do the sermon justice. It seemed as if every sentence uttered was a direct inspiration from on high. It was the eloquence of the Holy Ghost, and it came with power." Sometimes, however, in his sermons he indulged quite freely in speculation.[1] In a discourse preached before the Indiana Conference in 1836 he attempted to define the tendency of the natural capacities of man for good or evil. His brethren, less tolerant of heterodoxy than Methodist preachers are now, decided that he was unsound in the faith, that his doctrine was Pelagianism, and after a vote of censure by the conference, he retired from the itinerant to the local ranks, in which he remained, as stated above, until 1846. But his errors were of the head, not of the heart. He was a good man, and God greatly blessed his labors.

Whilst sustaining a local relation he engaged in the practice of medicine, in which he became quite successful. His zeal and industry were great, both as it regarded his professional engagements in the healing art and his duties as a preacher, being at all times ready to do good to the bodies and the souls of men.[2]

During his year on Illinois Circuit he crossed the Mississippi and spent some time in a tour of inspection among the new settlements in Missouri. He was probably the first Methodist itinerant to visit and preach in the country west of the Missis-

---

[1] Dr. Aaron Wood.   [2] Rev. J. B. Finley.

sippi; for, although John Clarke had preceded him there, it was first whilst he was a local preacher and afterwards a Baptist.

Under Mr. Oglesby's labors the membership in the Illinois Circuit was increased to one hundred and twenty.

CHAPTER IV.

1805.

CUMBERLAND DISTRICT—William McKendree, P. E.
Illinois—Charles R. Matheny.

IN 1805 CHARLES R. MATHENY was appointed to
the Illinois Circuit, which still remained in the
Cumberland District, of which William McKendree
was presiding elder. Mr. Matheny had just been
received into the Western Conference at its session
at Griffiths, Scott County, Kentucky. Of his labors
during the year we have no account. At the close
of the year he was discontinued at his own request,
and settled in the Ogle settlement, in St. Clair
County. In 1808 we find him present at a camp-
meeting held by Jesse Walker. He moved to Sangamon County in the Spring of 1821, and when
the county was organized in the same year he was
elected county clerk, and filled the office until his
death in 1839. His house was for some time the
preaching-place in Springfield, as well as a home
for the preachers. He married a Miss Ogle, and
was the father of a large and highly respectable
family, most of whom became leading members of
the Church. During the latter part of his life he
was an invalid, and seldom preached. He was but

a moderate preacher, but was highly esteemed as an honorable, upright Christian gentleman.

There was a slight decrease in the membership this year, only one hundred and ten being reported to conference. But the year was signalized by the erection of the first Methodist church in Illinois, the Bethel Church, in Goshen settlement, in what was afterwards Madison County, and where a good society has been maintained until the present time. The church was built on the land of Thomas Good, two and a half miles south of Edwardsville. A conference was held in it in 1817, and the old church, with the neighboring camp-ground, was the spiritual birthplace of multitudes of souls.

Of the presiding elder, WILLIAM McKENDREE, a volume might be written; but we can give here only a brief notice of him. He was a native of Virginia, born in 1757. His early education was quite limited; but in after life, by diligent study, he accumulated a large store of knowledge. During the War of the Revolution he enlisted as a private soldier, but was soon made adjutant, and afterwards, for his superior business qualifications, was placed in the commissary department. He was a man of fine appearance, with good features, and possessed of great physical strength. When thirty years old, under the preaching of John Easter, he was converted; and the next year, 1788, he was received in the traveling connection. After eight years of circuit work he was appointed presiding elder in Virginia, serving on four different districts in four successive years, until, in 1800, he was removed to the West, in which he continued to labor as presiding elder until his election to the episcopacy in 1808. Bishop Simpson says of him: "He was a man of great energy and genius, and was deeply pious, and modest almost to timidity. His mind was clear and logical, his knowledge varied and extensive, his imagination lively but well regulated, and his eloquence was unusually powerful. He was careful in the administration of discipline, and introduced system into all the operations of the Church. His influence was patent everywhere; but especially was he regarded as the father of Western Methodism, to which he had given years of earnest labor, and in the success of which he felt a deep and abiding interest. He died March 5, 1835, at the residence of his brother, near Nashville, Tennessee. One of his last expressions was, 'All is well.'"

CHAPTER V.

1806.

CUMBERLAND DISTRICT—Wm. McKendree, P. E.
Illinois—Jesse Walker.

FROM the session of the Western Conference
held at Ebenezer, Nollichuckie, Tennessee,
JESSE WALKER was sent to the Illinois Circuit.
To him Methodism in Illinois and Missouri is
doubtless indebted more than to any other single
individual; for throughout a large portion of both
States he was literally its pioneer. He was born in
Buckingham County, Virginia, June 9, 1766. His
parents were not religious, but moral, teaching him
to pray and attend divine worship, and abstain from
gross sin. He had but few educational advantages
in his youth, twenty days covering the whole of his
school life. When a child of nine years he was
awakened under the sermon of a Baptist preacher,
and soon afterwards was converted. But for want
of religious instruction and religious society he
backslid, and became very wicked. When about
twenty he was powerfully reclaimed, and in July,
1786, he united with the Methodists. He was immediately appointed class-leader, and in that work
became so useful that the preachers urged him to
accompany them on the circuit. For some years he

held back; but at length, whilst living in the neighborhood of Nashville, Tennessee, the command, "Go ye into all the world and preach the Gospel," came to him with such power that he yielded, and in 1802 united with the Western Conference at its session at Strothers, Sumner County, Tennessee. At the time he entered the itinerancy he was poor, with but little education and with a wife and several children. Of moderate preaching ability, he yet possessed a soul burning with desire for the salvation of the people; and though unable to discuss the doctrines of the Bible, he could yet tell the story of the cross with such pathos and power as to melt the hardest heart. Governor Reynolds says of him: "Mr. Walker was a man of great energy and courage, very warm and excitable, and producing great excitement in his congregations. He was a short, well-set man, walked erect, and was possessed of great firmness, energy, and perseverance. His complexion was sallow, his eyes blue, small, and piercing. He was not a profound scholar, but a student of the Scriptures and human nature." His first four appointments, which were in Tennessee and Kentucky, were Red River, Livingston, Livingston and Hartford, and Hartford alone.

In the Spring of 1806, in company with his presiding elder, William McKendree, he paid his first visit to Illinois. He was greatly delighted with the country, and felt that here God had a great work for him to do. He returned to his circuit, preached in it until conference, and then received his appointment to the Illinois Circuit. Reaching home about noon, by ten o'clock the next day he was ready to start with his family, a wife and two daughters, for his new field of labor, a distance of at least two hundred miles. Their only mode of travel was on horseback. After a tiresome journey through the wilderness, in which they were greatly detained by storms and high waters, and suffered much from cold and hunger, they at length reached the Turkey Hill settlement, in St. Clair County, a few miles from which he located his family, and where he continued to reside for a number of years. His parsonage was an old log cabin belonging to a Brother Scott. It had a plank floor and a stick chimney, with the hearth so low that the edge of the floor made seats for all the family around the fire. As soon as possible he entered on his labors, and it was not long before souls were converted. On New-Year's eve he held a watch-night meeting, probably the first ever held in Illinois, and in connection with the meeting he held also the first love-feast.

In April, 1807, he held the first camp-meeting ever held in the State, about three miles south of the present town of Edwardsville. It was the day of small things in numbers. There were only three preachers present,—Jesse Walker, Charles R. Matheny (who had traveled the circuit the year before), and Hosea Rigg. But the meeting was a powerful one, and many present were affected with that strange movement, the jerks. During the Summer another camp-meeting was held on the circuit at a place called Three Springs, afterwards known as

Shiloh. This was in connection with a quarterly-meeting. The meeting commenced on Friday morning, and continued until the following Monday. The presiding elder, William McKendree, was present from the beginning of the meeting. He was accompanied by Abbot Goddard and James Gwin. Some local preachers were also present. Mr. McKendree and his traveling companions had just visited John Travis, the only preacher then laboring in Missouri. After attending a camp-meeting on his work, where their labors were greatly blessed, they came to Mr. Walker's meeting, during which several interesting incidents occurred. The following is related by Mr. Beggs:

"On Friday morning the meeting commenced by the sounding of a horn, as a signal to rise; then, at the second sounding, they were to assemble at the altar for prayer before breakfast. Having assembled, a hymn was first lined, and then sung."

Whilst singing, they suddenly heard the sound of voices at a distance, as if also engaged in singing. It was the elder, who rode up in company with several preachers; and the singing was continued amidst hearty hand-shakings, tears, and smiles, and shoutings of hosannas, which lasted fifteen or twenty minutes before the preachers could get off their horses. Mr. Gwin has given so graphic an account of the meeting that we can not do better than quote his language:

"From the camp-meeting we returned, crossed the river to Judge L.'s, who refreshed us and sent forward our baggage in a cart to Brother Garrett's, where our next meeting was to be held, which was called the Three Springs. We arrived on Friday morning on the camp-ground, which was situated in a beautiful grove surrounded by a prairie. A considerable congregation had collected, for the news of the other meeting had gone abroad and produced much excitement. Some were in favor of the work and others were opposed to it. A certain major had raised a company of lewd fellows of the baser sort, to drive us from the ground. On Saturday, while I was preaching, the major and his company rode into the congregation and halted, which produced considerable confusion and alarm. I stopped preaching for a moment and quite calmly invited them to be off with themselves, and they retired to the spring for a fresh drink of brandy. The major said he had heard of these Methodists before; that they always broke up the peace of the people wherever they went; that they preached against horse-racing, card-playing, and every other kind of amusement. However, they used no violence against us, but determined to camp on the ground and prevent us doing harm. But at three o'clock, when Brother Goddard and I were singing a hymn, an awful sense of Divine Power fell on the congregation, when a man, with a terrified look, ran to me and said, 'Are you the man that keeps the roll?' I asked, 'What roll?' 'That roll,' he replied, 'that people put their names to when they are going to heaven.' I supposed he meant the class-paper, and sent him to Brother Walker. Turning to Brother Walker, he said, 'Put my name down, if you please,' and then fell to the ground. Others started to run off, and fell ; some escaped. We were busy in getting the fallen to one place, which we effected about sunset, when the man who wished his name on the roll arose and ran off like a wild beast. Looking around upon the scene, and listening to the sobs, groans, and cries of the penitents, reminded me of a battle-field after a heavy battle. All night the struggle went on. Victory was on the Lord's side; many were converted, and by sunrise next morning there was the shout of a King in the camp.

"It was Sabbath morning, and I thought it the most beautiful morning I had ever seen. A little after sunrise, the man that had run off came back, wet with the dews of the night, and with strong symptoms of derangement. At eleven o'clock Brother McKendree administered the holy sacrament; and while he was dwelling upon its origin, nature, and design, some of the major's company were affected, and we had a melting time. ·After sacrament, Brother McKendree preached to a large congregation, all the principal men of the country, and all in reach, who could get there, being present. His text was, 'Come, let us reason together ;' and, perhaps, no man ever managed the subject better or with more effect. His reasoning on the atonement, the great plan of salvation, and the love of God was so clear and strong, and was delivered with such pathos, that the congregation involuntarily arose to their feet and pressed toward him from all parts. While he was preaching, he very ingeniously adverted to the conduct of the major, and remarked:

'We are Americans, and some of us have fought for our liberty, and have come here to teach men the way to heaven.' This seemed to strike the major, and he afterwards became friendly, and has remained so ever since.

"This was a great day. The work became general, the place was awful, and many souls were born of God. Among the rest was our wild man. His history was a peculiar one. He lived in the American Bottom, had a fine estate, and was a professed deist. He told us that, a few nights before we passed his house, he dreamed that the day of judgment was at hand, and that three men had come from the East to warn the people to prepare for it; that so soon as he saw us he became alarmed, believing we were those men; and, having ascertained where we were from, who we were, and where going, he came to the camp-meeting. He became a reformed and good man.

"We went to Goshen camp-meeting. Here we had comfortable camps and an arbor large enough to shelter seven hundred persons, in the form of an L. The stand was in an unsheltered spot between the two squares. We had, also, a small, log meeting-house, in which our first quarterly-meeting was held. Preaching began on Friday, and was kept up regularly. The people having heard of the revival at the other camp-meetings, flocked out in great numbers, many to see the strange work. Some brought brandy and cards for their amusement during the meeting. On Friday and Saturday, the Word preached seemed to do little good. An awful cloud seemed to rest upon us. In passing the preachers' tent I saw Brother McKendree alone, bathed in tears. I stepped in, and he said to me, ' Brother, we have been preaching for ourselves, and not for the Lord. Go, brother, and preach Christ crucified to the people!' My heart was deeply affected. We fell upon our knees, and implored the help of God. This was about sunset. I preached at candle-lighting. My text was, ' Behold the man!' It commenced raining shortly after I began to preach, and as the audience was under shelter, I did not stop, although exposed to the rain. My heart was fired and my tongue loosened in an unusual manner. For a few moments nothing but sobs and sighs were heard among the people; at length the whole congregation seemed suddenly smitten with the power of God. Many fell as in battle, and were presently raised to tell of pardoning mercy and encourage others to seek the Lord.

"We continued all night in the work. On the next day, Sunday, at nine o'clock in the morning, the Lord's-supper was administered.

"It was a memorable day, and eternity only will reveal the result. One conversion deserves particular notice. An Indian, of the Chickamauga tribe, on a hunting-trip, fell in with us at our camp-meeting. I will give his own account of his conversion. He said: ' When I saw so many people, I thought I would stop and get some whisky; and while you were talking in the rain, I was standing by a sapling, and there came on me a mighty weight, too heavy for me to stand under. I caught the sapling, but my hands would not hold it, and I fell to the ground. While there, blackness came over me: I tried to get away, but could not until about daylight. I thought surely I had been drunk; but then I remembered I had nothing to drink. Although I concluded not to go back, yet, when they began to sing, something drew me back, and before I knew it I was among them again, and then the same weight came on me, and the darkness. I fell to the ground, and thought I was about to die. I tried to get up, but was too weak. At last a white man came and talked over me, and while he was talking I got lighter and lighter, and every thing looked whiter than the sun could make it look. The heavy load and the blackness all left me. I felt glad in my heart, and jumped up and felt light.' Arrangements were made to send this Indian to school. He soon learned to read and write, and at the last account of him he was trying to walk in the light. On Monday, the last day of the meeting, one hundred joined the Church."

The conference year closed successfully, Mr. Walker reporting a membership of two hundred and eighteen white, and two colored, this being the first report of colored members in Illinois. The Church has learned since that day that in Christ white and black are no more important distinctions than male and female.

This year was signalized also by the erection of the second church, in Illinois at Shiloh, in St. Clair County. It continued to be a place of worship until 1819, when a new church was built of brick.

In 1875 a third church was built on the same spot, costing $6,700.

Mr. Walker's subsequent appointments were as follows: 1807, Missouri; 1808, Illinois; 1809–10, Cape Girardeau, and 1811, Illinois Circuit for the third time. In 1812, falling into the Tennessee Conference, he was made presiding elder of the Illinois District, which he traveled the full term of four years. In 1816, at the formation of the Missouri Conference, he was placed on Missouri District, on which he remained three years. In 1819–20, he simply appears in the General Minutes as missionary. In 1821 his appointment was St. Louis. In 1822 he was conference missionary in Missouri, and in 1823 he was appointed as "missionary to the Missouri Conference, whose attention is particularly directed to the Indians in the bounds of said conference." In 1824 he was sent as "missionary to the settlements between the Illinois and the Mississippi Rivers, and to the Indians in the vicinity of Fort Clark." In the Spring of 1825 he accompanied Mr. John Hamlin, whose wife was a member of the Church, in his flat-boat, well-manned, to Chicago. It was a tedious trip, but he failed not to have family prayers on the boat every morning. It is probable that while in Chicago he preached the first sermon ever preached there.[1] For the three following years he was missionary to the Pottawattomie Indians. In 1828, his appointment was Peoria; 1829, Fox River; 1830, Chicago Mission, and 1831, Des Plaines. In 1832 he was appointed pre-

---

[1] Rev. S. R. Beggs.

siding elder of Chicago District, but traveled it only one year. The next year he was again sent to Chicago mission, and with this appointment his labors as an effective preacher closed. At the conference of 1834 he was placed on the superannuated list, on which he remained a little over a year until his death, October 15, 1835.

Mr. Walker "was five feet, seven inches high, of slender, but vigorous frame, sallow complexion, light hair, prominent cheeks, small blue eyes, a generous and cheerful expression, and dressed always in drab-colored clothes of the plainest Quaker fashion, with a light-colored beaver hat, nearly as large as a lady's parasol. He had extraordinary aptness to win the confidence and sympathy of back-woodsmen; his friendships were most hearty, his courage equal to any test, his piety thorough, his talents as a preacher moderate."[2]

His dress, however, was not always such as Dr. Stevens describes above. "I think," says Cartwright, "it was in the Fall of 1819 our beloved old Brother Walker, who had traveled all his life, or nearly so, came over to our Tennessee Conference, which sat at Nashville, to see us; but, O, how weather-beaten and war-worn was he; almost, if not altogether, without decent apparel to appear among us. We soon made a collection, and had him a decent suit of clothes to put on; and never shall I forget the blushing modesty and thankfulness with which he accepted that suit."

One of the most remarkable traits in the char-

____

[2] Dr. A. Stevens.

acter of Mr. Walker was his strong will. It was this, combined with his steadfast faith in God and his earnest love for souls, that inspired him with an energy that carried him through difficulties which to most men would have appeared insuperable, and that induced him to persevere when most others would have acknowledged defeat. His securing a foothold for Methodism in St. Louis in the face of the greatest obstacles is only an instance of what he accomplished by his unconquerable determination. Says Mr. Witten, "Soon after the first session of the conference that was held in McKendree Chapel in 1819 Jesse Walker determined to plant Methodism in the city of St. Louis. He engaged two young ministers to assist him in his apostolic work. When they reached the city the Legislature was in session, and every public house was crowded with guests. Literally, there was no room for them in the inn. When it became known who they were, and what their visit to St. Louis meant, they became the laughing-stock of all who saw them. They endured insult and scorn in various ways, and at last concluded to leave the place in disgust; and accordingly mounted their horses and rode into the public square, where they held a consultation. The young ministers resolved to leave, and thus the apostolic Walker was forsaken. The outlook was so poor that he concluded to go to Mississippi, and actually started and went eighteen miles; but his mortification over his repulse in St. Louis was so great that he resolved to go back and try it again, saying, 'Was I ever defeated in this blessed work? Never. Did any one ever trust God and get confounded? No. Then by the grace of God I 'll go back and take St. Louis.' With some difficulty he found entertainment, but at a high price. He obtained permission to preach in a place occupied occasionally by the Baptists. At his first meeting but few came out, the second was better attended and some interest was manifested, and then the place was closed against him. He then rented a room at ten dollars a month, and held divine service twice every Sabbath, teaching five days in the week gratuitously. He now began to take steps for the building of a church. Help from unexpected sources was found, and a plain house was erected and a membership was reported at the end of the year of seventy-five." But Mr. Walker did not confine his labors to St. Louis. No "pent-up Utica" could confine his powers. The pioneer spirit by which he was influenced led him to enter into every open door; and, during the years in which St. Louis was his head-quarters, he kept up an appointment at Alton, thirty miles distant, preaching regularly once a month in the house of Nathaniel Pinckard.

Mr. Scripps gives a striking account of his labors in Missouri at an earlier period. In 1809–10 he was on the Cape Girardeau Circuit. Indeed, he formed the circuit. Joseph Oglesby had traveled the Maramee Circuit the year before, and had reconnoitered the country and preached in the neighborhood. And Samuel Parker, the presiding elder, had preached the first sermon in the town. But "these preliminary efforts of Oglesby and Parker were only the harbingers of Walker's advent as preacher in charge of the Cape Girardeau Circuit. Bringing his deeply interesting family of wife, Sukey, and two daughters, Polly and Jenny, with him, he sat down with an unconquerable determination to make Methodists out of the most inauspicious, ungainly materials for such an operation imaginable, the most knotted, gnarled, twisted, and jagged specimens of the genus *homo* conceivable; the denizens of a region over which the sanctity of the Sabbath had not as yet cast a shred of its sacred mantle, and whose boast was that Sunday was impeded by the Mississippi, and could not get across the river to them. Yet among such he sat down to thunder the denunciations of the law, or herald the invitations of the Gospel, casting his unreserved confidence for a support amongst them on Him in whose cause he labored, who provideth for the young ravens when they cry, and without whom not a sparrow falleth to the ground. Indeed, he could depend upon no other, for his charge were pioneers, recent settlers, struggling for a hand to mouth livelihood themselves, and, if willing, too poor, and himself as poor in this world's goods as they were, if not more so." When he was on the Cape Girardeau Circuit he held the first camp-meeting ever held in Missouri. To give notice of it, he, with John Scripps, then a young man, crossed the swamp to New Madrid, and there he offered the first prayer ever offered at a family altar in the place. There were five camps on the ground. The audience never exceeded two or three hundred. There was good order and strict attention. Some had the jerks. There were many convictions, a few conversions, and some accessions to the Church. At the sacrament there were eleven communicants. The wine was squeezed from wild grapes. The communion-table was a puncheon, split from a log and smoothed a little on the upper side, laid on cross-ties on four forks stuck in the ground, and covered with a sheet, for there were no table-cloths then.[3]

Mr. Walker could not confine himself within the limits of any particular field. Like Mr. Wesley's, his motto was, "The world is my parish," and wherever he heard of those who needed the Gospel, he felt that it was his mission to bear it to them. To hundreds of the early settlers he was the first to carry the glad tidings of great joy, and that, too, not unfrequently before they had erected their cabins. When John Sinclair was appointed to Chicago District, he soon found that, "wherever he had been, Walker had been there before him, and, being ambitious to preach Christ first to some of the new-comers, and hearing of a family that had just settled at Root River, now Racine, he made all haste to bear them the offer of eternal life. Coming by the way of Chicago, he met Brother Walker. Inquiring after his health, he was told that he (Walker) was well, but very tired, as he had just been to look after a family recently settled at Root River. In despair, Sinclair gave up the hope of the honor he had counted upon as unattainable."[4]   Indeed, as Dr. A. L. P. Green says, Jesse Walker "was to the

----

[3] Rev. John Scripps.   [4] Rev. S. R. Beggs.

Church what Daniel Boone was to the early settlers—always first, always ahead of every body else, preceding all others long enough to be the pilot of the new-comer. His natural vigor was almost super-human. He did not seem to require food and rest as other men; no day's journey was long enough to tire him, no fare too poor for him to live upon. To him, in traveling, roads and paths were useless things; he blazed out his own course. No way was too bad for him to travel; if his horse could not carry him, he led him; and where his horse could not follow, he would leave him, and take it on foot; and if night and a cabin did not come together, he would pass the night alone in the wilderness, which with him was no uncommon occurrence. Looking up the pioneer settler was his chief delight, and he found his way through hill and brake as by instinct. He was never lost; and, as Bishop McKendree once said of him, in addressing an annual conference, he never complained, and as the Church moved west and north it seemed to bear Walker before it. Every time you would hear from him he was still further on; and when the settlements of the white man seemed to take shape and form, he was next heard of among the Indian tribes of the North-west."

When placed on the superannuated list he settled at the Desplaines River, twelve miles west of Chicago, and kept a kind of tavern or stopping-place for travelers. His step-daughter, Mrs. J. R. Gorin, of Decatur, says that he never omitted family prayer, morning and night, no matter who might be stopping with him. He was greatly beloved by the Indians, and often gave them the last morsel of food in the house. He was never known to be angry or to speak an impatient word. The cause of his death was a severe cold he took on his way to camp-meeting. In crossing Root River he found the water deeper than he had calculated on. He got very wet, took cold, and died in about six weeks, at the very time when his conference was in session. "His last moments were such as might be expected from his long and laborious life in the way of doing good. To a ministerial brother, who visited him shortly before his demise, he said that God had been with him from the time of his conversion, and was still with him. His last moments were tranquil, and he died in full and confident hope of a blessed immortality." [5]

It is believed that at one of Mr. Walker's camp-meetings this year ENOCH MOORE was converted. He was the first American male child born in Illinois, having first seen the light in a block-house at Bellefontaine, Monroe County, Illinois, February 17, 1783. "At a very youthful age he developed a thirst for knowledge and a great avidity for study. He eagerly sought after all kinds of books and literature of a practical and useful character, and, possessing a mathematical mind of high order, he, when comparatively young, became one of the most competent surveyors and civil engineers of his days, and much of the government surveying of that time was done under his immediate direction and

____

[5] General Minutes.

supervision."[6] In 1804 he married Miss Mary Whiteside, a native of Kentucky, but who had moved to Illinois in 1793. His wife was converted at the same camp-meeting as he. He was not at first satisfied with his conversion; but shortly afterwards, at a meeting held at a Brother Maee's, he was so powerfully blessed as to remain unconscious for a time. Soon after his conversion he was licensed to preach, but remained in the local ranks until his death. He labored quite extensively as a local preacher, and was regarded as one of the best in the region in which he lived. Though his house was not a preaching-place, yet it was a place to which the preachers delighted to resort, where they always met a cordial welcome, and where they had access to one of the best libraries in the country at that time. Though not an active politician, he was well versed in political science, and much of his life was in office. He was a member of the convention that formed the first constitution of Illinois. He was also a member of the Legislature. For ten or twelve years he was clerk of the circuit court of his county, and for about twenty years probate judge. He was a man of fine personal appearance, about six feet high and very straight. He had ten children, most of whom became active members of the Church. He died in 1848.

---

[6] Captain J. M. Moore.

CHAPTER VI.

1807.

Cumberland District—James Ward, P. E.
Illinois—John Clingan.

FROM the session of the Western Conference of 1807, which was held at Chillicothe, Ohio, John Clingan was appointed to the Illinois Circuit, with James Ward as presiding elder.

Of John Clingan we have no other account than that furnished by his appointments in the General Minutes. He was admitted on trial in the Baltimore Conference, but received his appointment to Guyandotte in the Western Conference. In 1807 he was appointed to Illinois, the next year to Licking, the next to Letart Falls, and in 1810 to Mad River. The next year his name does not appear in the Minutes. In 1812 he stands connected with the Ohio Conference as appointed to Zanesville, and at the close of the year is reported as located. Of his labors in Illinois we have no account. It is probable that he did not attend conference at the close of the year, as the report of members is the same as that made by Mr. Walker the year before.

James Ward, the presiding elder, was for more than half a century one of the most devoted and successful ministers in the Church. Born in Maryland in 1771, and converted in his seventeenth year, in 1792 he united with the Baltimore Conference. For eleven years he traveled circuits in that conference, chiefly in the valley and mountainous regions of Virginia; then for four years he was presiding elder of the Greenbrier District. In the Spring of 1807 he was transferred to the Western Conference, and appointed to Lexington. In the Minutes of the Western Conference for that year he appears to have been assigned to the Cumberland District as presiding elder, though it is probable that he did not actually receive the appointment until the election of Mr. McKendree to the episcopacy in the Spring of 1808. For the next two years he was on the Kentucky District; in 1811 he was assigned to Shelby Circuit; then for two years to the Salt River District; and in 1813 he located, and continued in that relation for fifteen years. In 1828 he was readmitted in the Kentucky Conference, continuing most of the time in the active work until 1840, when he was superannuated. On the division of the Church in 1845 he refused to go south with his conference, and in 1848, " without controversy and by a unanimous vote," [1] he was received as a member of the Baltimore Conference, and placed on the list of superannuated members, in which he remained until his death in 1855, in the eighty-fourth year of his age and the sixty-third of his ministry.

Mr. Ward was a man of great firmness and decision, carrying out his convictions of right and duty regardless of consequences to himself. Brought up

---

[1] General Minutes.

in the Church of England, of which his parents were members, in opposition to the wishes of his friends, he united with the Methodist Episcopal Church, through the instrumentality of whose ministers he had been led to the Savior. Then, impressed with the conviction that it was his duty to devote himself to the work of the ministry, despite his domestic claims (for his father had died and left to him the care of the family), and the strenuous opposition of his mother, constrained by the love of Christ, he resolved to devote himself to the itinerant work. So, fifty-three years afterwards, when he was called on to choose between the pro-slaveryism of the newly formed Methodist Episcopal Church South and the mother Church, with her anti-slavery principles, he unhesitatingly chose the latter, though his choice deprived him for a time of a conference home with its privileges and separated him from those with whom for more than forty years he had been in close and loving fellowship. He was remarkable, too, for his untiring zeal and energy. During the year in which he presided over the work in Illinois, "he astonished the people by his zeal." During the years of his location, his son tells us that, "working diligently with his hands, he embraced every opportunity of preaching. He spent no idle Sabbaths when it was possible for him to get to Church. He kept up regular appointments, and was always willing to assist the traveling preachers at camp-meetings and two days' meetings, and spent much of his time from home." Those who knew him in his early ministry in Virginia, "speak with rapture of his untiring zeal and his almost exhaustless energy."[2] His labors were greatly blessed. "In the various charges he filled, the most extraordinary revivals of religion were, under God, the result of his labors." While on the Cumberland District, "great displays of divine power were everywhere within its bounds seen and felt under his ministrations." Cartwright speaks of him as "a warm-hearted, lively, and zealous preacher; his labors were greatly blessed, and some very powerful revivals of religion followed." "As a preacher," says Redford, "Mr. Ward was not what the world would call eloquent. There was nothing rhetorical in his gestures, nor did he appeal to the sympathetic passions of the people. His preaching was Scriptural; and this, with the fact that he was a man of prayer, always trusting in God, was the basis of his great success."

[2] General Minutes.

CHAPTER VII.

1808.

INDIANA DISTRICT—Samuel Parker, P. E.
Illinois—Jesse Walker.

AT the session of the Western Conference held October 1, 1808, at Liberty Hill, Tennessee, the Indiana District was formed, Samuel Parker being appointed presiding elder of it. The district embraced two circuits in Indiana, three in Missouri, and the Illinois Circuit, to which Jesse Walker, after spending a year in Missouri, was appointed.

It was probably during this year that the following, related in "Morris's Miscellany," occurred. At a camp-meeting held by Mr. Walker during the Summer, "early in the meeting, a young lady of influence, sister-in-law of the territorial judge sent out by the general government, was so powerfully converted that her shouts of joy and triumph broke the silence of all the surrounding forest and sent a thrilling sensation through every heart in the encampment. This example of the power of saving grace cheered on the soldiers of the cross, and inspired all with confidence of success. After operating till, as Jesse Walker expressed it, 'the last stick of timber was used up,' that is, till the last sinner left on the ground was converted, the meeting adjourned." Bishop Morris relates this as occurring two years before, during Mr. Walker's first term on the circuit. But this is evidently an error, for it was not until 1809 that the Illinois Territory was organized, and a territorial judge appointed.

At the close of the year Mr. Walker reported a membership of three hundred and fifty.

SAMUEL PARKER was a native of New Jersey, born in 1772. With his parents he removed to what was afterwards Uniontown, Pennsylvania, and there, in his fifteenth year, under the preaching of James Lurton, he was converted. Removing to the neighborhood of Newcastle, Kentucky, for four years he labored faithfully, zealously, and successfully as a local preacher. In 1804 he was received in the Western Conference, and appointed to the Hinkstone Circuit. For three years he traveled in Kentucky, and one year on the Miami Circuit, in Ohio; and so efficient had he proved himself in these charges, and so remarkably had his labors been blessed, that, immediately after his ordination as elder, he was appointed to preside over the newly formed Indiana District, one of the most laborious and one of the most responsible appointments in the Church. This appointment alone, as it shows the estimate formed of him by that wonderful discerner of character, Bishop Asbury, proves him to have been one of the foremost men of his day. In the infancy of the Church, advancement from the diaconate to the presiding eldership was, in some cases, a necessity; but for many years before Mr. Parker's day the bishops had selected as their representatives only those who had served some time as elders; and since that time, this, with the rarest exceptions, has been their invariable practice. During the four years he was on the Indiana District he was in labors more abundant; and so greatly were his labors and those of his preachers blessed of the Lord, that, before the expiration of his term, the district was divided into two, and the membership increased more than fourfold. He labored afterwards in Ohio and Kentucky until the conference of 1819, when he was appointed, though in declining health, to superintend the work in Mississippi. He went to his field of labor, but it was only to die. Before three months had expired, consumption did its work, and he passed from earth to his heavenly home.

His personal appearance was prepossessing. His form was slender but well made, his forehead expansive, his eye black and piercing, and his voice musical and capable of the softest and sweetest intonations, and he was excelled by few in the power of song. In the pulpit he was often almost irresistible, and wherever he went, wondering and weeping audiences crowded to hear him. Such was his fame as a pulpit orator that many came from great distances to listen to him. In his Christian character he exemplified in an unusual degree the description of charity given by Paul in his first letter to the Corinthians. It was love that led him to perform such labors and endure such privations that before he reached his fiftieth year he had literally worn himself out in the work of the Lord.

The following account of a service in which he engaged shows the wonderful readiness and earnest zeal of the preachers of that day. At the conference in Cincinnati, at the close of his term on the Indiana District, no church being large enough to hold the crowds who attended on the Sabbath, services were held in the Lower Market, where the preachers occupied a butcher's block as their pulpit. Learner Blackman preached first from "Thy Kingdom come." He was followed immediately by Samuel Parker with another sermon from "Thy will be done." Then James Ward gave an exhortation. And after that John Collins gave a thrilling address, based upon their peculiar surroundings, offering salvation without money and without price, and invited all who desired religion to designate themselves, when a large number came forward and kneeled as seekers of salvation, and before the services closed many were happily converted.

7

CHAPTER VIII.

1809.

INDIANA DISTRICT—Samuel Parker, P. E.
Illinois—Abraham Amos.

THE session of the Western Conference of 1809 was held in Cincinnati, Ohio, Bishops Asbury and McKendree being both present. ABRAHAM AMOS was appointed to the Illinois Circuit. He had been received in the Western Conference in 1803 and appointed to Natchez in Mississippi. The next year his appointment was the Miami and Mad River Circuit in Ohio. In 1805 he was sent to Guyandotte in Virginia, the next year to Licking in Kentucky, and in 1807 to the Livingston Circuit in the same State; in 1808 he was appointed to the Missouri Circuit, and this year to the Illinois. At the close of the year he located. He was a native of Bourbon County, Kentucky. After his location he settled in that part of St. Clair which was afterwards set off as Monroe County, where he resided until his death. He married Mary Garrettson, the first American child in the State of Illinois who grew up to womanhood. After the death of Mr. Amos she married Nathaniel Pinckard, grandfather of John C. Pinckard and N. P. Heath, formerly of the Illinois Conference, and P. M. Pinckard, of the

Methodist Episcopal Church South. Mr. Amos was a large, muscular man, very vehement in voice and gesture, sometimes, whilst preaching, bringing his fist down with such violence as to split the book-board. He was a man of sterling worth, sustaining a good Christian and ministerial character as long as he lived.[1] He reported three hundred and forty-one members on the circuit, a slight decrease from the number reported the year before.

There were also reported from Massac fifteen members, though no such appointment appears on the Minutes of this year or the year after. It is probable that this was the beginning of the Cash Creek Circuit, to which an appointment was made the next year.

---

[1] Rev. J. A. Scarritt.

CHAPTER IX.

1810.

INDIANA DISTRICT—Samuel Parker, P. E.
Illinois—Daniel Fraley.
CUMBERLAND DISTRICT—Learner Blackman, P. E.
Cash Creek—Thomas Kirkman.

IN 1810 the Western Conference held its session in the brick chapel, about four miles north-east of Shelbyville, Kentucky. Two preachers were sent this year to the settlements in Illinois; namely, Daniel Fraley, to the Illinois Circuit; and Thomas Kirkman, to the Cash Creek Circuit, an appointment connected with the Cumberland District, of which Learner Blackman was the presiding elder.

This was DANIEL FRALEY'S first year in the conference. In 1811 he was appointed to Coldwater. The next year he was in the Ohio Conference, and was assigned to Madison; the next year to Salt River; in 1814 to Pickaway, and in 1815 to Whitewater. At the close of this year he located, and settled at Centerville, Indiana, where he remained until his death. In the Spring before his location the first execution in the eastern portion of Indiana took place. The criminal was a man who had been convicted of the murder of his son-in-law. At the gallows Mr. Fraley stood in the

wagon in which the murderer had been conveyed
from the jail, and preached a very impressive sermon to him as he sat on his coffin, and to the hundreds of people who had gathered from miles
around to witness the execution.[1]   Mr. Fraley's
year on the Illinois Circuit was a successful one,
the membership having increased to four hundred
and eleven.   A camp-meeting which he held at
Shiloh, in the month of August, was, according to
Governor Reynolds, who attended it, a time of
power and success.

He also organized the first society in Union
Grove, St. Clair County.   The place of meeting
was the house of William Padfield, where the first
session of the Illinois Conference was held, in 1824.
The present Summerfield society is a continuation
of the old Union Grove class.

That part of Illinois south and east of the Kaskaskia River was not settled by the whites quite as
early or as rapidly as that embraced in the Illinois
Circuit.   Yet settlements were gradually formed,
and the population increased so that more laborers
were needed to supply the spiritual wants of the
people.   In 1802 a few whites settled in Shawneetown, and by 1805 it had become a place of considerable trade.   The salt-works, twelve miles north-
west of Shawneetown, had been purchased of the
Indians by Governor Harrison, and were attracting
a considerable number of settlers.   Several families
had settled on Bigbay Creek about 1805.   Before
1809 the town of Newhaven, on the Little Wabash,

---

[1] Indiana Miscellany.

had been begun; and the population had increased so rapidly in the country along the Ohio and the streams running into it, that in 1812 three new counties were established—Gallatin, Johnson, and Pope—embracing the settlements about Shawneetown and the salt-works and those on Bigbay and Cash Creeks.

It is probable that the circuit of which Thomas Kirkman was the first preacher embraced all the settlements south of the mouth of the Kaskaskia River, around the Mississippi and Ohio to Fort Massac, if not to Shawneetown. He reported as the result of his labors a membership of seventy-one.

According to the General Minutes, THOMAS KIRKMAN was received on trial in the Western Conference in 1807, but his appointment for that year is not given. In 1808 he was sent to the Livingston Circuit, in Kentucky. The next year his name is again omitted, both in the appointments and the list of members. But in 1810 he appears again as appointed to Cash Creek. In 1811 he was sent to Roaring River, and at the next session of conference, owing to failing health, he located. He settled in the neighborhood of Hopkinsville, Kentucky. "His life was a reflection of the Gospel of Christ. He was a preacher of only moderate talents; but so consistent was he in his deportment that he attracted many to Christ by his walk and conversation. He lived to a good old age, an ornament to the Church and a blessing to the community in which he lived and died."[2]

___

[2] Dr. Redford.

Of the presiding elder, LEARNER BLACKMAN, a volume might be written. He was a native of New Jersey, born in Gloucester County, in 1781. In his sixteenth year, through the instrumentality of his brother-in-law, Rev. John Collins, under the first sermon he ever preached, he was soundly converted, and before he was nineteen was licensed to preach, and received in the Philadelphia Conference. His first appointment was to the Kent Circuit, in Maryland. His experience at the beginning of his pastorate on this charge was peculiar. The people had heard that the bishop had sent a *black man* as their preacher, and, of course, felt that such an appointment was an insult to them. His arrival amongst them, however, removed this difficulty; but his youthful appearance was an offense they could not overlook. At his first service a leading member of the society requested a local preacher to conduct the exercises, thus ignoring entirely their regularly appointed pastor. The local preacher consented, but at the close of his sermon called on the youthful pastor to exhort. Mr. Blackman's exhortation convinced them that, though a boy in appearance, in intellect and experience he was of full age. He became so popular in the circuit that, at the close of the year, a petition was sent to conference for his return. The request was not granted; for in the Spring of 1801 he was sent to the Dover Circuit in Delaware, and in the Fall of the same year was transferred to the Western Conference, and appointed to Russell Circuit, in Virginia. The next year he traveled the New River Circuit, in the same

State, and the next year the Lexington Circuit, in Kentucky.

At the close of his year there, as stated in his memoir in the General Minutes, "in compliance with the request of the bishops, he went on a mission to Natchez. Here a new scene of things presented itself to his view. He is now to face uncivilized nations and a wilderness of four or five hundred miles. After a journey of ten or eleven days, and lying out as many nights, making his saddle-bags his pillow, his blanket and cloak his bed, the heavens his covering, the God of Israel his defense, he arrived safe in the Territory." For the two following years he was presiding elder of the Mississippi District. In 1808 and 1809 he presided in Holston District, in Tennessee. The two following years he was on the Cumberland District, embracing parts of Kentucky, Indiana, and Illinois. Then, for three years, he was presiding elder of the Nashville District, and in 1815 was reappointed to the Cumberland District. This was his last appointment, as he was drowned in the Ohio River whilst returning from a visit to his brother-in-law in Ohio. In personal appearance, says the biographer of John Johnson, "he was tall, rather slender, but erect, gentlemanly, dignified, grave, and impressive, neat and tasteful in dress, and affable and polished in manners." Jacob Young says of him : "He was a man of extraordinary natural and moral courage. Of him it might be said in truth, as Rev. William Cravens from Virginia once said, 'The fear of man never once entered into his experience.' He feared no danger, dreaded not the tongue of slander, while he was doing and suffering for the glory of God. Whatever he thought *ought* to be done, he thought *could* be done, and, like General Jackson, he accomplished every thing he undertook. I have had a close acquaintance with many Methodist preachers, and truth binds me to say, although I have known greater, I know not that I ever knew a better man." The following from his own diary shows the completeness of his consecration to God: " This morning I entered into the following resolution, to ask myself twelve times in the course of each day this important question: Am I prepared to die? First, when I awake in the morn; second, third, and fourth, in private retirement before private devotion; .fifth, at family worship; sixth, when I arise on my horse to travel to appointments; seventh, when I alight off my horse at meeting; eighth, when I begin to preach; ninth, in class-meeting; tenth, in private devotion; eleventh, at family prayer; twelfth, when I lie down to rest at night." This resolution, as his diary shows, was faithfully observed. " Whenever he preached," says Dr. Redford, " he expected immediate results, and he was seldom disappointed. ' I am alarmed,' said he, ' when sinners are not converted.' No danger daunted him, no privations were shunned. In the pulpit, in the altar, in the social and family circle, everywhere he was the faithful ambassador of Christ, and counted not his life dear if he could be instrumental in the accomplishment of good. In every department of his work he excelled. If he preached upon the duties of Christianity, he impressed upon his hearers the paramount importance of a holy life. If he presented the great doctrines of the Bible, he handled error with a giant grasp. Frequently he bore down every thing before him. Inspired often with the grandeur of his theme, he arose to the loftiest heights of oratory, and in words of burning eloquence portrayed the exceeding sinfulness of sin and the fearful doom of the ungodly; and then, dipping his pencil in living light, he would paint the agonies that Jesus bore on Calvary, while the hundreds who sat before him would be melted to tenderness and tears." He "was a man," says Mrs. Johnson, "whom every body loved. No word but *love* will express the feelings with which all regarded him."

Among the accessions to Methodism in Illinois during the conference year one of the most important was Rev. JOSIAS RANDLE. He was born in Brunswick County, Virginia. After a severe struggle he was converted in North Carolina and united with the Methodist Episcopal Church in 1788. He was sent by R. Ellis, presiding elder, to superintend a mission school among the Cherokee Indians. He remained there about a year and formed a class of white emigrants who had settled in the neighborhood of the school. After supplying a circuit till conference in 1791, he was received in the traveling connection and sent to Broad River. In 1798 he located and settled in Warren County, Georgia. In 1802 he was readmitted and in 1809 again located. He was a member of the General Conferences of

1804 and 1808. In 1811 he removed to Illinois and settled near Edwardsville. He died there in triumph January 15, 1824.

Rev. Richard Haney, D. D., relates the following, which is inserted here as this was probably the year in which a preacher was sent to them, though the circumstance occurred many years before: "Not long after the time when Methodism was introduced into St. Clair County, a remarkable circumstance occurred in the south-eastern portion of the State. A party of eight or ten men were together assisting an emigrant to put up a cabin not far from the mouth of the Wabash, when it was proposed that they meet on the next Sabbath at one of the cabins for worship. To this they all agreed. On the Sabbath eight women and ten men were assembled. But amongst them there was no one who had ever conducted public worship. Indeed, of the men not one had ever made a profession of religion. A three-legged stool was placed in the midst of them, a Bible laid upon it, and then all waited for some one to begin the service. No one being willing to lead, the man of the house suggested that nine straws be prepared of equal length and one a little longer, and that he who drew the longer one should conduct the service. To this they all pledged themselves. The longest straw was drawn by George Davidson, who with great trepidation commenced the task. After reading a chapter in the Bible, they sang the hymn, beginning " Come, thou Fount of every blessing," and then he fell upon his knees to pray. As with sinking heart and trembling voice he began, the power of God fell upon the assembly; before he arose from his knees he was powerfully converted, and others were prostrate on the floor, crying for mercy. It was not long before some of them were converted, and the work went on until every adult in the settlement had become a child of God. They chose Mr. Davidson as their leader, who continued to lead them and minister to them until they were supplied with the services of an itinerant by Bishop Asbury."

CHAPTER X

1811.

ILLINOIS DISTRICT—Samuel Parker, P. E.
Illinois—Jesse Walker, George A. Colbert.
WABASH DISTRICT—James Axley, P. E.
Cash River—Baker Wrather.

THE Western Conference held its session for 1811 at Cincinnati, Ohio, commencing October 1st. To the Illinois Circuit Jesse Walker was appointed for the third time, with George A. Colbert as his colleague. We have no record of Mr. Walker's labors this year, but the increase in the membership during the year shows that it was both laborious and successful. He reported an increase of one hundred and thirty-five whites and two colored. The settlements were now rapidly spreading along the water-courses and into the interior of the State. As early as 1809 there were settlements on Shoal Creek as far up as where the flourishing town of Greenville now stands, and along the Okaw and smaller streams settlers were rapidly opening farms. The spirit of Mr. Walker would impel him, as it did afterwards in Northern Illinois, to follow up these settlements as fast as they were formed, no matter how great the labor or how severe the exposure, and we may safely assume that by this time his circuit included more than twice the territory that it covered when he was first appointed to it.

But Mr. Walker did not complete his year on the circuit. The presiding elder, Mr. Parker, having left the district early in the Spring to attend the General Conference, to which he was a delegate, Mr. Walker was taken from the Illinois Circuit to supply his place for the remainder of the year.

Of his colleague, GEORGE A. COLBERT, we know but little beyond the record of his appointments in the General Minutes. This was his second year in the Western Conference. His first year had been spent on Cold Water Circuit. At the close of his year in Illinois he was sent to Natchez. The next year his name does not appear in the Minutes, and at the conference of 1814 he was returned located. He probably settled in the Wabash District, for at the Illinois Conference of 1828, held at Madison, Indiana, his recommendation to elder's orders was presented from that district; and that he had maintained a good report is evident from his election to that office by the conference.

To Cash River (Cash Creek last year), Baker Wrather was appointed, with James Axley as presiding elder. The year was a prosperous one, two hundred and fifteen members being reported at its close—an increase over the previous year of nearly one hundred and fifty.

BAKER WRATHER was received on trial in the Western Conference in 1810 and appointed to Danville Circuit. His second charge was Cash River. The next year he was assigned to Abingdon, the next year to Dover, and in 1814 to Nashville. In the Minutes for 1815 he is reported as located. But this is probably an error, for at the conference of 1816 he was expelled from the Church. It seems that he had sold a slave and sent him to the South, thus separating husband and wife, and for this he was tried and expelled. It is said that he returned to the Church some years before he died.

JAMES AXLEY was one of the most remarkable men of his day. More anecdotes are probably related of him than of any other Western preacher save Peter Cartwright. And yet from the anecdotes current in regard to these men we learn but little of their true character. They give us the humorous or ludicrous, or uncouth or severe side of them, but fail to show us their real worth as faithful Christians and laborious ministers of the Gospel. Mr. Axley was a native of North Carolina, but removed with his parents to Kentucky in childhood. He was converted in early life and was received into the Church by Peter Cartwright when forming the Livingston Circuit whilst serving as a supply under the presiding elder. He united with the Western Conference in 1804, and continued traveling until 1822, when he located and settled on a farm in East Tennessee. During his itinerant life he was eight years on circuits in Tennessee, Kentucky, and Ohio, and ten years on districts, all save one in the Tennessee Conference.

Physically he was a large man, nearly six feet in height, with a large, strong, muscular frame with but little surplus flesh, with a chest broad and deep, and a voice so strong that he could frequently be heard distinctly at a distance of half a mile. His features were coarse, his countenance indicative of great firmness, and his walk erect and steady. His advantages for education were quite limited, but by his fidelity in study he became mighty in the Scriptures, and one of the most successful preachers of his day. As a Christian, he was noted for his strong faith, his intense earnestness, his deep devotion to the cause of Christ, and his uncompromising hatred of sin in every form.

As a preacher, he varied as much in manner as in matter. When unfolding the riches of the Gospel, he often moved his hearers to tears. But when denouncing sin, to quote from Dr. McAnally, he could use "such sharp-pointed irony, such biting ridicule, such withering sarcasm" as has rarely, if ever, been heard before or since. He was especially severe on slavery, drunkenness, the use of tobacco, and extravagance in dress. Such was his hatred of slavery, that, as preacher and presiding elder, he took decided ground against slaveholders having any thing to do in managing the affairs of the Church, and especially preaching. He was not willing even that a man who owned slaves should lead a public prayer-meeting. He had wonderful power over his congregations. Sometimes, by one of his odd remarks, the whole audience would be convulsed with laughter, and, in a few minutes, by his melting pathos, would be bathed in tears. No preacher of his day could command larger congregations than he. Generally he would take a text, and unfold and apply it in the orthodox manner. But sometimes he would take a whole paragraph denouncing some special sin, and, after dwelling on that until satisfied, would take another in which another sin is spoken of, and another, and another, until he felt that he had delivered his soul. "As a doctrinal preacher, Mr. Axley deservedly stood high. Few men ever better understood or could better expound the doctrines of the Methodist Church than he." Mrs. Johnson says of his preaching: "He usually began his sermons with natural strokes which were generally mistaken for humor, and seldom failed to excite his hearers to laughter. But before he had spoken long, his deep, sonorous voice became exceedingly impressive, and the weeping was as universal and as irresistible as the laughter had been at first."

In the social circle among his intimate friends, he was easy in his manners, free in conversation and quite communicative. In mixed society he was reserved and abrupt. At home he was kind, industrious, and economical. Of his wonderful power in prayer and the wonderful answers that were accorded to his prayers, many remarkable facts are recorded.

He died near Madisonville, Tennessee, in 1838. His end was peace. Though his sufferings for the three weeks of his last illness were great, he bore them patiently. Says Dr. Redford of him: "When asked by a member of the Church if it was convenient to have prayers, 'It is always convenient to have prayers in my house,' said the dying saint. Just before he passed away, he called first his wife, and afterwards his children, one by one, and laying his hands on their heads, imparted to them his last blessing, requesting each one to meet him in heaven. He then made the same request of his friends who were present, and in a few moments closed his eyes in death.".

There were many points of resemblance between Axley and his friend Peter Cartwright. The latter says of him: " Brother Axley was truly a child of nature, a great deal of sternness and firmness about him as well as oddity. But he was a great and good minister of Jesus Christ. He often said, a preacher that was good and true had a trinity of devils to fight—superfluous dress, whisky, and slavery. Brother Axley and myself were like Jonathan and David." And the friendship formed between them in early life continued unbroken until Axley entered into rest.

During the nine years in which the work in Illinois had been connected with the Western Conference, Methodism, at first confined to a narrow strip along the Mississippi, had spread over the southern portion of the State, keeping pace with the ever advancing settlements, so that instead of the one feeble mission, with which the work commenced, there were now two strong circuits with a membership of seven hundred and sixty whites and two colored. Instead of the one discouraged missionary, unvisited by a presiding elder during his whole term, there were now three circuit preachers, cheered by the frequent, if not quarterly, visits of two able and sympathizing presiding elders. And thus was the work begun that afterwards, by the divine blessing, spread over the whole State, and, indeed, over the whole North-west, divided already into four strong annual conferences in Illinois, and more than twice that number in Iowa, Wisconsin, and Minnesota.

Part II.

In the Tennessee Conference.

1812 to 1815.

Part II.

IN THE TENNESSEE CONFERENCE.

1812 to 1815.

CHAPTER I.

1812.

ILLINOIS DISTRICT—Jesse Walker, P. E.
Illinois—James Dixon.

WABASH DISTRICT—Peter Cartwright, P. E.
Little Wabash—John Smith.
Massac—David Goodner.

AT the General Conference of 1812 the Western Conference was divided into two: the Ohio Conference, embracing Western Pennsylvania, Ohio, Eastern Indiana, Western Virginia, and Northern Kentucky; and the Tennessee Conference, including Mississippi, Tennessee, Southern Kentucky, Western Indiana, Illinois, and all the territory west of the Mississippi River.

The first session of the Tennessee Conference was held at Fountain Head, Sumner County, Tennessee, November 12, 1812. Bishops Asbury and McKendree were both present, though the conference was under the superintendency of the latter. Some changes were made in the work in Illinois. The name of the Cash River Circuit was changed to Massac, and a new circuit was formed in the eastern part of the territory and named Little Wabash. It is probable that some societies had been formed in this region before this year, and had been supplied by the preachers on the Vincennes Circuit. These two circuits were placed in the Wabash District, of which Peter Cartwright was appointed presiding elder. The Illinois Circuit was connected with the Illinois District, of which Jesse Walker was made presiding elder. Though this district was called Illinois, five out of the six circuits composing it were in Missouri, and only one in the territory from which it took its name. To the Illinois Circuit James Dixon was appointed, John Smith to the Little Wabash, and David Goodner to Massac. There was some decrease in the membership this year. In the Illinois Circuit was a falling off of a hundred and eleven from the year before; the Massac Circuit had only one hundred and seventy-one instead of the two hundred and fifteen reported from Cash River; and the newly established Little Wabash Circuit reported only seventy-two, making a loss of eighty-three members in the three charges during the year.

Yet in other respects advancement was made. John Moore, son of James Moore, who was one of the first settlers in what is now Monroe County, built a large brick house a mile and a half north of Waterloo, cutting off two small rooms from one end for his family, and setting apart all the rest of the house for a preaching-place. Many protracted and quarterly-meetings were held there, and many souls were born into the kingdom. The meetings were wholly supported by Mr. Moore, but he never begrudged what he gave, and would have given more for the sake of the cause.

JAMES DIXON was a native of Ireland. When young he came to America with his father, who settled in Western Virginia. Mr. Dixon was admitted into the Western Conference in 1810. His first circuit was Tuscarawas, in Ohio, his next Green River, in Kentucky, and this year the Illinois Circuit. In 1813 he was sent to Goose Creek, in 1814 to Knoxville, and the next year to Claiborne and Natchez. Here his health failed, and for some years he sustained a superannuated relation to the conference. In 1820 he was appointed to Knoxville and Greenville; but the next year he was again placed on the superannuated list, and continued in it until his death, in 1849. Says Dr. McAnally: "He was finely educated and highly gifted. In his prime he was an able preacher and an able exponent and defender of the doctrines and polity of the Church to which he belonged." He gave evidence of this in a protracted newspaper controversy with Dr. I. Anderson, a leading member of the Presbyterian Church in Tennessee, who had attacked the peculiar doctrines and polity of the Methodist Church. Mr. Dixon ably defended them, and, in the opinion of many, was not worsted by his learned and able opponent. Whilst traveling the Knoxville and Greenville charge he was suddenly stricken down by disease, remaining for some weeks utterly helpless and almost unconscious. When restored to consciousness, it was found that his memory had completely failed, so that he could not even tell his own name. Some years afterwards he became entirely deranged, and was placed in the lunatic asylum at Nashville, where he continued until released by death.

JOHN SMITH was by birth a Virginian. This was his first year in the conference. The next year he was appointed to Red River Circuit, and at the close of the year was discontinued. But the following year he was again received on trial, and at the end of the year the conference gave him the benefit of his previous probation, and admitted him into full connection, and elected him to deacon's orders. He continued traveling until 1821, when he located. After his location he settled at Monticello, Kentucky, and engaged in the practice of medicine. In 1832 he removed to Springfield, Illinois, and formed a partnership with Dr. Todd, a leading physician of that place. He afterwards removed, first to Carlinville, where he also practiced medicine in partnership with Dr. Jayne, and thence to Edwardsville, where he died. He was a good preacher, a natural orator, of fine education, neat in his personal appearance, a faithful Christian, quite active for many years as a local preacher, and a man of influence in the community in which he lived. In his early ministry he was very popular and useful. But for some time before he died he ceased preaching altogether.[1] One of his daughters was married to Rev. L. L. Harlan, of Macoupin County.

____

[1] Rev. L. L. Harlan.

Of DAVID GOODNER, who traveled the Massac Circuit this year, we have but a meager account. He had united with the Western Conference in 1811, and had been appointed to Richmond and Flint Circuit. At the close of his year on Massac he located. In 1819 he was readmitted, and traveled the Caney Fork Circuit one year, at the close of which he located again, and we have no further account of him.

Much has been written of PETER CARTWRIGHT, who was this year presiding elder of the Wabash District, and much more might be written. But as this was the only year in which he was connected with Methodism in Illinois until his permanent connection with it by transfer to the conference, it will be more appropriate to postpone an account of his life and character until we reach the organization of that body. This was the first of his fifty years in the presiding eldership. He says of his appointment in his autobiography: " I told Bishop Asbury that I deliberately believed that I ought not to be appointed presiding elder, for I was not qualified for the office; but he told me there was no appeal from his judgment. At the end of six months I wrote to him, begging a release from the post he had assigned me; but when he returned an answer he said I must abide his judgment, and stand in my lot to the end of the time. I continued accordingly in the service; but the most of the year was gloomy to me, feeling that I had not the first qualification for the office of a presiding elder. Perhaps I never spent a more gloomy and sad year

than this in all my itinerant life; and from that day
to this I can safely say the presiding elder's office
has had no special charm for me; and I will remark that I have often wondered at the aspirations
of many, very many Methodist preachers for the
office of presiding elder, and have frequently said,
if I were a bishop, that such aspirants should always
go without office under my administration. I look
upon this disposition as the outcropping of fallen
and unsanctified human nature, and whenever this
spirit, in a large degree, gets into a preacher, he
seldom ever does much good afterward." To those
who knew Dr. Cartwright, and especially to those
who were associated with him in the presiding eldership, and witnessed the scene with Bishop Waugh,
described by Mr. Daniels in the *National Repository*
for April, 1880, these remarks appear very singular,
to say the least.

CHAPTER II.

1813.

Illinois District—Jesse Walker, P. E.
Illinois—Ivy Walke.
Little Wabash—James Porter.
Massac—Josiah Patterson.

THE conference held its session of 1813 at Rush Chapel, Williamson County, Tennessee, beginning on Friday, October 1st, and continuing six days. The work in Illinois was placed in one district, under the superintendence of Jesse Walker, the circuits remaining the same as last year. To the Illinois Circuit Ivy Walke was appointed, James Porter to the Little Wabash, and Josiah Patterson to Massac. On the Illinois Circuit there was a decrease this year of twenty-eight members; but on the Little Wabash there was an increase of eighty-two, and on Massac of one hundred and eleven, making an increase in the Territory of one hundred and sixty-five.

Of Ivy Walke we have no information save that afforded by the General Minutes. This was his first year in the conference. The next year he traveled Goose Creek Circuit, in Tennessee, and the next year Clinch Circuit. In 1816 his name does not appear on the Minutes, and the next year he is reported located.

JAMES PORTER was born in Washington County, Virginia. He united with the Tennessee Conference in 1812, and was appointed to Wayne Circuit. After leaving Illinois he continued traveling in the Tennessee Conference until 1820, when he fell into the Kentuky Conference, in which he remained until 1823, when, on account of ill-health, he located. He was, says Dr. McFerrin, a faithful servant of the Church.

JOSIAH PATTERSON's experience as an itinerant was peculiar for the time in which he lived, and very different from that of most of his associates. Whilst other preachers were changed through all the States and Territories from Illinois to Mississippi, and from Virginia to Missouri, his labors for his whole itinerant life were confined to Illinois; and, though connected with three conferences, he never received an appointment out of the territory to which he was first appointed. He was a native of South Carolina, born May 12, 1793. In 1812 he removed to Tennessee, where he was converted and united with the Church. Soon after he was licensed to preach, and in 1813, when he was only in his twenty-first year, he was received into the Tennessee Conference.

His appointments were as follows: 1813, to Massac; 1814, St. Mary's; 1815, Bigbay; 1816, Cash River and Bigbay; 1817-18, Okaw; 1819, Cash River; 1820, Shoal Creek; 1821, Okaw; 1822, Wabash and Mt. Vernon; 1823-24, Cash River. In 1825 he was granted a supernumerary relation, and assigned to Brownsville alone, and in 1826, in the same relation, to Kaskaskia with James Hadley. During all these years he labored with great acceptability and usefulness. At the conference of 1827 he was granted a superannuated relation, in which he remained until his death, October 15, 1829. His memoir in the General Minutes says of him : " He was eminently a man of faith and prayer, punctual in attending his appointments, faithful in preaching and visiting from house to house, and wherever he went God owned and blessed his labors. Few men among us have been instrumental in bringing more souls to the Lord Jesus Christ than Brother Patterson." " In personal appearance he was not very prepossessing, being low in stature, somewhat stoop-shouldered, and in repose apparently thoughtless; but when aroused in preaching, as was usually the case with him, every muscle seemed instinct with life. He was a man of strong religious emotions, and was sometimes affected with that strange disease, the jerks. In his pastoral visitations he was accustomed to pay particular attention to the children, and made it a rule to teach them the catechism of the Church wherever he visited."[1] In severe labor and exposure probably none of the pioneers of Methodism in Illinois, save Jesse Walker, endured more than Mr. Patterson. The writer has heard from his descendants, who resided in Bloomington, many stories of his sufferings from high water and storms, and lodging on the ground whilst traveling his vast circuits in Southern Illinois.

---

[1] Mrs. Mitchell.

CHAPTER III.

1814.

ILLINOIS DISTRICT—Jesse Walker, P. E.
Illinois—James Noland.
St. Mary's—Josiah Patterson.
Fort Massac and Little Wabash—John C. Harbison.

OF the year 1814 but a brief account can be given. The session of the Tennessee Conference was held at New Chapel, Logan County, Kentucky, beginning September 29th, and continuing eight days. Jesse Walker was reappointed to the district, James Noland was sent to the Illinois Circuit, Josiah Patterson to a new charge called St. Mary's, and John C. Harbison to Fort Massac and Little Wabash, which were united this year. The St. Mary's Circuit was a part of the old Cash River Circuit, embracing the territory from the mouth of the Ohio to the Okaw. Several changes seem to have been made in the work during the year by the presiding elder, as indicated in the reports of charges and numbers made to the next conference. Some of the charges formed in 1814 were not reported at all, and some new ones are mentioned. The Illinois Circuit reports 462 members against 408 last year. A new circuit, the Okaw, formed from the south part of the Illinois Circuit, is returned with thirty-three members. The Cash River Circuit, which was not mentioned last year, reports 286 whites and 38 colored members. Bigby or Bigbay, as it should be written, which was probably the Fort Massac of last year, reports 317 whites and 29 colored, and Wabash returns 261 whites. The entire membership in Illinois this year, as reported, was 1359 whites and 67 colored, an increase of 582 in all over the membership of the year before. There is probably some error in these reports.

JAMES NOLAND traveled only this year, having been received by the Tennessee Conference at the beginning, and discontinued at the close of the year. He was a native of North Carolina, born about 1790. He came to Illinois in 1793 with his parents, who settled in Monroe County. He was converted in early life under the ministry of John Clarke. He was more than an average preacher, and at times was wonderfully eloquent. He was very zealous, quite independent, and somewhat disposed to controversy. There was a Dunkard settlement at Whiteside Station, two miles south of Columbia, with the elders of which he discussed the restorationist doctrine, and utterly discomfited them. He was a great peace-maker, was very industrious, and stood high as a Christian. It is believed that he started the first Sunday-school in the State, in Columbia, Monroe County, in 1816 or 1817. He retired from the itinerancy to attend to his temporal matters, and spent the rest of his life on his farm near Columbia.[1]

---

[1] Capt. J. M. Moore.

This was also the first year of JOHN C. HARBI-SON in the itinerancy. He had been a lawyer, and gave up a good practice for the sake of the ministry. The next year he was on Cash River Circuit. In 1816 he was elected as the first secretary of the newly formed Missouri Conference, into which he had fallen, and was sent from it to Belleview and Saline. The two following years he was on the Buffalo Circuit, in Missouri. In 1819 his name does not appear on the Minutes, and in 1820 he is reported expelled. At the joint session of the Illinois and Missouri Conferences, in 1824, " Thomas Wright introduced a motion, seconded by Jesse Walker, that John C. Harbison, late a deacon in the traveling connection, but expelled, should be restored to his official standing; which motion was lost. It was then moved by John Dew that the presiding elder be instructed to demand his parchments, which motion prevailed."[2] It is evident from this that the justice or propriety of his expulsion was questioned by some of the best men in the Conference.

---

[2] Journal of Illinois Conference.

CHAPTER IV.

1815.

ILLINOIS DISTRICT—Jesse Walker, P. E.
Illinois—John Scripps.
Okaw—To be supplied.
Cash River—John C. Harbison.
Bigbay—Josiah Patterson.
Wabash—Daniel McHenry.

THE session of the Tennessee Conference of 1815 was an important one in many respects. It was held at Bethlehem meeting-house, Wilson County, Tennessee, beginning October 20th. It was the last session at which the preachers from Indiana, Illinois, Missouri, and Mississippi met with those from Tennessee and Kentucky; for, at the General Conference in the following Spring, the first three were formed into the Missouri Conference, and the fourth into the Mississippi. It was also the last visit of Bishop Asbury to the West. During the session he preached a discourse on the death of Bishop Coke, and delivered also his own farewell address to the conference. Bishop McKendree was also present at the session. Some changes were made in the work in Illinois, the three appointments of the year before being increased to five. Only four preachers, however, were appointed, one of the charges, the Okaw, being left to be supplied. But, instead of continuing it as a separate charge, the presiding elder reunited it with the Illinois Circuit, of which it had once formed a part, and appointed the same preacher, John Scripps, to travel the whole work, embracing the counties of Madison, St. Clair, Monroe, and Randolph. The returns at the end of the year show a great falling off in the membership, so great, indeed, as to lead to a suspicion that there must be some error in the figures of the preceding year. This year, from all the circuits, only nine hundred and sixty-three white and five colored members were reported, a loss for the year of three hundred and ninety-six whites and sixty-two colored.

But, although there was such a large decrease in the membership of the Church, the country continued to improve; new settlements were constantly made, and new opportunities thus afforded for the spread of the Gospel. It was during this year that the first settlements were made in what are now the counties of Macoupin and Greene, a Mr. Coop, being the first to settle in the former, and Thomas Carlin and Thomas Rollin in the latter. The settlements, however, did not increase very rapidly in these counties until after the withdrawal of the Kickapoo Indians, in 1818. During this year the first Methodist society was formed in Alton, by John Scripps, who was then traveling the Illinois Circuit.[1] "At Kaskaskia, the then seat of government, there had been occasional preaching, but these occasions had been few and far between."[2]

____
[1] Rev. J. Scripps.   [2] Dr. McAnally.

The itinerancy had entirely neglected this place. "At my first appointment," says Scripps, "Sunday, April 14th, I was much annoyed by the French Catholics, who crowded the court-house door, with noisy disturbances, while their chapel bell, in immediate contiguity, commenced ringing, and its clattering reverberations filled our room, till Governor Edwards went out and procured silence. Through the residue of the year we had quietness, a respectable, attentive, feeling congregation, and much prospect of doing good; but I made no efforts towards raising a class."

Up to this time, the only organized Protestant Churches in the Territory had been the Methodists, the Regular or Hardshell, as they were termed, and the Separating Baptists. But on July 1, 1816, the first Presbyterian sermon was preached by a traveling minister at the house of a Mr. Alexander, near Shiloh, in St. Clair County. His text was 1 Peter iv, 18. Soon afterwards, Rev. Mr. Giddings moved to the country and organized the first Presbyterian Churches. Many of that denomination scattered through the country, had put themselves under the watch-care of the Methodists until their own societies could be organized. Some of them became so attached to our usages that they preferred remaining with us permanently; but most, as opportunity was afforded, returned to the mother Church, and aided in the establishment of Presbyterianism in the land.

As a specimen of the labors of some of the early itinerants in Illinois, the following description of a round of quarterly-meetings by the presiding elder, Jesse Walker, as given by John Scripps, is worth preserving:

"He commenced this round at Goshen meeting-house, near the site of the present town of Edwardsville, Illinois, on Friday, the 1st of April. Closing his meeting on Monday, the 4th, he traveled a zig-zag route, filling daily and nightly appointments in different neighborhoods in the Illinois Circuit, till he arrived at the Big Spring meeting-house on Friday, the 8th, where, in a protracted meeting, he labored till Monday, the 11th. A second week of similar services, through otherwise destitute settlements, brought him to Davis's school-house, below the confluence of the Big Muddy River with the Mississippi, probably one hundred miles south of his starting-point. I found him here on Saturday, the 16th, accompanied by Jacob Whitesides (then just putting on the itinerant harness). At this place there were some conversions, and a class of sixteen persons was formed. Jacob Whitesides was sent back to labor in the field of the last week's operations, with directions to form a new circuit, which was eventually effected, and it was denominated the Okaw Circuit.

"On Monday, the 18th, Jesse Walker, J. Patterson, and myself set out for the Massac camp-meeting, to be held at the Rock and Cave, on the Ohio River. We traveled this day in an easterly direction, through a generally uninhabited country and almost pathless woods, thirty-two miles, to Thomas Standard's, where a congregation, previously notified by Brother Patterson, awaited our arrival. The exercises of the evening were thrillingly interesting, and continued till midnight. About noon the next day we separated, still tending onward in devious paths to hold night-meetings six or eight miles apart, to meet again the next day, probably again to part for the night, to hold as many meetings as our numbers and the localities of the neighborhood would admit of. On Friday, the 22d, we arrived at the camp-ground. Services commenced immediately upon our arrival, and during the entire progress of the meeting we had precious seasons of refreshing from the presence of the Lord, several conversions, and many accessions to the Church. Brother J. Johnson was with us one of the nights, and preached for us. This meeting broke on Monday. Brother Walker closed the services with an interesting discourse; but Monday night found him several miles on his way to his next appointment, again holding forth to a large congregation in Proctor's meeting-house. But to particularize his labors would swell this account to too great an extent. Suffice it to say that, crossing the Big Wabash near its mouth, we ascended that river in the then Territory of Indiana, crossed the Black River, Patoka and White Rivers, to Brother Johnson's, about twelve miles from Vincennes. By the next Friday, April 29th, the quarterly-meeting for Vincennes Circuit was held. It was a time of power, and closed Monday morning. We made a short travel that day of six or eight miles, and held a night-meeting at Dr. Messick's; the next day, noon, at Harrington's Tavern; at night at Anthony Griffin's,

on Black River. We recrossed the Wabash, and
commenced the Wabash Quarterly-meeting, Friday,
May 6th, at Brother Hannah's, in a block-house,
from which our next appointment was one hundred
and seventy or eighty miles south-west across the
Mississippi, to New Madrid Circuit, Missouri Territory, commencing Friday, the 13th; thence sixty
miles north to Cape Girardeau Circuit, May 20th.
At both these appointments, and all subsequent to
them through the Summer, camp-meetings were held,
the necessity for which grew out of the fact that no
one-room, or even two-room, log-cabin (and we had
no other sort of houses) was capable of entertaining
one-half or even one-fourth of Jesse Walker's quarterly-meetings; for his regular Sabbath congregations collected, far and near, from ten, twenty, or
thirty miles around, to these attractive centers of
religious services. From Cape Girardeau Brother
Walker proceeded, by himself, to hold a camp and
quarterly meeting on Saline Circuit, commencing
Friday, 27th; on the Maramec Circuit, June 3d;
Cold Water, 10th; and Missouri Circuit, June 17th;
to which appointment, following the circuitous route
he had to travel, it was upwards of two hundred
miles north; and here, on Monday, the 20th of
June, he concluded his second round of meetings,
about eighty miles north-west of home, and sixty
from Goshen, the commencement of this round,
where he again preached in returning to his family,
there to enjoy a few day's respite, to repair his
itinerant gear, and prepare for the still more extensive operations of the Summer campaign, under the
more favorable auspices of shallow streams, better

roads, longer days, and the sweltering fervor of a
July sun.

"Such labors as I have recounted would, in these
times of good roads, bridged waters, wealthy friends,
comfortable accommodations, and table luxuries, be
deemed great; but the circumstances under which
Jesse Walker performed them were characterized by
difficulties, dangers, privations, and sufferings almost
inconceivable in the present improved state of
things. Our roads were narrow, winding horse-
paths, sometimes scarcely perceptible, and frequently
for miles no path at all, amid tangled brushwood,
over fallen timber, rocky glens, mountainous preci-
pices; through swamps and low grounds, overflowed
or saturated with water for miles together, and consequently muddy, which the breaking up of the
Winter and the continued rains gave a continued
supply of; the streams some of them large and
rapid, swollen to overflowing, we had to swim on
our horses, carrying our saddle-bags on our shoulders. It was a common occurrence, in our jour-
neying, to close our day's ride drenched to the skin
by continually descending rains, for which that
Spring was remarkable. Our nights were spent,
not in two but in one room log-cabins, each generally constituting our evening meeting-house, kitchen,
nursery, parlor, dining and bed room,—all within
the dimensions of sixteen feet square, and not unfrequently a loom occupying one-fourth of it, together
with spinning-wheels and other apparatus for man-
ufacturing their apparel—our congregations requiring our services till ten or twelve o'clock; our sup-

per after dismission, not of select, but of just such
aliment as our hospitable entertainers could provide
(for hospitable, in the highest sense of the word,
they were; corn-cakes, fried bacon, sometimes but-
ter, with milk or herb-tea, or some substitute for
coffee. At the Rock and Cave camp-meeting, the
measles being very prevalent in the congregation, I
took them. Very high fevers were the first symp-
tom: but, unconscious of the cause and nature of
my affliction, I continued traveling through all
weathers for upwards of two weeks, before the complaint developed its character. My stomach became
very delicate, and through a populous part of our
journey I inquired for coffee at every house we
passed, and was invariably directed to Mr. L.'s, several miles ahead, as the only probable place for the
procurement of the grateful beverage. On making
known my wants to Mrs. L., she searched and found
a few scattered grains at the bottom of a chest, of
which she made us two cupfuls.

"We have sometimes sat in the large fire-place,
occupying the entire end of a log cabin, and plucked
from out the smoke of the chimney above us pieces
of dried and smoked venison, or jerk, the only pro-
vision the place could afford us, and the only food the
inmates had to sustain themselves, till they could
obtain it by the cultivation of the soil. Our horses
fared worse, in muddy pens, or tied up to saplings or
corners of the cabin, regaled with the refuse of the
Winter's fodder, sometimes (when we could not restrain over-liberality) with seed-corn, purchased in
Kentucky at a dollar per bushel, and brought in

small quantities, according to the circumstances of the purchaser, one hundred miles or more at some expense and trouble. This, when they had it, our remonstrances to the contrary could not prevent being pounded in mortars to make us bread. Our lodgings were on beds of various qualities, generally feather-beds, but not unfrequently fodder, chaff, shucks, straw, and sometimes only deer-skins, but always the best the house afforded, either spread on the rough puncheon floor before the fire (from which we must rise early to make room for breakfast operations), or on a patched-up platform attached to the wall, which not unfrequently would fall down, sometimes in the night, with its triplicate burden of three in a bed. Such incidents would occasion a little mirth among us, but we would soon fix up and be asleep again. Now, I would here remark, that many of these privations could have been avoided by keeping a more direct course from one quarterly-meeting to another, and selecting, with a view to comfort, our lodging-places. But Brother Walker sought not personal comfort so much as the good of souls, and he sought the most destitute, in their most retired recesses, and in their earliest settlements."

Severe as was this it was surpassed by a trip of Walker and Scripps the Winter before. Says the latter:

" The indefatigable Walker was then preparing for a Winter's campaign through cold and storm and snow on his district, extending to Vincennes and Evansville, Indiana. So inclement was the season that I thought it dangerous for him to travel alone, and therefore procured substitutes from among my equally sympathizing local brethren to supply my place on the circuit while I accompanied him. The weather, on this tour, was in general intensely cold; nor were the means then in the country of procuring habiliments adequate to the season, as at present. The prairies, where the cold north-easter raged with unchecked fury, were settled only on their margins; and, at whatever time of day we entered on one, however extensive, we could have no comfortable hope of seeing a fire, or shelter from the most pitiless storm, till we had crossed it. On one occasion we entered a twelve-mile prairie at about four o'clock in the evening, with our upper garments completely saturated—the effects of an afternoon's hard rain. At about five o'clock the wind changed and the residue of our way we traveled in a sleet, or rather, more literally, a storm of ice, while the darkness of the night compelled us to yield the reins to our horses; and, on our arrival at the house we were obliged to require assistance to help us off our horses, as our clothes were so inflexible with ice that we could scarcely move in them, and could not, without help, have dismounted. But, if the cold was uncomfortable, the thaws were more dreaded, as more dangerous, by flooding the streams. In one of these thaws we came to a large stream, the ice on which was sufficiently strong to have borne us; but, raised by the flood and thawed next the shore, we could not get our horses on it. In meandering the stream in quest of a more pro-

pitious place to cross, we found one where the lower
ice had been separated by the flood from the upper,
leaving between the two-a space of about three feet.
Not knowing whether the stream here was swim-
ming or not, with some difficulty I restrained Brother
Walker from going foremost, while I precipitated
myself and horse, by sliding down an almost per-
pendicular bank, into the water. He followed close
behind. It was very deep, but fordable; and, while
scrambling up the opposite bank, we barely escaped;
the whole mass, loosened from above, jammed with
a violent concussion against the lower, and the whole
rushed on with the stream.

" After closing a very fatiguing and disagreeable
day's ride, on the eighth of February, we put up
at the Ohio Saline Tavern, a center of resort for all
the young bucks and other more exceptionable characters of a dissolute community. After supper we
were favored with a separate room and a cheerful
fire. A privilege so seldom enjoyed, we thought to
improve by a recourse to Wesley's Notes (by the
by, the only commentary we had access to in those
days in our far West); but we were scarcely seated,
before a fiddle in an adjoining room struck up a
solemn tune of sacred music, followed by livelier
and still more lively airs, hurrying onward to
catches, jigs, glees, and still more exceptionable
music, with an accompaniment, at first, of sup-
pressed titters, but rising with the music to loudest
bursts of uproariousness. Being satisfied, in my own
mind, that they were peepers, anxious to witness
the effects of the unhallowed sounds on the preach-

ers, I wished my companion not to seem to notice
it, but in vain. He either could not, or would not,
restrain his feelings. He laid aside his book and
appeared engaged in silent and devout ejaculations
till, an opportunity offering, by the landlord's coming into our room, he asked him to request these
merry gentlemen to suspend their mirth a few minutes, and to invite them in for worship before we
should retire for repose. I believe they all—a large
company—acceded to the request, accepted the invitation, and behaved with the greatest decorum,
while Brother Walker very appropriately read and
paraphrased a chapter, gave out and sang a hymn
(in which most that could sing, joined), and then,
in a most fervent prayer, acknowledged the mercies
of the day, and implored the pardon of all offenses,
and supplicated the Divine protection through the
night. All kneeled, and some of them remained
after the services, in interesting and profitable conversation, until late bed-time, and no further dis-
cordant sounds annoyed us."

John Scripps was a native of England, having
been born in London, August 26th, 1785. When
he was six years old his father removed to America,
settling first at Alexandria, and afterwards in the
neighborhood of Morgantown, Virginia. John, who
was a sickly child, was not sent to school, but was
allowed to avail himself of his father's excellent
library, which he did to such advantage that, when
in his twentieth year he entered the Virginia Academy, with the exception of the dead languages, he
was found the best scholar in the institution. On

his eighth birthday, under the direction of his mother, he began reading the Scriptures consecutively—a practice which he kept up as long as he lived. And yet, in spite of this, he early imbibed infidel notions, of which he did not get rid until he read "Grotius on the Truth of the Christian Religion." He now became a firm believer in the truth of Christianity, and united with the Methodist Episcopal Church, of which his mother had already become a member. But he could never give the exact date of his conversion. In 1809 he removed to Cape Girardeau, Missouri, and established a tanyard. He was soon after made class-leader, and was then given license to exhort, and afterwards to preach. In the Fall of 1814 he was employed by the presiding elder to travel the Illinois Circuit whilst the preachers went to conference; and on their return found, to his surprise—for he had not been consulted—that he had been received into the conference and appointed to Patoka Circuit, in Indiana. He went to his charge, however, resolved to do his duty. Up to this time no society had been formed in Columbia, the only town in his circuit; but Mr. Scripps not only formed a class there, but extended his circuit so as to include Evansville, on the Ohio River, where he also formed a good society, in which nearly every family in town was represented. In 1815 he was appointed to the Illinois Circuit, to which, as stated above, the Okaw Circuit was attached. In it was Kaskaskia, the capital of the Territory, which Mr. Scripps made one of his preaching-places, and where he had good success.

At the close of the year he had to prepare for the session of the newly formed Missouri Conference, which was to be held at Shiloh, in his circuit. He was to meet Bishop McKendree at a camp-meeting near Vincennes, to conduct him to the seat of the conference. But, instead of taking the circuitous route down the Mississippi and up the Ohio and Wabash, which was usually taken in order to avoid danger from the Indians and keep within the settlements, Mr. Scripps resolved to take a straight course for Vincennes, though it would compel him to travel one hundred and thirty miles through a country infested with Indians and uninhabited by a single white settler. In company with several others, he made the trip in safety, preached four times at the camp-meeting, and then returned by the same route with the bishop, starting from the camp-ground on Tuesday and reaching Shiloh on Saturday, after resting four nights under the open canopy of heaven. Before this, Mr. Scripps had often doubted his call to the ministry; but after conversing with Bishop McKendree on the subject whilst on this trip, the bishop told him that if John Scripps had not been called to preach, neither had William McKendree. After the first session of the Missouri Conference, Mr. Scripps was its secretary until the formation of the Illinois Conference, in 1824. In 1816 he was appointed to Coldwater, afterwards called St. Louis Circuit. He took the city into his charge, and made his *début* in an old, dilapidated log building used as the court-house, legislative hall, and theater, which was the only

public building in the place, except the Roman
Catholic cathedral. He stood on the stage, surrounded by the comic scenery, and preached to a
large and attentive audience, composing the entire
American population. He continued to preach
there and in a school-house, which was built during
the year; but his successors abandoned the place,
and there was no more Methodist preaching in St.
Louis until Jesse Walker re-established it in 1820.
During this year Mr. Scripps visited Kaskaskia,
where he had preached the year before. He was in
rough pioneer costume, with knees, toes, and elbows
out. Two other well-dressed missionaries from the
East were in the place. But when the time for
preaching came, Governor Edwards selected Mr.
Scripps, who had been tried, in preference to the
untried strangers, and put him in the sheriff's box,
a small platform above the heads of the audience,
for a pulpit. His next appointment was Boonslick.
In 1818 he was sent to Cape Girardeau, in 1819 to
Boonslick and Lamoine, and in 1820 to Blue River.
For the two following years he was on the Arkansas District, and in 1823 on the St. Louis Circuit.
At the close of the year, his health having failed,
he was granted a superannuated relation to the Missouri Conference, in which he continued until the
division of the Church in 1845. Refusing to go
South with his conference, he was transferred to the
Illinois Conference in 1846, and placed on the superannuated list, and continued in it until 1850,
when he withdrew from the Church. In 1854 he
reunited with the Church, was restored to the min-

istry, and remained a local preacher until his death, July 26, 1865. He was a member of the General Conferences of 1820 and 1824.

Soon after his superannuation he married Miss Agnes Corrie, of whose conversion an account is given in the history of 1820. In 1825 he settled in Jackson the county-seat of Cape Girardeau County, Missouri, and engaged in the mercantile business. But, being unwilling to lead his children into temptation by bringing them up in a slave State, in 1830 he removed to Illinois, and settled in Rushville, where for a time he engaged in merchandising. He afterwards published a county paper, and held several county and township offices. Soon after his removal to Rushville he organized a Sunday-school, of which he was superintendent for seventeen years, and was afterwards a teacher in it for ten years.

Mr. Scripps was a man of more than ordinary ability. Small in stature, he was yet possessed of remarkable energy and determination. Sometimes, indeed, the strength of his will and his adherence to his own convictions of right impressed others with the belief that he was obstinate, and occasionally brought him into collision with his pastors or presiding elders. He could not endure oppression in any form, nor would he submit to be dictated to by others. Having made up his mind in regard to right or duty, it was with difficulty he could be induced to change his course, and the slightest exercise of compulsion would excite in him the most determined opposition. Having done so much to build up Methodism in Rushville, having shown his love to the Church by a life of labor and sacrifice in her behalf, and having a vastly wider experience than most of those appointed as pastors of the Church there, he felt that his views of Church polity were entitled to some consideration from them,—more, indeed, than they were always disposed to give them.

At the conference of 1848 his character was arrested on the ground that he had imprudently indulged in the use of intoxicating liquors. The matter was referred to his presiding elder, Dr. Akers, who investigated it, and concluded that there was no ground of complaint in the case. Mr. Scripps, on the recommendation of his physician and for a disease from which he suffered greatly, and which eventually caused his death, did of necessity use spirituous liquors, but only as a medicine. And so well satisfied was the presiding elder of the groundlessness of the charge, that he employed him for six months of the year to fill a vacancy in the station where he lived. But in 1850 his pastor, W. W. Mitchell, took such strong ground in opposition to him that he withdrew from the Church, and surrendered his ordination parchments to the conference. Yet, during the four years in which he was out of the Church, he kept up the family altar, and attended to all the outward duties of religion; and was frequently called on to officiate at funerals. After his reunion with the Church he seems to have become much more spiritual, and in March, 1860, he writes in his journal: " This month I obtained a second blessing." Mr. Scripps "possessed an iron will, never tired till his object was accomplished, and clung to his opinions with a tenacity that commanded admiration, if not assent. Self-educated, a close student in early life, he maintained the same habit to the close of his days. While a mere boy in the wilds of Virginia, with no schools and but few facilities for acquiring knowledge, he commenced the work of self-instruction, and though his time was all occupied in labor, except at night and on the Sabbath, yet, by the light descending through an old-fashioned chimney by day and pine splinters by night, he learned to write by epitomizing two large volumes of the History of Rome. A careful observer of particulars and generals, with a strong, retentive memory, the incidents of his early career were ever fresh in his mind in all their details, thus rendering him a most delightful companion. Industrious and methodical in all his habits, both secular and religious, he accomplished an amount of labor equaled by few, and surpassed by fewer still. Given to hospitality, with enlarged Christian benevolence, much of his time and means were employed for the good of others, and many a young man has gone forth to bless the world who owes his aspirations and success in life to the early and long-continued training received from him."[3]

Dr. Stevenson well says of him: "To an intellect naturally vigorous there was added a culture that was extensive, accurate, and intensely practical. A close and critical examination of his numerous

---

[3] Schuyler Citizen.

papers failed to discover a misspelled word, a sentence faulty in construction, or a sentiment that would not bear the closest scrutiny."

To his pastor and other friends, who were with him in his last moments, he expressed himself as assured of a blissful immortality. A short time before his death he called his family around his bedside, gave to each of them his dying admonition, bade them an affectionate farewell, and then, in full possession of his mental faculties, quietly sank to rest in Jesus his Savior.

He was a careful observer and faithful recorder of passing events. He was a good preacher, his sermons being always thoroughly evangelical and indicative of much thought. In doctrine he was sound. He was very fluent in conversation; and his habits of close observation and his very retentive memory, made him, in his old age, one of the most delightful of companions. He was an excellent business man, careful, correct, and yet prompt and ready. The writer knew him well during the last years of his life, being often entertained by him at his quarterly visitations to Rushville, and learned to esteem him highly for his intelligence, geniality, and piety. He had the sad privilege of visiting him on his death-bed and preaching at his funeral. He died well, in the full faith of the Gospel.

One of his contemporaries and fellow itinerants, Rev. John Hogan, thus writes of him: "I have been acquainted with him for many years. I have traveled several circuits that had been traveled long before by John Scripps, and the recollections of. him by all the people were very vivid and pleasant. He was very strict and particular in all the minutiæ of a Methodist preacher's duty. I have often been shown, as a relic, treasured by the old class-leaders, the class papers prepared by Brother Scripps. How singularly neat they were! He wrote a beautiful, plain hand. He made no flourishes, no extras, every thing so clean and neat; and then, the state of life and state of grace were so particularly noted; the attendance on the means of grace regularly noted; and, on the front leaf, clearly written out, the disciplinary requirements as to the regular quarterly fast. He was very careful to have all these matters regularly attended to. This was his method.

"In his day there were but few public roads, and in most places not even a pathway from one settlement to another. Sometimes the preachers traveled by the use of the pocket-compass. Sometimes they took along a little hatchet, and, being shown the way, blazed or notched the trees to point out the road, or rather course, afterwards. John Scripps had a sharp iron with which he would scratch the trees in the course he was to pursue in going from one appointment to another. And these remained plain for years afterwards. When the trees had not been disturbed, I have often followed those marks upon such parts of his original circuits as remained in my bounds. I have heard many anecdotes of his manner of preaching, of study, and devotion to his work. The people loved him, and his ministry was profitable to them, and his memorial was written on their hearts. No wonder, then, that his memory was cherished, and that they loved to speak of his work of faith and his labors of love."

Of DANIEL McHENRY, who traveled the Wabash Circuit this year, we have no other account than his appointments in the General Minutes. He had just been received into the Tennessee Conference, and this was his first appointment. The next year he was sent to Patoka; in 1817 he again traveled the Wabash Circuit; in 1818 he was appointed to Patoka and Pigeon, in 1819 to Vincennes, and at the next session he located, and settled near Carmi, Illinois.

During the four years in which Illinois was connected with the Tennessee Conference, the membership had increased from seven hundred and sixty-two to nine hundred and sixty-eight, and the appointments from two to five.

PART III.

IN THE MISSOURI CONFERENCE.

1816 to 1823.

Part III.

IN THE MISSOURI CONFERENCE.

1816 to 1823.

CHAPTER I.

1816.

ILLINOIS DISTRICT—Samuel H. Thompson, P. E.
Illinois—Jesse Haile.
Okaw—Jacob Whitesides.
Cash River and Bigbay—Josiah Patterson, Wm. Jones.
Wabash—John Harris.

THE first session of the Missouri Conference
was held at Shiloh, St. Clair County, Illinois,
beginning September 23d. Bishop McKendree presided, and John C. Harbison was secretary. Several changes were made in the work in Illinois, both
in the circuits and the men. The Cash River and
Bigbay Circuits were united and two preachers sent
to it, so that the five charges of the year before
were reduced to four this year. Of the preachers
laboring in the Territory, Josiah Patterson was the
only one who had traveled in it before; all the
others were new men.

The presiding elder, SAMUEL H. THOMPSON,
who from this time occupies a prominent position
in connection with Illinois Methodism, was born in

Westmoreland County, Pennsylvania, March 15,
1784. His parents were Presbyterians, and in their
faith he was carefully instructed. He received in
youth a good English education, to which by diligent study he added in after life. In his eighteenth
year he united with the Methodist Episcopal Church
as a seeker of religion, and two years afterwards,
while engaged in secret prayer, it pleased God to
give him an evidence of the pardon of his sins;
and shortly after, in family prayer, he obtained a
clear and abiding evidence of the regeneration of
his nature."* He was received in the Western Conference in 1806, and appointed to Whitewater Circuit in Indiana, with Thomas Nelson as his colleague, and John Sale as his presiding elder.

During the Summer of 1807, in connection with
his colleague and presiding elder, he held the first
camp-meeting ever held in the State of Indiana.
It was in what is now Wayne County, about a mile
south-east of where Salisbury was afterwards laid
out. "The country being new, and the inhabitants
few, the number of persons in attendance was not
large, but it was a time of power and great glory.
A goodly number of the unconverted who attended
this meeting were, before its close, happily brought
to a knowledge of sins forgiven. The conversions
were clear and satisfactory."†

In 1810 he was sent to Nollichuckie in Tennessee, the next year to Clinch, and in 1812, falling
into the Tennessee Conference, he was appointed to
Knoxville, and in 1813 to Christina. During these

---

*General Minutes. †Rev. W. C. Smith.

years his labors were greatly blessed, and he was the means of leading many souls to Christ. In 1814-15 he was on the Missouri District, and at the organization of the Missouri Conference in 1816 he was appointed to the Illinois District, which covered all the inhabited parts of Illinois and the western and southern portions of Indiana. In 1818 he traveled the Shoal Creek and Illinois Circuit, and in 1819 the Illinois Circuit. For the next two years he was on the Missouri District, and in 1822 he was reappointed to the Illinois District, on which he remained four years—two years in connection with the Missouri Conference, and two years in the Illinois Conference. The district, says Cartwright, "covered more than two-thirds of the geographical boundaries of the State; but with unfaltering steps he traveled night and day, seldom missing his appointments, through cold and heat, floods or snow-storms. His labors were greatly blessed, and there is very little doubt that he was the most popular and useful preacher in the State. Hundreds, if not thousands, from the Illinois District, in the great day of judgment, will hail our beloved brother, and call him blessed."

Near the close of his term on the district he was nominated for lieutenant-governor of the State; but his position as a candidate for political office was irksome to him, and nothing could induce him to seek success by the electioneering tricks, then as now, practiced by candidates. As Governor Reynolds says: "He possessed an irreproachable character, and he would not tarnish it by any electioneering act." Fortunately, perhaps, for him, he was not elected.

His health having failed through his incessant labors, he was granted a supernumerary relation at the conference of 1826, and for the two following years he served as such on the Illinois Circuit. The next year he traveled the Shoal Creek Circuit; in 1829 he was appointed to the Kaskaskia District, which he traveled for three years; in 1832 he served as agent for the newly established Lebanon Seminary (afterwards McKendree College), and the next year he was on the Lebanon Circuit. In 1834 he was appointed to Vandalia, but at the close of the year was placed on the superannuated list. The next year his position was changed to supernumerary, and as such he labored as he could on Vandalia and Hillsboro, Lower Alton and Belleville charges successively. But his health having failed completely, in 1841 he was again placed on the superannuated list, and on March 19th of the next year he was released from his sufferings by death.

Mr. Thompson was a man of fine personal appearance, and in manners was the polished Christian gentleman. He was possessed of fine social qualities, and was an admirable conversationalist. As a preacher he was very popular. His style was rather hortatory than didactic, and his discourses abounded in anecdote and illustration. He seemed, indeed, to possess an inexhaustible fund of anecdotes, and could tell them with a grace and force that impressed strongly those who heard him. He was very sympathetic, and, like Jeremiah, his head was a fountain of tears. His sweet spirit endeared him to all who knew him. No member of conference was more highly esteemed by his brethren than he. He was five times elected by them to the General Conference, twice from the Missouri, and three times from the Illinois Conference, and at the session of the latter at Vincennes, in 1830, no bishop being present, Mr. Thompson was unanimously called to the chair; and from the journal it appears that the business was transacted with as much dispatch and correctness as though under the direction of a bishop. He was for many years the leading spirit in the conference, serving on the most important committees, and impressing himself upon the whole body. Dr. Redford says of him, "He was one of the most indefatigable preachers of his day. And to the labors of no preacher is the Church in Illinois more indebted than to Mr. Thompson." His memoir in the General Minutes says:

"While his zeal for the divine law and his love for the souls of men impelled him to express his disapprobation of every form of moral evil, and fearlessly to administer the discipline of the Church, the exquisite sensibility of his own feelings made him a model of courtesy to all men, and tempered the edge of his reproof with the most affectionate tenderness. The duty of praying with his family was never, after his marriage, omitted by him but once; and so highly did he value the privilege of uniting with them around the domestic altar, that he uniformly requested whoever might be a visitant at his house to permit him once a day to lead in their devotions. Eminently a man of peace himself, he breathed the peaceful spirit of Christianity everywhere around him; and especially upon his family, and upon the Church in his vicinity, he impressed this characteristic mark of Christianity in a very high degree. Full of sympathy, his generosity and hospitality abounded toward all men, but especially toward that body of men in connection with whom he had suffered so much in the cause of their common Master. A few days before his death God was pleased to give him such a view of the heavenly world as filled his soul with joy unspeakable and full of glory; and he continued until his death glorying in tribulation, and rejoicing in hope of the glory of God."

The following confirms what is said in his memoir in regard to his attachment to family prayer. As Mr. Beggs was on his way from his father's in Indiana to his circuit in Missouri, to which he had been appointed from the conference of 1823, he says: "I was not a little comforted to meet Brother Samuel H. Thompson, presiding elder of Illinois District, late one evening on his way to a quarterly-meeting. He insisted on my stopping over night with him. After some religious conversation, in which he gave me very good advice, he led the family prayers, in which he remembered not only me, but my horse, suggesting what Mr. Wesley said, that when he prayed for his horse he never lost any. He then gave me a way-bill to my circuit, being acquainted with the whole five hundred miles I had to travel."

Mr. Thompson excelled in raising funds for Church and benevolent objects, and was so frequently engaged in that work that he was called by some "the beggar general." Says Mr. Beggs: "His strong appeals were almost resistless. On one occasion he closed his appeal by telling the people to come forward and lay their offerings on the table. Among those who responded was a gentleman who put his hand deep into his pocket, and took out a handful of silver to get some change. Thompson saw him, and, as if supposing that he intended to lay all upon the table, exclaimed at the top of his voice, 'Thank God for one liberal soul!' By this time all eyes were fixed on the 'liberal' gentleman, who could not help laying down the entire handful. But Thompson illustrated his precept in this respect by example. He generally headed the contribution, and so generous was he in his offerings that he not unfrequently had to borrow money to get home with. The liberality of the Methodist preachers was remarkable. Giving beyond their means, they yet realized it was **more blessed to give than to** receive."

"Brother Thompson," says Cartwright, "labored hard and suffered much for more than thirty years. His field of labor for these years embraced large portions of Ohio, Indiana, Tennessee, Kentucky, Illinois, Missouri, and Arkansas States, most of which was new and on the outskirts of civilization, destitute of means of comfortable support. In these respects his zeal, like a quenchless fire, urged him on night and day, over desert wastes, towering mountains, rapid rivers. He often suffered hunger and almost nakedness in quest of lost and wandering sinners, to bring them back to God; and thousands now in heaven will praise God forever that this self-sacrificing Methodist preacher taught them the way to life in their mud hovels and smoky cabins. The last year of his eventful life his health almost entirely gave way, and while confined to his bed, from which he never rose, such was his ardent thirst for the salvation of souls that he requested to call in the neighbors, and to be propped up in his bed, and to preach one more sermon to them before he left for heaven. His desire was granted; the room was crowded, and such a sermon hardly ever fell from the lips of mortal man. The power of God fell on the congregation; they wept aloud, and fell in every direction; and many will date their start for heaven from that sermon. And now, having delivered his last message, he said : ' My work is done, and I am ready to go at my Master's bidding.' "

After his superannuation he was appointed receiver at the United States land office at Edwardsville, and retained that position until his death.

Of the early history and conversion of JESSE HAILE, who this year traveled the Illinois Circuit, we have no information. He sought admission to the Tennessee Conference of 1812, but for some cause was not received. He then bought a rifle, and proposed to enter into the service of his country in the war with Great Britain, saying that in serving his country he would be in the service of God and

his fellow-men. In 1813 he was received on trial
in the Tennessee Conference, and appointed to Missouri Circuit, which he traveled for two years. In
1815 he was sent to Cape Girardeau, and in 1816
to the Illinois Circuit, which he also traveled two
years. The next year he was on the Illinois District, and the following year on the Missouri District. In 1820 he was appointed to New Madrid,
in 1821 to Shoal Creek, and in 1822 to the Illinois
Circuit again. The next year he was sent to Indianapolis Circuit, in 1824 he was again appointed to
the Missouri District, and for the four following
years he traveled the Arkansas District. In 1827
he was transferred to the Illinois Conference, and
appointed to Bloomington Circuit, Indiana. S. R.
Beggs was his colleague for three-quarters of this
year, and he speaks of it as a prosperous year, with
a number of conversions. The preachers visited several camp-meetings, everywhere meeting with great
success. Each of them received his full allowance
of quarterage ($100) from the charge. The next
year Mr. Haile was sent to Sangamon Circuit, the
next year to Paris, the next to Pekin, and in 1833
was placed on the superannuated list. The year
following he was appointed to Carrollton; but, his
health being still insufficient, he was again for two
years kept in the relation of a superannuate. In
1837 his relation was changed to supernumerary,
and he was appointed to Carlisle, in 1838 to Hillsboro, and in 1839 to Shelbyville. His appointment
in 1840 was Big Creek, in 1841 Newhaven, in 1842
Livingston, and in 1843 Paris. This was his last

appointment. He died at Nashville, Illinois, just after the session of conference of 1844. His end was peace. His memoir in the General Minutes says: "On all of the above fields Brother Haile labored faithfully and usefully, and we know not that any wrong was ever charged against him. He was a good, plain, pointed, and practical preacher and minister, and studied to do every thing by rule and at the time. The circuits he traveled in the early part of his itinerancy embraced extensive territory, thinly peopled, in which he endured much fatigue and exposure, but was never known to say, 'My work is hard.'"

"Mr. Haile was a man of medium size, always grave and dignified in his bearing. He was seldom known to laugh, but his countenance would give out an expression of inward pleasure. He was quite polite in his manners, and, though a man of few words, his conversation was always interesting. He was never light or trifling in word or manner, nor could any one indulge in levity in his presence. As a preacher, he was sensible and instructive, understanding well his subjects, and discussing them with system. In the pulpit he was always dignified and self-possessed, speaking as though conscious that he had authority. He was a very modest man, as far as possible from self-seeking, accepting without a murmur whatever the Church gave him to do, and doing it to the best of his ability. He never made any attempt to accumulate property. It is said, though this must be a mistake, that he owned but two horses during his long career as a traveling preacher; but it was true that, when he died, his horse, saddle, and bridle, with a few books, composed the sum of his earthly possessions. He had been suffering from chills before he went to conference;. but on reaching Nashville he was stricken down with bilious fever, and, despite the efforts of physicians and friends, sunk under it in a few days after the session closed. As he neared his end, after conversing pleasantly with some brethren who had called on him, he became so happy in view of the prospect before him that he broke out into triumphant shouts of praise, and soon after passed to his reward." [3]

Mr. Haile was one of a class of preachers of whom but few remain, thoroughly devoted to his work, strictly conscientious, and believing Methodism to be the divinely appointed agency for the conversion of the world, he was strict in observing and enforcing every feature of the Discipline, as well as in believing and proclaiming all its doctrines. He had no compromise to make with sin in any form. It is said that he once had a member arraigned and excluded from the Church on the sole charge of not maintaining family worship. And in his preaching he feared not to tell men plainly that they were sinners, and that if they did not repent they would go to hell. While on the Arkansas District, he boldly denounced the prevalent sins. Rev. J. C. Berryman says of him: "He was an Abolitionist of the Garrison type, and did not hesitate to preach against slavery, publicly as well as privately." Like

---

[3] Gen. J. H. Moore.

many of the fathers, he was very severe on dram-drinking, and made it his special business by preaching and discipline to rid the Church of the evil practice. And so with conformity to the world in dress or fashion. He believed that to insure heaven, the Christian must be crucified to the world. Of course, his plainness of speech and fidelity in preaching the Word and administering discipline made him unpopular with worldly-minded and nominal Methodists, but by the faithful ones few ministers were more highly esteemed than Jesse Haile. " He was very plain in his apparel, usually wearing a Quaker coat and a broad-brimmed hat. His eyes were small, eyebrows heavy, nose large, and hair thin and straight. He was an able debater, particularly strong on the baptismal controversy, and never releasing an opponent until he had completely demolished him. He was very firm and unyielding."[1]

Like Asbury and McKendree, and many of the early preachers, he never married, deeming it his duty to give to the Church his whole time and effort.

Jacob Whitesides, who was this year appointed to Okaw Circuit, was born in North Carolina in 1788, and with his parents moved to Illinois in 1793. He was converted at an early age under the ministry of Rev. John Clark, and was received in the Tennessee Conference in 1814, and appointed to Cold Water and Maramec, and in 1815 to the Missouri Circuit. At the close of his year on the Okaw Circuit he was sent to Cash River and Big-

---

[1] Rev. N. P. Heath.

bay, and the next year to Shoal Creek and Illinois as supernumerary. He continued in this relation and in that of a superannuate until 1822, when he located. Being impressed with the belief that he was providentially called to Arkansas, he removed to that country in 1823, and in 1836 was readmitted in the Arkansas Conference, and appointed to Mount Prairie Circuit, on which he labored two years; in 1838, he was sent to Sulphur Fork, and at the close of the year located. "He had married a Miss Clark, a most estimable and worthy lady, and finely adapted to itinerant work. He was a man of medium height and rather spare. He was full of sympathy and wept much while preaching. As a minister, he was of about average ability, but in piety, zeal, and efficiency, he excelled. He was a good singer, and deeply devoted to the spiritual interests of the young. He was a decided opponent of American slavery; and, after his settlement in Arkansas, he did not cease advocating the cause of the oppressed."[5]

WILLIAM R. JONES, the junior preacher on Cash River and Bigbay Circuit, had just been received in the conference. He was returned to the charge the next year. In 1818 he was sent to Lamoine Circuit, Missouri, and, at the session of 1819, was expelled from the Church.

This was also the first year in the conference of JOHN HARRIS, who was sent to the Wabash Circuit. The next year he was appointed to Hot Springs, and in 1818 to Cash River. He contin-

---

[5] Capt. J. M. Moore.

ued to travel in Missouri and Arkansas, save two years, when he was superannuated, until 1833, when he located. Mr. Beggs relates the following concerning Mr. Harris and his work on the Fishing River Circuit, to which he was appointed in 1823: "It was some time in July that I went up to assist Brother Harris, of the Fishing River Circuit. It was the first camp-meeting held on Brother Baxter's camp-ground, near Liberty, about one hundred miles up the Missouri. Brother Harris and myself were the only Methodist preachers present, and we both preached and exhorted, each in turn. The meeting grew in interest till Monday. I tried to preach on that day, and Brother Harris was to preach a funeral sermon. When I closed, he commenced giving out the hymn,—

> ' And am I born to die,
> To lay this body down?'

When he came to the second verse,—

> 'Soon as from earth I go,
> What will become of me?'

the power of the Almighty came down in such a wonderful manner as is seldom witnessed. Brother Harris fell back in the pulpit, overcome by the influence of the Holy Spirit, and called upon me to invite the people forward for prayers. During my sermon I had noticed that one powerfully built man in the congregation was so filled with the power of God that it was with difficulty he restrained his feelings. Now was the time for him to give vent to his feelings, and his shouts of 'Glory to God in the highest,' were such that the whole congregation seemed thrilled with the power of God. It was as if a current of electricity ran through the assembly, setting on fire with the love of Jesus each soul in divine presence. It was a memorable time; the whole camp-ground was convulsed, and the invitation was no sooner extended than the mourners came pouring forward in a body for prayers till the altar was filled with weeping penitents. It was as if the shouts of his sacramental hosts were heard afar off. The meeting continued that afternoon and all night. Late in the night I went to Brother Baxter's house to get some rest, but the work was so urgent, sinners weeping all over the camp-ground, that I was sent for to come back and continue my exertions; and there we wrestled, the Christian and the sinner, in one common interest, like Jacob of old, till the break of day. On Tuesday morning scarcely a soul remained unconverted or not seeking pardon."

The year was one of only moderate prosperity. On the Illinois Circuit there was a gain of 63 members, on the Okaw of 39, and on the Wabash of 33, whilst on the Cash River and Bigbay Circuit there was a decrease of 95, making a net gain in Illinois for the year of only 41. The entire membership was 998 whites and 11 colored.

CHAPTER II.

1817.

Illinois District—Samuel H. Thompson, P. E.
Illinois—Joseph Pownall.
Okaw—Josiah Patterson.
Cash River and Bigbay—Jacob Whitesides, Wm. R. Jones.
Wabash—Daniel McHenry.

THE Missouri Conference for 1817 was held at Goshen, in the Bethel meeting-house, Madison County, Illinois, October 6th. Bishop Roberts presided and John Scripps was secretary. No changes were made in the plan of the work in Illinois, the circuits remaining the same as they were the year before. The year was one of some prosperity. On the Illinois Circuit, under the labors of Joseph Pownall, there was an increase of 94 members. On the Okaw Circuit, under Josiah Patterson and William Sterrett, there was an increase of 101. The Cash River and Bigbay Circuit, however, traveled by Jacob Whitesides and William R. Jones, reported a decrease of 58; and the Wabash, of which Daniel McHenry was pastor, a decrease of 26. The whole number of members in the territory was 1,107 white and 13 colored.

There were some very valuable accessions to the Methodist population of Illinois this year. Amongst them was, SAMUEL MITCHELL, who settled near

Belleville. He had been a resident of Botetourt County, Virginia. For more than half a century he labored as a local preacher. He was a man of great natural endowments, of prepossessing and dignified personal appearance, of most winning and affable manners, and a very able, acceptable, and useful preacher. Before leaving Virginia he manumitted his slaves, and selected a home in a free State, where his children could grow up free from the contaminating influence of slavery.[1] He was the father of John T. and James Mitchell.

Another of the notable accessions to the Church this year was ZADOC CASEY, who settled at Mt. Vernon, in Jefferson County. He was born in Georgia in 1798, but at an early age removed to Tennessee. He enjoyed but few educational advantages in his youth, having attended school but three months, and not learning to write until manhood. Yet by his own efforts he became a well-read and intelligent man, and was honored by his fellow-citizens with some of the most important offices in the land. In 1828 he became a member of the State Legislature. In 1830 he was elected lieutenant-governor, and was said to be one of the best presiding officers the senate ever had. In 1832 he was elected to Congress, in which he served ten years, and where he acquired an honorable reputation for attention to business, for punctuality in attending the sessions, and for his sound mind and judgment. He was afterwards a member of the State Constitutional Convention of 1848, and often

---

[1] General Minutes.

afterwards a member of the Legislature. For over forty years he was a faithful and useful local preacher. At the conference at Madison, Indiana, in 1828, he was elected to elder's orders. He was a natural orator, always commanding large congregations, and making a favorable impression on his hearers. He was a man of fine personal appearance, of remarkable suavity of manners, yet modest, retiring, and unassuming. He died September 12, 1862.

An amusing anecdote is told of the influence Methodism was already exerting in the country, and illustrating the zeal and fidelity of the pioneer preachers. A Pennsylvanian of German descent, named Richard Wilhelm, had settled this year in what is now Staunton Township, in Macoupin County. He and his family lived for some time in the hollow of a sycamore-tree ten feet in diameter. He had a great dread of Methodists. Soon learning, however, that the preachers were coming, he sold out his claim and moved southward. When asked what was his destination, he declared that he was going until he found a country a good deal hotter than this, but that he would get away from the Methodists. He was last heard from in Texas.

Of JOSEPH POWNAL, who labored in Illinois for the first time this year, we have but little information. He was received on trial in the Ohio Conference in 1814 and appointed to Marietta, and in 1815 to Steubenville. In 1816 he appears in the Missouri Conference, and was sent to Silver Creek, the next year to Illinois, the two following years to

Blue River, and at the conference of 1820 he located. At the session of the Illinois Conference, held at Charleston, Indiana, in 1825, he was elected to elders' orders.

WILLIAM STERRETT, who this year traveled as junior preacher on the Okaw Circuit, but whose name does not appear on the Minutes, deserves more than the mere mention of his name. He was born in Pennsylvania about 1790, and while yet a boy, came with his parents to the Territory of Illinois, and settled in the American Bottom near Kaskaskia. He was converted in early life. His conversion was so clear and powerful as to give tone to all his after life. Possessed of rare natural gifts and enjoying much of the grace of God, his father, who was then a Presbyterian, resolved to educate him for the ministry of that Church. But a great revival occurring under the auspices of the Methodists in the neighborhood, both father and son were led to become members of the Methodist Episcopal Church. Young Sterrett served in the war with Great Britain from its beginning to its close as a private soldier in Captain Moore's company of mounted rangers. Whilst in the service he was detailed with a squad as guard to a boat load of provisions destined for some point on the upper Mississippi. Whilst on their way, entering a group of islands thickly covered with willows, they were suddenly assailed by a deadly fire from savages in ambuscade, whilst a heavy wind was driving them directly into the power of the foe. So sudden and unexpected was the assault, and so perilous the situation, that the pilot, pale with terror, deserted his post, leaving the boat to drift before the wind. Mr. Sterrett, amid whizzing bullets, some of which penetrated his clothing, sprang to the helm, and succeeded by his coolness and courage in saving the boat and crew from destruction. He was naturally very diffident, and it was only at the earnest solicitation of the Church that he consented to receive license to preach. During this year, whilst serving as junior preacher under Josiah Patterson on the Okaw Circuit, his zeal impelled him to labors beyond his strength, and he was compelled at the close of the year to retire from the itinerant field, and henceforth labor only in a local sphere. This he did efficiently and usefully. After some years he removed to St. Louis, where he faithfully served the Church as local preacher, class leader, and financial agent, until his death. He was the father of S. T. Sterrett, formerly of the Illinois, but now of the California Conference.[2]

---

[2] Capt. J. M. Moore.

CHAPTER III.

1818.

ILLINOIS DISTRICT—Jesse Haile, P. E.
Shoal Creek and Illinois—S. H. Thompson, Thomas
    Hellums, Jacob Whitesides, Sup.
Okaw—Josiah Patterson.
Cash River—John Harris.
Bigbay—Thomas Davis.
Wabash—Charles Slocumb.

THE year 1818 was an important one in the history of Illinois. The State was that year admitted into the Union. The population had increased to about forty-five thousand; fifteen counties had been already organized, and settlements were spreading more rapidly than in any previous period of its history. The treaty of Edwardsville, entered into this year, by which the Kickapoo Indians ceded to the United States ten million acres of land, embracing all the central portion of the State, opened up for the settlement a vast region, unsurpassed in fertility, and directed to Illinois a stream of emigration from most of the older States of the Union. To keep up with the advancing population, the bishop, presiding at the session of the Missouri Conference, which was held at the Bethel meeting-house, where the previous session had been held, and not at Mt. Zion meeting-house, in Murphy's settlement, as announced in the General Minutes, made several changes in the circuits. The number was increased to six, though two of them were united, and, instead of the five preachers of the year before, seven were now employed. A Shoal Creek Circuit was formed, embracing the settlements on both sides of that stream and on the Upper Okaw, though connected for the time with the Illinois Circuit, and Cash River and Bigbay were separated. Jesse Haile, who had traveled the Illinois Circuit two years before, succeeded Samuel H. Thompson on the district, whilst Mr. Thompson was put in charge of the combined Illinois and Shoal Creek Circuits, with Thomas Hellums as assistant, and Jacob Whitesides, supernumerary. Josiah Patterson was returned to the Okaw Circuit; John Harris, who had traveled the Wabash Circuit two years before, was appointed to Cash River; Thomas Davis, a new man in the State, was sent to Bigbay; and Charles Slocumb to Wabash. There was an increase in the membership this year of three hundred and thirty-two, mostly in the Illinois, Shoal Creek, and Okaw charges, the membership for the year being reported at 1435 whites and 17 colored.

THOMAS HELLUMS was brought up by pious parents, who from childhood taught him the way of the Lord. In 1805 he was received on trial in the Western Conference, and appointed to Red River Circuit; the next year he was sent to White River; in 1807 to Shelby, and in 1808 to Natchez. His appointment in 1809 was Nashville, in 1810

Tennessee Valley, the next year Cumberland, and
in 1812, falling into the Ohio Conference, he was
sent to Licking. At the close of this year, says
Redford, " worn down by constant toil and exposure, he was compelled to seek for rest, and in 1813
asked for a location. In a local sphere he first engaged in teaching school as a means of support, but,
compelled to relinquish this for want of health, he
entered upon the practice of law, having previously
studied that profession. Impressed, however, with
the belief that it embarrassed his ministerial and
Christian standing, he abandoned it." In 1818 he
was readmitted in the Missouri Conference, and appointed, as stated above, to the Illinois and Shoal
Creek Circuit as junior preacher. At the close of
the year he again located. The remainder of his
sad history is given by Rev. Jonathan Stamper in
the Home Circle, Vol. 3:

"Under protracted affliction of body his mind
became a ruin, and the remainder of his life was
spent in a state of partial insanity. During this
period he traveled extensively and preached often ;
and it is remarkable that no trace of derangement
could be seen in his discourses. He investigated
subjects with clearness and force, but immediately
after leaving the pulpit exhibited signs of his mal-
ady. He was fearful of all who came near, imagining them to be enemies who were trying to injure
him, and often exhibited defensive weapons as a
means of deterring them. The end of this good
brother was melancholy. While traveling in what
was then the Territory of Arkansas, he fell in with

some acquaintances, who induced him to attend a camp-meeting. But he seemed to be greatly harassed by fear from the time he reached the camp-ground, and could not be persuaded to preach until some time of the day on Sunday, when he took the stand, and preached one of the most lucid and powerful sermons those present had ever heard. On leaving the pulpit he became deeply deranged, manifesting alarm at the approach of his best friends, whom he forbade to come near him, at the same time showing in his hand a large knife. He at length got his horse and started from the meeting (which was held on the border of an immense prairie) out into the trackless waste, and has never been heard of since."

THOMAS DAVIS, who was this year on Bigbay Circuit, united with the Tennessee Conference in 1815, and was appointed to Vincennes. The next year, from the Missouri Conference, he was sent to Patoka, and in 1817 to Little Pigeon. In 1819–20 he traveled the Wabash Circuit; for the two following years he was on the Cape Girardeau Circuit, in Missouri; in 1823, he labored on the Shoal Creek Circuit; and, in 1824, he was appointed from the Illinois Conference to Mt. Carmel. In 1825 he was again on the Wabash Circuit. For the four following years he labored in Indiana, and at the conference of 1830 he located. He afterwards united with the Methodist Protestant Church.

CHARLES SLOCUMB was received on trial at the first session of the Missouri Conference, and appointed to Vincennes and Harrison, and the next year to Patoka. In 1819 he was sent to the Mt. Carmel Circuit, but his health failing, he was placed on the superannuated list at the end of the year, and in 1821 he located. Six years afterwards he was readmitted in the Illinois Conference, and sent to Patoka Circuit, but at the close of the year he again located. In 1833 he was once more readmitted, and appointed to Shawneetown, and at the expiration of the year was again granted a location, and in this relation he continued until his death. He settled in White County, near Carmi. One who knew him well, says of him: "He was deeply religious. He was very popular as a preacher, and preached the funeral sermons for all the country for miles around. In his manner he was very pathetic, his sermons often producing a powerful effect on his hearers. He was especially strong on the baptismal controversy. He was considered by the people as a great preacher." "Mr. Maffitt, in describing the Eastern preachers," says Mr. Beggs, "spoke of their method as being, as a general rule, systematic and phlegmatic; but the Western preachers—their voice was like a mountain horn. Our camp-meetings were peculiarly the school of this style, in which the appeals had all the freedom of the open air and the winds and the directness and speed of the lightning. I attended such a meeting at Mt. Carmel, in 1825, over which S. H. Thompson, presiding elder, presided. The converts in those days were born strong into the kingdom, and entered it shouting.

"Charles Slocumb, who labored in the Wabash region, was such a preacher as I have described, a local preacher, yet his ministrations were invariably attended with great power. At the above camp-meeting, a most hardened sinner was forced to cry for mercy under one of his powerful sermons. He was portraying the misery of the damned, when this man, an old Revolutionary soldier, who had been standing on the outskirts of the throng, came rushing towards the altar, crying at the top of his voice, 'Quarter! quarter!' Falling on his knees, he exclaimed, 'I am an old soldier; I fought through the Revolutionary war, I have heard the cannon roar in battle, and seen the blood pour forth in streams; but since God made me, I have never heard such cannonading as that. I yield! I yield!" Mr. Slocumb " was a fine, spirited man, a strong, useful, and popular preacher. He died in 1844. His death was peaceful and triumphant."[1]

[1] Rev. J. H. Dickens.

CHAPTER IV.

·1819.

ILLINOIS DISTRICT—David Sharp, P. E.
Illinois—Samuel H. Thompson.
Okaw—James Lowry.
Cash River—Josiah Patterson.
Wabash—Thomas Davis.
Mt. Carmel—Charles Slocumb.

THE fourth session of the Missouri Conference was held at McKendree Chapel, Cape Girardeau County, Missouri, beginning September 14, 1819. The chapel in which the conference was held was probably the first church edifice erected west of the Mississippi River. It was built of poplar logs, under the direction of Jesse Walker, in 1807 or 8, and in 1882 was still standing and in good repair, though some alterations had been made in the arrangement of the building. Some changes were made in the work in Illinois. The name of Shoal Creek disappears, and the Illinois Circuit stands as before 1818. The Bigbay Circuit also disappears, probably connected with Cash River, and a new charge, Mt. Carmel, was formed from the Wabash Circuit.

The town of Mt. Carmel, from which the circuit was named, had been settled by a Methodist colony from Ohio. A company, of whom Thomas S. Hinde, Wm. McDowell, and Dr. Stubbs were the chief, had purchased, in 1817, a tract of land from a Mr. Greathouse, on the bank of the Wabash, three miles below the Grand Rapids, and sent out REV. WILLIAM BEAUCHAMP, as their agent, to lay off the town. Mr. Beauchamp, after laboring with great success as a traveling preacher for several years in New England, New York, and Pittsburg, and as a local preacher in Western Virginia, had for one year been editing the *Western Christian Monitor*, at Chillicothe, Ohio, the only religious paper then published in the Church. With his family and assistants, he moved in a boat down the Scioto and Ohio and up the Wabash, holding family prayer regularly, observing the Sabbath, and traveling as befitted a Methodist colony. In the first cabin that was erected after their arrival he organized a Church, composed of his own family, the carpenter, the blacksmith, some laborers, and two colored boys. Soon afterwards their number was increased by the addition of other Methodist families who removed to the town. Mr. Beauchamp himself was preacher, doctor, and surveyor for the colony. Dr. Stevens says of him: "He showed himself the truly great man in all the details of this new business, planning public measures and economical arrangement; devising mechanical improvements, for which he had a rare genius; directing the instruction of the youth, and simplifying its modes; ministering as pastor to the congregation, and meanwhile advancing in his own studies and improvement." Before leaving Chillicothe, he had drawn up a charter for the government of the colony which was adopted by the Illinois Territorial Legislature at its session in 1817, and, under this old charter, the municipal government has ever since been administered. It is a remarkably well-planned document for the design of the proprietors.

In 1821 Mr. Beauchamp retired to his farm, three miles from Mt. Carmel. Soon after this he lost his only son, a promising boy of fourteen. He then re-entered the itinerant ranks, and was stationed one year in St. Louis, at the end of which he was appointed presiding elder of the Indiana District. He was a member of the General Conference of 1824, and such was the estimate his brethren had of his talents and piety that he came within a few votes of being elected bishop. He returned from the General Conference in feeble health, and died at Paoli, Indiana, just before the first session of the Illinois Conference, in his fifty-third year. Mr. Beauchamp was about five feet, eight inches in height, slender but well-proportioned, with dark hair, sallow complexion, and thin visage. " His features were regular and oval, his head, forehead, and face well-proportioned. There was nothing remarkable in his appearance, even his eye in repose seeming languid and uninterested. But when aroused all this was changed, and every feature was eloquent. Usually, he impressed one with a reserve bordering on austerity; yet in conversation none could be more interesting or adaptive. In a company of select friends his soul expanded as at a mental feast. In public speaking his voice was uniform, remarkably soft, but became loud and energetic in argument. His gestures were natural and easy. One of his much-admired traits was that, in preaching, when dwelling on the promises and invitations of the Gospel, there was a soft tenderness, a sweetness in his voice, interrupted frequently by gentle breaks, as if the swelling sympathies of his heart obstructed his utterance, when a gentle, thrilling sensation appeared to move the listening multitude, all bending forward to catch every word as it fell from his lips. But when he became argumentative, and especially when assailing false doctrines, his tone was elevated, his whole system nerved, his voice assumed a deep, hollow tone, was elevated to its utmost pitch, and fell like peals of thunder on the assembly. On one occasion, while engaged in controversy, his antagonist, who had sat and listened for some length of time to arguments too powerful for him to answer, began to look terrified, as if the voice which he now heard came from another world. He arose, apparently with the design of leaving the house, but was seemingly so overcome that he had no power to do so; he staggered, caught by the railing, reeled and fell into his seat, and there remained, overwhelmed and confounded, until Beauchamp had concluded, when he quickly left the house." [1]

"He was a man of refined taste and gentlemanly manners. He was possessed of great versatility, and could adapt himself to all classes. As a preacher, he was attractive and impressive, solemn and eloquent, and very popular. Besides his numerous essays and newspaper articles, he was the author of

---

[2] *Methodist Magazine.*

a work on the 'Evidences of Christianity,' that was widely and deservedly popular. Besides his son, he had three daughters, who were married, one of them to Aaron Wood; but all died childless. When Mr. Beauchamp lived in Virginia, and his sister married a slaveholder, he uttered the following prayer: 'O God, write all my children childless rather than the latest generation from me should ever own a slave.' "[2]

At the time Mt. Carmel was laid out, Wabash County, of which it is now the county-seat, was not organized, but constituted a part of Edwards County. Its county-seat was Palmyra, a town of about three hundred inhabitants, at the Wabash Rapids, three miles above Mt. Carmel. There was the United States Land-office, and there, before 1820, was a branch of the old State Bank of Illinois. Afterwards the county-seat was removed to Albion. The growing town, Mt. Carmel, drew off the population from Palmyra, and where was once a flourishing village is now a forest.

It is worthy of note that this was the first circuit in Illinois named after the chief town and post-office in it. Generally the circuits were called by the names of the streams upon which they were situated; and as some of these streams are two or three hundred miles long, it is not always easy to ascertain the location or boundaries of the circuits named from them. It is only recently that the importance has been seen of naming the charge after the chief town in it.

------

[2] Dr. A. Wood.

The year was a very prosperous one. The country was settling more rapidly than ever, and new Methodist societies were formed in every direction.

REV. JOSEPH CURTIS, who had just removed from Ohio, formed the first class this year in what is now Edgar County, in the house of Col. Jonathan Mayo, the first settler in that region. The class consisted of seven persons; namely, Jonathan Mayo and wife, John Stratton and wife, Joseph Curtis and wife, and Sallie Whitley. Three of these—Mr. and Mrs. Mayo and Mrs. Curtis—were still living in 1882.

Mr. Curtis was also first to proclaim the Word of God in Edgar County. He was a man of moderate preaching ability, but a consistent Christian and an industrious local preacher, enjoying the confidence of the community.

The Pinckard family moved from Ohio this year, and settled at Alton in the Fall of 1819. NATHANIEL PINCKARD, the father, was a native of Virginia. He was a very acceptable and useful local preacher. In early life he had been a missionary to the West Indies under Dr. Coke, and for several years had charge of an academy at Kingston, Jamaica. He was a man of fine education, and spent much of his life in teaching. As soon as his cabin was erected in Upper Alton, he commenced preaching in it on the Sabbath, and soon it became the regular preaching-place for the appointment. One of his sons, William G., and his son-in-law, Mr. Heath, erected the first cabin in what is now Alton City. Three of his grandsons became Methodist preachers,—

N. P. Heath and John C. Pinckard, of the Illinois Conference, and P. M. Pinckard, of the Methodist Episcopal Church South. One of his granddaughters became the wife of C. P. Baldwin, of the Illinois Conference, and another the wife of T. W. Chandler, who died a member of the Southern Illinois Conference. In the Spring of 1820 BENNETT MAXEY, a local preacher from Ohio, settled near Mr. Pinckard, and alternated with him in preaching to the people. Amongst the new-comers to Sangamon County were the Husseys, who settled on Fancy Creek, and were, indeed, the first settlers in that part of the county. For many years the house of Nathan Hussey, the father, was a preaching-place; and most of his large family of children became active and useful members of the Church. His eldest son, William, has long been a pillar in the Church on Williamsville Circuit. A camp-ground was established in the neighborhood, where many souls found the Savior, and where the writer of these sketches experienced his second birth.

This year the Ross family moved from New York and settled at Atlas, in what is now Pike County. Some of them were, or afterwards became, Methodists, but a society was not formed there for some time.

JOHN D. GILHAM settled this year on the Piasa, in what is now Jersey County, and it was not long until a flourishing society was formed in his neighborhood.

In the Spring of 1820 several persons who were, or afterwards became, Methodists, settled in Morgan

County. Amongst them were the Wyatts, James Deaton, Jesse Ruble, and James Gilham, who all became leading members of the Church in different parts of the county.

Amongst the visitors to the country this year was the eccentric Lorenzo Dow. Paying a visit to Fort Clark, he preached quite extensively in the State as he was going and returning, attracting everywhere huge congregations, and making impressions upon his hearers that have never been forgotten.

The increase in the number of members reported this year was 419, a gain of nearly thirty per cent. The whole number at the close of the year was 1864 whites and 7 colored.

During this year the first missionary society in the State was formed. The following detailed account of it is taken from the *Methodist Magazine;* "At a meeting of the citizens of Mt. Carmel, in Edwards County, Illinois, Saturday afternoon, July 22, 1820, to take into consideration the establishment of an Indian free school and Indian mission, Elias Stone, a traveling preacher, was chosen chairman, and Thomas S. Hinde, secretary. After an address by W. Beauchamp, a Methodist Missionary Society was organized, and a constitution adopted. The president elected was David Sharp, P. E.; Wm. Beauchamp, vice-president; Thomas S. Hinde, secretary; Scoby Stewart, treasurer, and John Ingersoll, John Tilton, Edward Ulm, Thomas Gould, Joshua Beall, managers."

Two new men appear as connected with the work

this year, David Sharp as presiding elder of.the district, and James Lowry, sent to the Okaw Circuit.

DAVID SHARP was born of Quaker parents in the State of New Jersey, September 5, 1787. In 1800 he removed with them to Logan County, Ohio. When in his twentieth year he was converted and united with the Methodist Episcopal Church. This step brought on him the displeasure of his parents, and, though they afterwards became reconciled to it, he was compelled, for a time, to find a home away from his father's house. In his twenty-third year he was licensed to preach, and employed by the presiding elder to travel a circuit. He united with the Ohio Conference in 1813, and was appointed to Whitewater Circuit in Indiana. During the four following years he traveled successively White Oak, Lawrenceburg, Piqua, and Milford Circuits. The following year he was transferred to Missouri Conference and appointed to Silver Creek; and the next year, as stated above, he succeeded Jesse Haile on the Illinois District, on which he remained two years. In 1824 he was transferred to the Ohio Conference and appointed to Grand River. The next year he fell into the Pittsburg Conference, in which he remained until 1849. For four years of this time he was on the Pittsburg District, and during the remainder in some of the most important stations and circuits in the conference. In 1849 he was transferred again to the Ohio Conference, in which he continued until his death. For the last six years of his life he was on. the superannuated list. He died April 21, 1865, in his seventy-eighth year. As a preacher " his discourses were respectable, but not extraordinary. It may be said, however, of his performances and of himself, that he never made great pretensions, and never wearied his hearers with long discourses. It has often been said that his sermons were like trees with more fruit than blossoms or foliage. He was punctual. It was a rare occurrence for him to be absent from, or too late at, an appointment. It is said that his judgment of law and the order of business in quarterly conferences commanded universal respect. He was an unassuming, modest man, clothed with humility, uniformly pious. Indeed, we think, what was said of Barnabas might in truth be applied to him, ' He was a good man, full of the Holy Ghost, and of faith.' He died well. The religion he had so long and faithfully preached to others was his theme and solace in the chamber of his sickness and on his dying bed. While his vigorous constitution and retentive memory were yielding to the weight of years and the power of disease, his inner man, unimpaired, not only retained but magnified the grace of God in Christ. The same cheerfulness of mind which had alleviated the burdens and sweetened the sorrows of life, now imparted its hallowing influences to the closing scene." [3]

JAMES LOWRY traveled but two years. He was received into the Missouri Conference in 1818, and appointed to Mt. Prairie and Pecan Point. At the close of his year on Okaw Circuit he was discontinued, and we have no further account of him.

---

[3] General Minutes.

CHAPTER V.

1820.

Illinois District—David Sharp, P. E.
Illinois—Alexander McAllister.
Okaw—Hackaliah Vredenburg.
Cash River—Francis Moore.
Wabash—Thomas Davis.
Mt. Carmel—John Stewart.
Sangamo—James Simms.
Shoal Creek—Josiah Patterson.

THE year 1820 was a very prosperous one for Methodism in Illinois. It began with a revival, and revival influences were felt in most of the districts throughout the entire year. The session of the Missouri Conference was held at Shiloh, in the Illinois Circuit, beginning September 13th. Bishop Roberts presided. In connection with the conference session, as was then the almost universal practice in the West, a camp-meeting was held, which continued for nearly two weeks. Over one hundred persons were converted. It was, as S. H. Thompson declared, " a grand jubilee," and the preachers went out from it to their new fields of labor, " strong in the Lord and in the power of his might." The number of circuits in the district was increased from five to seven. The Shoal Creek Circuit was now established as a permanent charge,

and a new circuit was formed in the rapidly settling
Sangamon region. The name of this circuit was
first written Sangamo, then Sangamaugh, then San-
gama, and finally Sangamon. This region began to
be settled about 1817. In that year Henry Fun-
derburk settled on Horse Creek. The next year
the Drennans, William and Joseph, whose house was
afterwards a preaching-place, settled on Sugar Creek,
a few miles from where Chatham now stands. In
1819 JOSEPH DIXON, who had settled at Shiloh, in
St. Clair County, as early as 1806, moved to Sangamon County, and settled on Horse Creek. His
home was also one of the first preaching-places,
and he became one of the most efficient stewards in
the circuit. His conversion was under peculiar circumstances. He was a great hunter, and frequently
made long trips to the unsettled portions of the
country, returning from them laden with peltries.
In connection with two others, he had gone on a
trapping expedition several hundred miles up the
Missouri River. He spent two Winters there—the
first with his companions, in a cave dug out of the
side of a hill, and the second alone; for his companions had quarreled with him and deserted him.
Whilst there in solitude, his eyes became inflamed,
and he eventually lost his sight. In this helpless
condition, reflecting upon his past life and his want
of preparation for death, he fell upon his knees and
asked God to have mercy on him and deliver him,
promising that if he would deliver him, he would
serve him all the rest of his life. His prayer was
heard; he was directed to the use of means by

which his sight was restored; and as he recognized
in this the hand of God, and fell before him to return thanks for the cure that had been wrought, he
felt a sweet peace filling his soul, and then realized
that his sins were forgiven and he was made a child
of God. In the Summer, after a successful season
of trapping, after many narrow escapes, he returned
to St. Louis, sold his furs for several thousand dollars, and then, with his family, from whom he had
been absent nearly three years, removed to the Sangamon country, and became a useful and active
steward and exhorter in the Church. In the Spring
of 1821, a church, to which the name of Zion
Chapel was given, was built chiefly by his agency,
and to which he afterwards deeded five acres of
ground for church and cemetery purposes. It continued to be used for worship until 1843, when it
was burned down. Mr. Dixon died at the residence of a daughter, in Morgan County, in 1844.

Another person who settled in Sangamon County
this year, and became an active and influential
Methodist, was JOHN COOPER. He was born in
South Carolina, June 3, 1794, but with his parents
moved to Tennessee in childhood. He was a faithful, laborious, and useful local preacher, preaching
nearly as much as the traveling preachers, and with
great acceptability to the people. He was a justice
of the peace and county commissioner for many
years. He died in June, 1860.

In the Fall of this year NATHAN SCARRITT and
his wife Latty moved from New Hampshire to Edwardsville, Illinois. He was born in Connecticut,

she in New Hampshire. They were married about 1812. Both were religious before marriage. They were the parents of ten sons and two daughters. In 1821 they moved from Edwardsville to Scarritt's Prairie. When he went to the spot he had selected to build a house, he laid down his tools and knelt upon the prairie-grass, and invoked God's blessing. The family altar was a fixture in his dwelling, and incense ascended as regularly as the morning and evening meal were eaten.[1] He died fully conscious, and in great peace and holy triumph, December 12, 1847. He was, during most of his religious life, an officer in the Church, and as a class-leader he had few superiors. His wife lived a widow twenty-eight years, and died at her son's, in Kansas City, December 7, 1875. Of their sons, Dr. N. Scarritt is an honored member of the Methodist Episcopal Church South, and Jotham A. Scarritt has been for many years an active and influential minister in the Southern Illinois Conference.

Other settlements were formed about the same time on Rock Creek and Spring Creek. The newly formed circuit embraced the settlements on both sides of the Sangamon River and the streams running into it; and as this was for some time the most northern circuit in the district, the preachers followed up the rapidly extending settlements, until in 1824 the circuit reached as far north as Randolph Grove, in what is now McLean County.

On most of the charges there was an increase in the membership this year, Cash River being the

---

[1] Rev. J. A. Scarritt.

only one reporting a decrease. The camp-meeting season was especially prosperous. A large number were held in the district, two or three in each charge, and at most of them large numbers were converted. Two of these meetings were held on the Mt. Carmel Circuit this year, of which Mr. Beauchamp gives an account that is quoted by Dr. Bangs in his history of the Church. The first was held about thirty-five miles south-west of Mt. Carmel, commencing on Friday and closing on the following Monday. About twenty professed faith in Christ. The second was held near Mt. Carmel, continuing for the same time, and resulted in the conversion of about forty-five, twenty-three of whom united with the Church. Among the converts were the CORRIE family, who had removed from Kircudbright County, Scotland, the year before, and had settled some miles north of Mt. Carmel, in what was afterwards Lawrence County. The family had been raised Presbyterians; but the mother only knew any thing of experimental religion. At the camp-meeting, the father, his son John, then a youth of seventeen, three daughters, and two cousins, who had come to America with them, were all converted in the course of a few hours, and united with the Church. John, in 1834, removed to Schuyler County, and for many years has been a pillar in the Church. The eldest daughter, Agnes, married John Scripps, and was long a mother in Israel, and all the family, so far as known, held fast their confidence unto the end.

The Gospel continued to spread and new societies to be formed as the settlements extended. This year the first sermon was preached in what afterwards became Macoupin County. The preacher was Parham Randle, a local preacher, who was then living near Edwardsville, and the place was the cabin of Richard Chapman, in what is now Dorchester Township. Mr. Chapman's house continued to be a preaching-place for several years.

This year Jacob Lurton moved from Kentucky, and settled on the Piasa, a few miles from Alton, where he became an active laborer. He had entered the traveling connection in 1786, and had traveled in succession the West Jersey Circuit, in New Jersey; Berkeley, in Virginia; Redstone, in Pennsylvania; Clarksburg and Kanawha, in Virginia; Baltimore and Harford, in Maryland; Salt River, in Kentucky; and Cumberland, in Tennessee and Kentucky. While in this circuit he preached in the cabin of the father of Peter Cartwright with great power, while the congregation were melted to tears. His health having failed, he retired from the itinerant work, and spent the rest of his days in a local relation, preaching, however, whenever his health would permit. He was an original genius, a real son of thunder, and a faithful and useful minister of the Gospel. He died at his home in Illinois in great peace.

The increase in membership for the entire district was 530, and the whole number of members reported was 2,401 whites, and 20 colored.

Alexander McAllister, who was this year sent to Illinois Circuit, was a native of Kentucky.

He was converted in the Fall of 1812, was received in the Missouri Conference in 1816, and appointed to Cape Girardeau and New Madrid. With the exception of his year in Illinois, his whole itinerant life was spent in Missouri. Between his admission and 1832, when he finally located, he was seven years on circuits, four years presiding elder, two years superannuated, one year supernumerary, and two years local. After his last location he entered into the mercantile business in Rushville, Illinois, in partnership with John Scripps, and died at the residence of Mr. Scripps, in March, 1834, while his family were still residing in St. Louis. Mr. McAllister was tall and rather slender in form, very pleasant and affable in manner, a preacher of more than ordinary ability, always well received in his charges, and popular with those to whom he ministered. "Though a mechanic, with a very limited education at the beginning of his ministerial career, he very soon attained a high position as a preacher of the Gospel. Indeed, he seems to have had few equals, and fewer, if any, superiors in his field and day. His strong mind, original power of thought, clear perception, and cool judgment soon made him the favorite champion of the cause he had espoused; and this, combined with his indomitable energy, decision of character, and strict habits of study and business, placed him in the front rank of the ministry, where he made a deep and lasting impression on the public mind."[2]

This was HACKALIAH VREDENBURG'S first year

____

[2] Dr. McAnally.

in the itinerancy. He was born in Westchester County, New York, May 10, 1790. In 1817, he settled in Terre Haute, Indiana, and three years afterwards united with the Missouri Conference. After filling his appointment on Okaw Circuit, he was sent in 1821 to Wabash, and in 1822 to Honey Creek. In 1823 he formed the Vermillion Circuit, to which he was returned from the Illinois Conference the next year. In 1825 he was appointed to Crawfordsville, and at the close of the year was granted a location. In 1831 he was readmitted and appointed to Logansport. The next year he fell into the Indiana Conference, and continued to travel until 1840, when he was granted a superannuated relation, in which he continued until his death, with the exception of one year, when he traveled Prairieville Circuit. In 1844 he fell into the North Indiana Conference, and in 1852 into the North-west Indiana, and thus was a member of five different annual conferences without ever having been transferred. "Most of Brother Vredenburg's itinerant life was spent in the valley of the Wabash. From its mouth almost to its source he preached, organizing new societies and circuits, carrying the Gospel message to the scattered settlements, and enduring all the exposures and privations of pioneer life. In one of his charges no house could be found to shelter his wife and children while he traveled his circuit of three or four hundred miles round. Rather than leave his work, he took possession of a deserted log stable, and, fitting it up with his own hands, made that the parsonage for the year. At other times, he was compelled on his rest days to cultivate a small piece of ground to supply his family with food, the pittance received being barely sufficient to furnish them with clothing. But amid all these privations and dangers, this faithful minister was always at his post, rarely missing an appointment, and never deserting his trust."[3] One who knew him well for nearly fifty years, says: "He was a good, plain preacher, and an energetic, good man. He died at the residence of his son-in-law in Wisconsin, January 23, 1869. Before his death his sight had become dim and his body exceedingly feeble; yet his mind was clear and strong, and his memory of the incidents and labors of his itinerant life unimpaired. When told by his physician that he could live but a little while, and that he had better prepare for death, he replied, "I have been doing so all my life."

The itinerant career of FRANCIS MOORE began and closed on the Cash River Circuit. He was received on trial in the conference this year, returned to the circuit in 1821, and at the close of the year discontinued. We have no further account of him.

JOHN STEWART was born in Sussex County, New Jersey, in 1795. In his twentieth year he was converted and joined the Methodist Episcopal Church. In 1817 he was received in the Ohio Conference and appointed to Little Kanawha Circuit. In 1818 he was sent to Mahoning, and in 1819 was transferred to the Missouri Conference, and appointed to Blue River. At the close of his

---

[3] General Minutes.

year at Mt. Carmel, he was assigned to Vincennes, and the next year was transferred again to the Ohio Conference, of which he remained a member until death. For fifty years he sustained an effective relation to the Church, serving as presiding elder for eleven years, and laboring on circuits and stations thirty-nine years. In 1866 he was placed on the superannuated list, and continued in that relation until his death, March 10, 1876. "He was a good preacher and a wise administrator. Truly devoted to God and the interests of the Church of his choice, he gave full proof of his calling as a minister of the Word. On some of his charges he was eminently successful in winning souls to Christ."[4] His year on the Mt. Carmel Circuit was a very laborious one, as well as a very successful one. His labors may be seen in the fact that his circuit embraced four county seats, those of Edwards, Crawford, Clark, and Wayne Counties, and his success is seen in the increase of the membership from 146 to 310.

JAMES SIMMS was a native of Virginia. In early life he moved to South Carolina, where he married. He afterwards removed to Kentucky, thence to St. Clair County, Illinois, and in the Spring of 1820 to Sangamon County. He settled on Sugar Creek, where he built a horse-mill, quarrying the stone and preparing the burrs for his mill himself. He was converted when young, and licensed to preach while in Kentucky. He labored as a traveling preacher only this year, and was discontinued at its

---

[4] General Minutes.

close. On the organization of Sangamon County he was appointed treasurer, but refused to qualify. He was the first representative from the county in the State Legislature. He afterwards moved to Morgan County, where in February, 1829, he aided in forming the first Methodist Protestant Church in Illinois, of which he became the first circuit preacher. He was a tall venerable looking man, mild in his manners, kind-hearted, very devout, and possessed of the qualities that made men popular in those early days. He was said to be a powerful preacher. He died of consumption February 20, 1844.

CHAPTER VI.

1821.

Illinois District— David Sharp, P. E.
Mt. Carmel—Robert Delap.
Wabash—Hackaliah Vredenburg, Thomas Rice.
Cash River—Francis Moore.
Okaw—Josiah Patterson.
Illinois—James Scott, Parham Randle.
Shoal Creek—Jesse Haile, Jacob Whitesides, Sup.
Sangamon—John Glanville.

THE sixth session of the Missouri Conference
was held at McKendree Chapel, Cape Girar-
dean County, Missouri, beginning October 17th.
Bishop George presided. The appointments in Illinois remained the same as they were the year before,
but more laborers were employed. To the Wabash,
Illinois, and Shoal Creek Circuits were assigned two
men each. The year was not marked by extensive
revivals, no circuit reporting a large increase, and
only thirty-six additional members being returned
in the entire district. Yet there was some progress
made in the organization of new societies, and the
spread of Methodism in the new settlements. The
first society was formed this year in Jacksonville.
John Glanville, who was on the Sangamon Circuit,
formed a class in the house of John Jordan in the
east part of the town, and this continued to be the

preaching place for several years. It was afterwards moved to the log school-house, which was used by Methodists and Presbyterians alternately, until church edifices were erected by them. But the honor of introducing the Gospel into Jacksonville belongs to JOSEPH BASEY, a local preacher, who had settled south-west of Jerseyville, but who afterwards removed to Morgan County. In 1821 he preached the first sermon in the county, and continued his labors as a pioneer to the new-comers until the settlements were organized into a circuit. He was elected to deacon's orders at the conference of 1835. He afterwards removed to Platteville, Wisconsin, and entered upon the practice of medicine, to which he had been educated. He was a very useful and successful local preacher, and quite successful in his profession as a physician. He lived and died respected by all who knew him.[1]

The first society was also formed this year in Springfield through the instrumentality of James Simms. The society worshiped in the house, and sometimes in the office of C. R. Matheny, the county clerk; afterwards in a school-house, and it was not until 1830 that a church was erected. This year, too, the Sharon Society was organized in Fayette County, about a mile east of the present town of Vera. Here WILLIAM PADON was converted this year, who was licensed to preach in 1835, and has ever since been a most laborious and successful local preacher.

The whole number of members reported for the

____
[1] Rev. N. P. Heath.

year was 2,417 whites and 40 colored. Several new names appear in the district this year.

ROBERT DELAP united with the Ohio Conference in 1819. His first appointment was Miami. The next year he traveled the Scioto Circuit. In 1821 he became a member of Missouri Conference and was appointed to Mt. Carmel. The next year he was on the superannuated list, and the following year he was changed to supernumerary and sent to the Vermillion Circuit with H. Vredenburg. In 1824 he fell into the Illinois Conference and was returned to Vermillion, the following year he was sent to Carmi, in 1826 to Wabash, and in 1827 he was again placed on the superannuated list, on which he continued two years. He was appointed to Paris in 1829, and then for seven years was superannuated. In 1837 he was sent to Buffalo Grove Circuit; at the close of the year he was again superannuated. In 1840 he fell into the Rock River Conference, remaining in a superannuated relation until 1843, when he was appointed to Sugar River Circuit. At the close of the year he located. He was a man of medium size, somewhat odd in his manners, an independent thinker, and always presenting something original in his sermons.[2]

THOMAS RICE united first with the Baltimore Conference in 1819. After traveling the Pendleton and New River Circuits, he was transferred to the Missouri Conference, in which he labored in succession on Wabash, Sangamon, and Flat Rock circuits. In 1824 he fell into the Illinois Conference,

---

[2] John Corrie.

but remained in it only one year on the Rushville Circuit in Indiana, when he was transferred to the Holston Conference, in which he continued to travel until 1837, when he located.

JAMES SCOTT was received on trial in the Missouri Conference in 1819, but his appointment does not appear in the General Minutes. In 1820 he was sent to Cedar Creek, in 1821 to Illinois Circuit, and in 1822 to Indianapolis. At the close of the year he located. In 1826 he was readmitted in the Illinois Conference and appointed to Madison, the next year to Whitewater, and the next to Charlestown. With the exception of three years in which he was local, he continued in connection with the conferences in Indiana until 1860, when he was deposed from the ministry by the North-west Indiana Conference.

PARHAM RANDLE was received in the Missouri Conference in 1821, traveled two years on the Illinois and Shoal Creek Circuits, and in 1823, at his own request, was discontinued. He was a son of Richard Randle of Montgomery County, North Carolina, and afterwards of Richmond, Virginia, where he kept a tavern. His house was the first Methodist preaching place in Richmond. Richard Boardman and Bishop Whatcoat held the first Methodist meeting there, and the landlord, Richard Randle, was converted at it. Parham, his son, moved to Illinois in 1818 or 1819, and settled first near Edwardsville, in Madison County. He was then thirty-five or forty years old, and was a local preacher of some ability. Whilst traveling the

Shoal Creek Circuit he lived in a leaky house, and his wife took a severe cold in it, which resulted in consumption, and, after a few years, caused her death. She died in triumph. But her illness compelled Mr. Randle to cease traveling. After his wife's death he deeded his property to his children, and lived with his son-in-law at Lebanon. In 1829 we find him elected to elder's orders by the annual conference at Edwardsville. He continued to be a useful and acceptable local preacher as long as he was able to preach. On his death-bed, when asked by Rev. T. Peeples, "Uncle Parham, where are you going when you leave us?" his answer was, "Why, direct to heaven." He was a good man, full of the Holy Ghost, and loved by all who knew him.[3]

This was JOHN GLANVILLE's first year in the conference. After a successful year on the Sangamon Circuit, he traveled in Missouri until 1829, when he located. The next year he was readmitted, and continued in the work, filling many of the most important appointments, and serving two years as presiding elder until 1845, when, with his conference, he went into the Methodist Episcopal Church South. "He was an Englishman of a good type, a man of superior preaching ability and Christian character,"[4] "a companionable, intellectual, able minister of the Gospel, distinguished for his originality."[5]

___

[3] Rev. G. D. Randle.
[4] Rev. J. C. Berryman.   [5] Rev. S. G. Patterson.

CHAPTER VII.

1822.

ILLINOIS DISTRICT—Samuel H. Thompson, P. E.
Mt. Carmel—Samuel Hull.
Wabash and Mt. Vernon—Josiah Patterson, Wm. H. Smith.
Kaskaskia—Anthony W. Casad.
Illinois—Jesse Haile, Cornelius Ruddle.
Cash River—John Blaisdell.
Shoal Creek—Parham Randle, William Townsend.
Sangamon—Thomas Rice.
Mississippi—Isaac N. Piggott.

THE session of the Missouri Conference for 1822 was held in the city of St. Louis, commencing October 24th. Samuel H. Thompson and David Sharp exchanged districts, the former being again appointed to the Illinois District and the latter taking Mr. Thompson's place on the Missouri. Two new circuits were formed this year in Illinois, the Mt. Vernon and the Mississippi, and the name of the Okaw Circuit was changed to Kaskaskia. The Mt. Vernon Circuit, however, remained connected with the Wabash, of which it had formed a part, though the members are reported from it at the end of the year as from a separate charge. That region had been settled for a number of years. The Caseys, Johnsons, and Maxeys, and various other Methodist families among the early settlers, made that one of the strongest circuits in the district. The

Mississippi Circuit was formed from the north part of the Illinois Circuit, and included the rapidly extending settlements now embraced in the counties of Green, Macoupin, Jersey, Scott, and Morgan. The year, like the preceding, was a year of only moderate success. Yet some new societies were formed. Among them was one which afterwards became an important and influential one, the Hopewell society, north of Carrollton, which was this year formed in the house of John Dodgson, who had moved to the country from Yorkshire, England, the year before. Several new societies in Morgan County were also organized this year by I. N. Piggott. There was an increase in the membership of 270, the report at conference being 2,687 white and 40 colored.

Among the new settlers in the country this year who became influential members of the Church, was REUBEN HARRISON, a native of Rockingham County, Virginia, who had moved to Kentucky in 1818, and in November, 1822, settled on Richland Creek, in Sangamon County. For many years he was a faithful steward and leader and active worker on the Sangamon Circuit, and his house was a preachers' house. He was a man of considerable energy. In 1826, in company with W. B. Renshaw, whose house for years was a preaching-place, he started for New Orleans from the mouth of Richland Creek with a flat-boat load of produce, being the second that ever went out from the Sangamon River. Mr. Harrison lived to a good old age, and died highly respected by all who knew him.

The following brethren appear in connection with the work in Illinois for the first time.

Samuel Hull, who was this year on the Mt. Carmel Circuit, had just been received in the Missouri Conference. In 1823 he was assigned to Honey Creek. During the year a charge of immoral conduct was presented against him. The case was investigated by a committee, and he was suspended until conference. The following extract from the Journal of the Illinois Conference at its first session in 1824, will show the merits of the case, and is inserted as an act of justice to Mr. Hull: " The case of Samuel Hull being taken up, charges of an immoral nature, on the testimony of Elizabeth Wallace, amounting to an attempt on her chastity, and for which he now stands suspended, were laid before the conference. The circumstances of the case being duly considered, together with the character of the woman and the manner of her acting on the occasion, the conference was fully convinced of his innocence; and, on motion of Brother Monroe, seconded by Brother Glanville, the sentence of the committee who had suspended him was reversed. His character was examined, approved, and he was admitted into full connection and elected to deacon's orders." He was returned to the Honey Creek Circuit the next year; and, before its close, his innocence of the charge that had been made against him was fully established. A young man, who was dying, confessed that it was he who had been guilty in the affair, and that the preacher was entirely innocent. At the close of the year he located and settled in the Vincennes Circuit in Indiana. He was a large, good-looking man, and an excellent preacher; very emotional, weeping much while preaching, and very zealous and faithful in his work.

William H. Smith, the junior preacher on Wabash and Mt. Vernon Circuit, commenced this year an itinerant career that continued for fifty-six years. He was a native of Georgia, born in 1796. His parents were elevated Christians. His mother died when he was only two years old; but his godly father trained him in the doctrines of Christianity. When he was seven years old his family removed to Kentucky, and when he was fifteen he was converted and received into the Church by Marcus Lindsay. Having removed to White County, Illinois, he was licensed to preach, and recommended to the Missouri Conference in 1822, and received his appointment as junior preacher to the circuit in which he lived. He was returned as preacher in charge of the same circuit the next year. In 1824 he fell into the Illinois Conference, and was sent to Patoka, and the next year to Booneville. In 1826 he was appointed to Paoli, a six-weeks' circuit, and during the year several hundred were converted. During his term on Eel River Circuit, which he traveled in 1827–8, six hundred souls were converted and brought into the Church. The next year he was sent to Carlisle, and in 1830 to Paris Circuit, which then included Edgar, Coles, and Clark Counties, in Illinois, and Vigo and Vermillion Counties, in Indiana. He continued to travel in the Indiana, North Indiana, and North-west Indiana Conferences, into which he successively fell by the division of the work, until 1866, when he finally ceased his labors in the active ranks of the ministry, and waited as superannuate until his change should come. " During his last days he delighted to speak of the past, with its labors and triumphs. He never seemed happier than when talking of the noble and glorious band of men with whom he had labored and won so many victories for God and the Church."[1] His death, which occurred at Greencastle, Indiana, September 28, 1878, was quiet, peaceful, and triumphant.

ANTHONY W. CASAD was a native of New Jersey. He removed first to Greene County, Ohio, and about 1820 to Illinois. In 1821 he was received on trial in the Missouri Conference. His first appointment was Buffalo, and his second Kaskaskia. At the conference of 1823 he was ordained deacon, received into full membership, and then granted a location. He settled in St. Clair County, near Lebanon. In 1828 he was elected to elder's orders as a local preacher. He afterwards resigned his ministerial authority, and surrendered his certificates of orders to the Church, and remained during the rest of his life a lay member. As a preacher, he was logical and instructive, but slow and tedious. He was naturally very fond of metaphysics. He was a good preacher, but not a revivalist. As a citizen, he was highly esteemed. After his retirement from the ministry he engaged in the practice

---

[1] General Minutes.

of medicine, and, as his services were demanded, served also as surveyor, school-teacher, and tailor. For many years he was a trustee of McKendree College. He died in great peace, full of faith and the Holy Ghost, at his residence near Summerfield, Illinois, about 1860. One of his daughters was married to Rev. C. D. James, of the Illinois Conference.

CORNELIUS RUDDLE was received on trial in the Missouri Conference in 1822, and appointed to Illinois Circuit. The next year he was sent to Wabash and Mt. Vernon, and the following year he was returned from the Illinois Conference to the Wabash Circuit. In 1825 he located. Three years afterwards he was again received on trial—though why he was not readmitted the journal does not show—and assigned to Madison, and at the close of the year was discontinued, at his own request.

JOHN BLAISDELL united with the Missouri Conference in 1821, and was sent to Lamoine. After his year on Cash River he continued traveling in the Missouri Conference until its session in 1826, when he located.

WILLIAM TOWNSEND had been traveling in the Missouri Conference since 1817. At the close of his year on Shoal Creek he located. He was recommended for readmission to the conference of 1827, but was not received, though the presiding elder had liberty to employ him, should he deem it expedient.

ISAAC N. PIGGOTT was received on trial in the Missouri Conference in 1819, traveled two years in

Missouri, and was discontinued. This year he was received again, and appointed, as stated above, to the Mississippi Circuit, to which he was returned the following year. In 1824 he located, and settled in the circuit he had been traveling. Mr. Piggott was for some years a prominent man in the State, as well as in the Church. Having settled south-west of Jerseyville, he obtained from the Legislature a ferry license across the Mississippi between Grafton and Alton in 1821. He afterwards entered the political field, and ran against Thomas Carlin (subsequently governor) for State senator, and both received certificates of election. The senate ordered a new election, and Mr. Piggott was defeated. He was possessed of strong native talent, and was a forcible speaker. After his location he turned his attention to law, and left the Church. When J. B. Wollard traveled the Grafton Circuit he professed to be reclaimed, reunited with the Church, and was again licensed to preach. But he was shorn of his strength, and after remaining in the Church for a few years, he again left it. In 1858 he removed to St. Louis, where he resided until his death, in 1874, at the age of eighty-two.

CHAPTER VIII.

1823.

ILLINOIS DISTRICT—Samuel H. Thompson, P. E.
Mt. Carmel—William McReynolds.
Wabash and Mt. Vernon—William H. Smith.
Kaskaskia—Frederick B. Leach.
Illinois—John Dew, Orceneth Fisher.
Cash River—Josiah Patterson.
Shoal Creek—Thomas Davis, Jesse Green.
Sangamon—John Miller.
Mississippi—Isaac N. Piggott.
Vermillion—Hackaliah Vredenburg, Robert Delap, Sup.

IN 1823 the Missouri Conference sat again in St. Louis, beginning its session October 23d. A new circuit, the Vermillion, was formed this year in the Illinois District, embracing the settlements on the west side of the Wabash above the Mt. Carmel Circuit. This region began to be settled in 1817. In that year Colonel Jonathan Mayo came to the country from Kentucky, and settled on North Arm Prairie, then included in Edwards County; and, as has been stated before, the first class in that region had been formed in his house by Joseph Curtis. Previous to the formation of the Vermillion Circuit, in addition to the ministrations of the local preachers, the settlements had been occasionally supplied with circuit preaching, first from the Harrison, and afterward from the Honey Creek Circuits, in Indiana. Haekaliah Vredenburg, who then traveled this circuit, preached first at Colonel Mayo's in February or March, 1823, and in August of that year held, near the same place, the first camp-meeting ever held in the Upper Wabash region in Illinois. He was assisted by Rev. J. W. McReynolds, who had formerly traveled in Kentucky, but was then local, and had recently moved to the neighborhood; by Dr. James; by a local preacher named Robinson, and by Alonzo Lapham, then an exhorter and class-leader. Dr. James, father of Rev. C. D. James, of the Illinois Conference, was a tall, straight man, and an excellent preacher. Mr. Robinson was also a good preacher. One of his sermons is remembered to this day. It was from the text, " The Lord knoweth how to deliver the godly out of temptation." Mr. Lapham afterwards moved to Macon County, where he received license to preach. Two of his sons became traveling preachers. About eighteen persons were converted at the camp-meeting, and amongst them was Colonel Mayo.

Mr. Vredenburg also formed the first class this year in the village of Paris, which had been laid off during the Summer as the county-seat of Edgar County. The society was formed in the house of Smith Shaw, father of Rev. H. S. Shaw, which continued to be the preaching place until the courthouse was built.

This year the Gospel was introduced into what is now McLean County. The first sermon was preached by Rev. James Stringfield whilst on a visit from Kentucky; this was in the Fall of 1823, and the next Summer the first class was formed by Jesse Walker in the house of John Hendricks, who was the first white settler in Blooming Grove. This was the beginning of the flourishing Churches in the city of Bloomington.

The first camp-meeting in what was afterwards Morgan County was held this year by S. H. Thompson on Walnut Creek, near Lynnville.

The year was a more prosperous one than the district had known for some time. In every charge there was some increase, the aggregate being 485; making in all 3,155 whites and 57 colored members in Illinois. During the eight years in which the work had been connected with the Missouri Conference the membership had increased from 968 to 3,212, and the preachers from six to fourteen.

Six new men were assigned to the work in Illinois this year.

WILLIAM McREYNOLDS was born in Washington County, Virginia, March 7, 1798, but with his parents moved to Kentucky whilst he was yet a child, and settled in Allen County. His parents were devoted Christians and brought up their children in the nurture and admonition of the Lord. In 1819, in a powerful revival under the labors of Charles Holliday and others, he was converted, and soon after entered upon the life of a traveling preacher. He was employed for a few months under the presiding elder on the Bowling Green Circuit with Andrew Monroe; and in 1820 he was received into the Tennessee Conference and assigned as junior preacher to the Christian Circuit, with

Peter Cartwright as his colleague. The next year he labored on the Middle Island Circuit in Virginia, and in 1822 he appears in the Missouri Conference as appointed to Blue River Circuit in Indiana. The following year, as stated above, he was on the Mt. Carmel Circuit, and at the close of the year was re-transferred to Kentucky, where he labored until 1833, when he located, and during the remainder of his life he served the Church as a local preacher. He died at Portsmouth, Ohio, March 4, 1868. Dr. Redford says of him, " In the several fields of ministerial labor he occupied he made full proof of his ministry, discharging his duty with commendable zeal. Epistles, known and read of all men, were to be found in the vales and mountains through which he passed as an ambassador of Jesus Christ." "A man of commanding personal appearance, of talents above mediocrity, ardent in his piety, and of popular manners, in the morning of his ministry he promised much to the Church. Retiring, as he did, from the active duties of an itinerant, in the full strength of manhood, however useful he was as a local preacher, the sphere of his labors was too circumscribed to give to his ministry that efficiency for which it was designed. During the twenty-six years that he sustained the relation of a local preacher it is gratifying to record that his zeal and labors in behalf of the cause of Christ, whether in the pulpit or presiding over institutions of learning, entitled him to the confidence of his brethren; while his consistent piety challenged the criticism of the enemies of the cross." "He closed his eventful career as the pastor of the Seamen's Bethel at Portsmouth, Ohio. On the Sabbath previous to his death he preached twice with great power. On Monday and Tuesday evenings, though complaining of indisposition, we find him again in the pulpit, calling sinners to repentance. On the following Saturday, in great peace, he breathed his last."

FREDERICK B. LEACH was received on trial in the Missouri Conference in 1822, and appointed to Lamoine Circuit. After his labors on the Kaskaskia charge, he continued to travel in Missouri until 1828, when he located. Nine years afterwards he was readmitted, traveled one year, and again located in 1838. "He was gifted, pious, devoted to his work, and eminently useful. Though quite popular in the pulpit, he did not become vain or proud of this, but by a humble and consistent life, and a chaste conversation, seasoned with grace, he made one of the most consistent and effective traveling preachers his presiding elder had ever seen."[1]

JOHN DEW was a native of Virginia, born July 17, 1789. In early life he was converted and united with the Methodist Episcopal Church. In 1812 he was received in the Ohio Conference and appointed to Salt River Circuit in Kentucky. Then he traveled in succession the Jefferson, Madison, and Guyandotte circuits in the same conference. In 1816 he fell into the Tennessee Conference and was sent to Holston Circuit, and at the close of the year he located. In 1823 he was readmitted in the Missouri

---

[1] Dr. McAnally.

Conference and appointed to Illinois Circuit, to which he was returned the next year from the Illinois Conference. In 1825 he was transferred to Missouri Conference and appointed presiding elder of Missouri District. The next year he was stationed in St. Louis, and in 1827 was retransferred to the Illinois Conference and appointed superintendent and conference collector for the Pottawattomie Mission at Salem. In 1828 he was appointed to Galena, in the extreme north-west corner of the State, and at least four hundred miles from his residence; "and such," says Cartwright, "was the poverty of the country at that time, for it was new and just in its forming state, that he provided for his family where they were, and spent most of this year almost entirely from home. His labors were blessed in this new field of toil, and he was instrumental in planting Methodism firmly there." During this year Mr. Dew formed a class in Galena, which disputes with the one at Walker's Grove (now Plainfield), the honor of being the first class formed in the Rock River Conference, though Mr. Beggs thinks the latter entitled to precedence. In 1829 Mr. Dew was sent to Lebanon, in 1830 to Shoal Creek, with Edward R. Ames as his junior, and the next year to Lebanon again. Then for two years he labored on Kaskaskia Circuit, and in the Fall of 1834 located. Two years afterwards he was readmitted and appointed president of McKendree College. In 1837 he was assigned to the Carlisle District as presiding elder, and for the two following years to the Lebanon District. He died after an illness of about two weeks on the 5th of September, 1840, a few days before the session of the annual conference.

"As a minister," says his memoir, " he was able and useful; as a circuit preacher, stationed minister, and presiding elder, his services will be long remembered by those who enjoyed the benefits of his ministry. As a man, he was honest; as a citizen, he was public-spirited; in the domestic circle he was kind and affectionate; as a Christian, his walk and conversation recommended the religion of the meek and lowly Redeemer." Dr. Cartwright says of him : " He had a fine order of talent as a preacher, was a strong theological debater, had a clear and sound mind, and was well qualified to defend the doctrines of the Bible against infidelity, and the doctrines of Methodism against all sectarian assailants. He was popular and useful as a preacher, labored hard, suffered much in spreading the Gospel, lived beloved, and died lamented by thousands." Mr. Dew was about five feet and a half in height, heavy set, dark-skinned, with black hair and black and piercing eyes, and of fine personal appearance. He was a man of strong and cultivated intellect, a hard student, and an able and instructive preacher. His voice was very musical, and in reading the Scriptures and lining the hymns, as was then the custom, he often produced a powerful effect upon his hearers.[2] He was a member of the General Conference of 1828.

Orceneth Fisher had just been received in

____
[2] Rev. N. P. Heath.

the Missouri Conference. The next year he was appointed from the Illinois Conference to Boonville, Indiana, and the following year to Mt. Vernon, Illinois. At the close of the year, his health having failed, he was granted a superannuated relation, in which he continued three years. Then, in 1829, he was sent to Brownsville Circuit as a supernumerary; but, his health being still inadequate to the work of the itinerancy, he was again placed on the superannuated list, in which he remained until 1834, when he located. He settled at Nashville, in Washington County, and engaged in the practice of medicine. In 1838 he was readmitted in the conference, and sent to Waterloo Circuit, to which he was returned the next year. In 1840 he was stationed in Springfield, and at the close of the year was transferred to the Texas Conference, and appointed to Washington, where he labored for two years. In 1843 his appointment was Brazoria. The next year he fell into the West Texas Conference, and was granted a superannuated relation; and in the division of the Church in 1845 he went into the Methodist Episcopal Church South. The writer heard him preach at a camp-meeting on the Athens Circuit, in the Summer of 1841. By request he discussed the subject of baptism, and it was certainly one of the most able, interesting, and forcible presentations of the subject ever heard in that region. One who was his pastor during his location (Rev. J. H. Dickens) says of him: "He was one of the most profound, critical, and brilliant preachers of that day. He was controversial, yet practical and deeply experimental. His pulpit efforts were always powerful, and sometimes almost irresistible. I scarcely ever saw his equal in power over the masses. His prayers seemed to enter heaven." Mr. Dickens relates the following anecdote of him. There was in the town of Nashville a wealthy merchant, who was also a State senator, a very popular and influential man, though wicked and skeptical, who had become so incensed at Dr. Fisher that he had sworn to whip him the first time they met. One day, as the doctor was passing his store, certain lewd fellows of the baser sort, who had heard the threat, told the merchant that Fisher was passing. Hastily pulling off his coat, the merchant, who was a very stout man, confronted the doctor, who was small and quite feeble, and telling him that he intended to thrash him, bid him throw off his coat and defend himself, for he intended he should have a fair chance. Dr. Fisher at once fell on his knees in the dust of the street, and prayed, as scarcely any other man could, that God would bless and save the merchant. This was too much for him. He turned and retreated to his store, saying that he could fight a man in any other position than on his knees. His wicked comrades laughed at him and taunted him; but they could not get him to fight a man in prayer.

This was the only year JESSE GREEN labored in Illinois. He had united with the Tennessee Conference in 1817, and traveled in connection with it until 1823, when he was transferred to the Missouri Conference, and appointed, as stated above, to Shoal

Creek. The next year he was assigned to the Cape Girardeau District, and continued traveling in the Missouri Conference, mostly as presiding elder, until 1845, when he went, with the majority of his conference, into the Methodist Episcopal Church South. He died in the Spring of 1847. From the General Minutes of his Church we learn that "he entered the ministry in early life, with qualifications for extraordinary usefulness; and during the whole period of thirty years, to his death, his course in the itinerancy was alike laborious, self-sacrificing, holy, and successful." A writer, quoted by Dr. McFerrin, says: "He was small of stature, erect and manly in form and bearing, and looked like one ordained to lead and govern among the hosts of spiritual Israel. He was a good preacher. His sermons often contained the rare combination of the metaphysical and the emotional. He commanded the attention and challenged the intelligence of his congregations. He spoke as one having authority from God, and his appeals to sinners to repent and be converted were sometimes terrific. He was a man of zeal and faith and power, and finally died in full expectation of a crown of righteousness."

He was, says Dr. McAnally, "superior as a preacher of strong and sound doctrine. He devoted himself to doctrinal studies, and became very able and successful in assaulting errors and defending the faith of Methodism. Calvinism and Campbellism, however, were his specialties, and he dealt them many a hearty and damaging blow. In the discussion of questions involving the freedom of the will he attained distinguished success, and was regarded as the strong doctrinal preacher of the conference. He was, moreover, of pleasant and agreeable manners and very popular on his work."

JOHN MILLER was a native of Kentucky, born in 1802. When he was about eighteen he was converted in the State of Indiana, and in 1823 united with the Missouri Conference, and was appointed to Sangamon Circuit. The next year, from the Illinois Conference, he was sent to Indianapolis, in 1825 to Paoli, and the next year to Illinois Circuit. In 1827 his appointment was Vincennes, and in 1828, Washington. For the two following years he was on the Mt. Carmel Circuit. In 1831 he was assigned to Corydon, and in 1832 fell into the Indiana Conference, in which he continued to labor for twenty years, eleven of them on districts, when he fell into the South-east Indiana Conference, of which he remained a member until his death. For fifteen years he continued filling circuits and stations, but in 1869 he was placed on the superannuated list, on which he continued until his death, in 1874. For some years before he ceased traveling, he lived in Madison, Indiana, which continued to be his home until he died. Mr. Miller was a very genial, companionable man, fond of jokes and anecdotes. He was remarkably self-possessed; one who knew him well for many years declares that he never saw him lose his self-control. He was a fine business man, and, without any apparent effort to make money, died possessed of a large property, the result of his prudent investments in real estate. He was a good preacher, somewhat slow of speech, but usually drawing good congregations. His sermons were not flowery nor rhetorical, but rather argumentative and convincing. His voice was distinct and musical, and he was a remarkably fine singer.[3]

[3] Dr. A. J. Miller.

Part IV.

·

The Illinois Conference

TO

The Separation from Indiana.

1824 to 1831.

Part IV.

THE ILLINOIS CONFERENCE

TO THE SEPARATION FROM INDIANA.

1824 to 1831.

CHAPTER I.

1824.

INDIANA DISTRICT—James Armstrong, P. E.
Vermillion—Hackaliah Vredenburg, Robert Delap.

ILLINOIS DISTRICT—Samuel H. Thompson, P. E.
Mt. Carmel—Thomas Davis, Samuel Bassett, sup.
Wabash—Cornelius Ruddle.
Cash River—Josiah Patterson.
Mt. Vernon—William Moore.
Kaskaskia—Thomas Randle.
Illinois—John Dew, James E. Johnson.
Mississippi—William Medford.
Sangamon—Peter Cartwright.
Shoal Creek—Ebenezer T. Webster.
Jesse Walker, missionary to the settlements be-
tween the Illinois and the Mississippi Rivers,
and to the Indians in the vicinity of Fort Clark.

AT the session of the General Conference of 1824
the Missouri Conference was divided into two,
the Missouri and the Illinois; the former including
the State of Missouri, and the latter the States of
Illinois and Indiana, that part of Indiana previously

connected with the Ohio Conference being now included in the Illinois. The two conferences held their sessions together at the house of William Padfield, St. Clair County, Illinois. The joint session began on Saturday, October 23, 1824, and closed on the following Thursday.

The journal of the session is signed by Bishop Roberts, though Bishops McKendree and Soule were also present. John Scripps was elected secretary, and James Bankson, assistant. At the opening session only eleven members were present, but on the Monday following thirty-three members of both conferences answered to their names. A camp-meeting was held in connection with the conference, at which, on Sunday, Bishop Soule preached a funeral sermon on the life, character, and labors of Rev. William Beauchamp, who had died about two weeks before. The sermon was afterwards requested for publication. Bishop Roberts was requested to preach a sermon on the death of Samuel Glaze, but as he could obtain no information in regard to him, the sermon was not preached.

The usual conference business was transacted, though the mode of conducting conference business then was very different from the present mode; and the amount of business done was trifling compared with that of an annual conference now. Then, the first business after the opening and organization of the conference was the election of stewards, three or five, and this was deemed so responsible an office that the elections were usually by ballot. Then, there were no examinations of under-graduates before the beginning of the session, and no appointment of committees of examination the year before. The candidates for admission into full connection were merely examined by a committee appointed at the beginning of the session, and the examination was rather on the soundness of their faith than on an extended course of study. Then, the preachers were required to report in open conference the amount of their claims and receipts; and at this session a resolution was adopted that "every brother who should fail to render his account on the second day after the commencement of the conference should not be a partaker of the dividend," that is, a sharer in the conference dividend from the profits of the Book Concern and the income of the Chartered Fund. At this session the Illinois Conference received one hundred and fifty dollars from the former, and eighty dollars from the latter; and the Missouri Conference received a like amount. Then, the examination of character was usually conducted with closed doors; and, instead of the "nothing against him," of the present day, an account of the labors of each preacher and a brief sketch of his character were given by the presiding elder. The effect of this upon the preachers was a better knowledge and a higher appreciation of each other, and a deeper interest in each other's welfare. Then, the bishops seemed to consider themselves, far more than now, the PASTORS of the conference, the spiritual counselors and instructors of the preachers; and many were the godly admonitions given by them during a conference session. Their deep piety, their commanding talents, their wide experience, and, above all, their hearty sympathy with the preachers in their labors, privations, and sufferings, for they had endured and were still enduring the same themselves, secured for them an affectionate reverence that is now seldom accorded by a conference to its presiding officer. In theory a bishop was then, as now, "*primus inter pares;*" but then, not in the estimation of the bishop, but of the preachers, *primus* was the emphatic word; whereas, in these days, the emphasis is generally on *pares.* Then, a committee was elected in each conference to unite with the bishops in estimating the probable expense of sustaining them. Then, at least in the West, a camp-meeting was usually held in connection with the conference session, and it was not uncommon for scores of souls to be converted during the conference week. The time of the preachers not spent in the transaction of necessary business was spent on the camp-ground in laboring for the salvation of souls; and, as an effect of this, they went to their new charges full of zeal for God and love for souls. Now, the numerous anniversaries and specialties of an annual conference, and the work imposed on the various committees, divert attention from the work of soul-saving, so that the conversion of a soul during a conference session now is the exception rather than the rule; and it requires no small degree of watchfulness and effort on the part of the preachers to avoid a decrease of spirituality while together at conference.

The members of the Illinois Conference at this, its first session, were the following: James Armstrong, Samuel Bassett, Peter Cartwright, John Cord, William Cravens, Thomas Davis, Robert Delap, John Dew, Nathaniel S. Griffith, James Havens, George K. Hester, Thomas S. Hitt, Samuel Hull, James Jones, William Medford, Josiah Patterson, Thomas Randle, Edwin Ray, Thomas Rice, Cornelius Ruddle, Calvin W. Ruter, William H. Smith, Peter Stephens, John Strange, James L. Thompson, Samuel H. Thompson, Hackaliah Vredenburg, Jesse Walker, Ebenezer T. Webster, Allen Wiley, Dennis Willey, Aaron Wood—in all thirty-two. Of these Peter Cartwright and Edwin Ray were transferred this year from the Kentucky Conference.

The class of the second year consisted of Orceneth Fisher, James E. Johnson, John Miller, William Moore, Edward Smith, Thomas Hewson, the last-named a probationer transferred this year from the Ohio Conference.

The following persons were received on trial: Daniel Anderson, John Fish, James Garner, Richard Hargrave, Samuel Low, George Randle, Jacob Varner.

When the case of Richard Hargrave was before the conference for admission on trial, it was stated that he had traveled in the Indiana District the year before under the presiding elder, William Beauchamp, but in consequence of his death there was no recommendation for Brother Hargrave at the conference. William Medford and James Armstrong assured the conference that a recommendation for him to travel had been obtained, and pledged themselves to produce it at the next session of the conference if he should be admitted; and on their assurance and pledge he was admitted.

Two of the preachers were placed on the superannuated list, William Cravens and Calvin W. Ruter; and four were granted a supernumerary relation, Samuel Bassett, John Cord, Robert Delap, and Dennis Willey.

Two districts were formed in Indiana, the Madison, with John Strange as presiding elder, and the Indiana, with James Armstrong. All the appointments in Illinois were in one district, with Samuel H. Thompson as presiding elder, with the exception of Vermillion Circuit, which was connected with the Indiana District.

The most important changes in the work this year were the separation of the Wabash and Mt. Vernon Circuits, and the appointment of Jesse Walker as missionary to form a circuit between the Illinois and Mississippi Rivers. This region began to be settled soon after the close of the war with Great Britain. In 1819 the Ross family, from New York, settled near Atlas in what was afterwards Pike County. In 1820 Abner Gads, with others, settled in Peoria, and soon afterwards the government established an Indian agency there. In the Fall of 1821 John Wood, afterwards governor of the State, with two others, visited the site of Quincy and selected that as his residence, and the next year took up his abode there. In February, 1823, Calvin Hobart, father of Chauncey and Norris Hobart,

now of the Minnesota Conference, with his family
and William H. Taylor, settled in what is now Schuyler County; and soon after Levin Green, a local
preacher from Missouri, settled in the same region,
and preached the first sermon in the house of Mr.
Hobart in the Fall of 1823. The country had settled so rapidly that in 1821 Pike County was organized with Atlas as the county-seat; and in 1825 the
whole military tract, as it was termed, was divided
by the Legislature into counties, nearly as they
exist now.

As nearly as can be ascertained, the ten circuits,
with the mission just mentioned, into which Illinois,
or rather the settled portion of it, was then divided,
covered territory about as follows:

VERMILLION CIRCUIT included the settlements
west of the Wabash in Indiana and Illinois, from
the mouth of Big Creek on the south, to Warren
County, Indiana, on the north, and extending west
to the Grand Prairie. This charge covered what
are now Edgar, Vermillion, and part of Clark
Counties in Illinois, and Vermillion and part of
Vigo Counties, Indiana.

MT. CARMEL CIRCUIT embraced the territory
now included in Wabash, Edwards, Lawrence, Richland, Crawford, and parts of Clark and Clay Counties, reaching from below Mt. Carmel to Darwin,
and including Maysville on the west side of the
Little Wabash.

WABASH CIRCUIT took in the settlements on the
Big and Little Wabash Rivers below the Mt. Carmel Circuit, and those on the Ohio to the Cash

River Circuit, including probably the counties of White, Gallatin, Hardin, Saline, and perhaps part of Pope.

CASH RIVER CIRCUIT included all the settlements on the Ohio and Mississippi and their tributaries, between the Wabash and Kaskaskia Circuits, and covering probably what are now the counties of Alexander, Pulaski, Massac, Johnson, Union, and Pope.

MT. VERNON CIRCUIT embraced all the territory between the Mt. Carmel Circuit on the east, Wabash and Cash River on the south, and Kaskaskia and Shoal Creek on the west.

KASKASKIA CIRCUIT included probably the counties of Randolph and Jackson, and parts of Perry and Monroe.

ILLINOIS CIRCUIT covered St. Clair County, and parts of Monroe and Madison.

MISSISSIPPI CIRCUIT included Greene, Jersey, Scott, Macoupin, and parts of Morgan and Madison Counties.

SANGAMON CIRCUIT embraced Sangamon and a part of Morgan Counties, and all the territory as far north as the settlements extended.

SHOAL CREEK CIRCUIT took in all the settlements on both sides of Shoal Creek, and on both sides of the Okaw above the mouth of Crooked Creek, covering what are now the counties of Clinton, Bond, Fayette, Montgomery, and Shelby.

Several camp-meetings were held this year, at which many souls were converted. Mr. Beggs relates that on his way from the Missouri to the Illinois Conference, to which he had been transferred, "I fell in with Samuel H. Thompson and Jesse Walker, at a camp-meeting near Padfield's, and a most glorious time we had there. On our way, near Mt. Carmel, Illinois, we attended another camp-meeting, and the gracious out-pouring of the Spirit converted many souls, and quickened the believers."

Another camp-meeting was held at Shiloh in September of this year, at which many souls were converted, amongst whom was one, Elihu Springer, who afterwards became a useful traveling preacher.

During this year Jesse Walker, in his missionary labors, formed the first class in Peoria, numbering sixteen members. And it was probably during this year that the following incident, recorded by Bishop Morris, occurred. He "visited one neighborhood near the Illinois River, containing some sixty or seventy souls. They all came to hear him, and having preached three successive days, he read the General Rules and proposed that as many of them as desired to unite to serve God according to the Bible as expressed in those rules should come forward and make it known. The most prominent man among them rose to his feet, and said, 'Sir, I trust we will all unite with you to serve God here,' then walked forward, and all the rest followed."

The year was one of prosperity. There was an increase in the work in Illinois of 530 white members, and a decrease of thirty colored—an aggregate increase of 520. The entire membership was 3,705 white and 27 colored.

The following brethren were this year connected with the work in Illinois for the first time:

JAMES ARMSTRONG was a native of Ireland, born in 1787, and was brought by his parents to America when but a child. When about nineteen he was converted in the city of Philadelphia, and united with the Methodist Episcopal Church. Some years afterwards he was licensed to preach, and in 1821 removed to the State of Indiana, and was received in the Missouri Conference, and appointed to Charleston Circuit, which he traveled for two years. The following year he was on Bloomington Circuit; and in 1824, though only entering upon his fourth year in the itinerancy, he was placed on the Indiana District as presiding elder. He traveled in all thirteen years, eight of which were spent in the presiding eldership. He was a member of the General Conferences of 1828 and 1832. Aaron Wood says of him: "He was of medium height and weight; his chin, lips, and nose sharp, eyes small, eyebrows heavy, forehead square and high, and hair thick and dark. He was always neatly dressed in plain black. He had a good voice, with a free use of plain English words of Saxon origin; nothing of the Irish brogue, but much of the fire, which, as he felt himself, he failed not to impart to others who gave him audience, till the bond became so strong between the speaker and hearer that both were carried along with the force and beauty of the subject before them. Having been presiding elder over all the State of Indiana, from the Ohio to the lakes, he was a herald of the Gospel whom

God had owned and blessed, and his untiring industry and influence, devoted as they were entirely to the organizing of the Church in the then new settlements, place him on the page of our history as the leading evangelist." In his memoir it is said: "He was an able minister of the New Testament; he labored with indefatigable diligence to promote the prosperity of Zion. God gave him many souls to his ministry." He died September 12, 1834, at his own residence, at Door Village, Laporte County, Indiana, where he had, two years before, formed the first society in the county.

Of SAMUEL BASSETT, who was this year appointed as a supernumerary to Mt. Carmel Circuit, we have only the record of his appointment. He was received in the Missouri Conference in 1820, traveled three years in Missouri, and in 1823 was placed on the superannuated list. In 1824, at the first session of the Illinois Conference, his relation was changed to supernumerary, and at the next session to effective. In 1825 he was assigned to Madison, Indiana, and at the end of the year was granted a location, at his own request.

"WILLIAM MOORE," says his memoir in the General Minutes, "was esteemed a very good man, about whose life and labors we have but little information. It appears, however, that he embraced religion in the prime of life, entered the traveling connection in 1823, and, after traveling a number of circuits with some degree of usefulness to the Church, he died in peace at his own house in Charleston, Indiana. "Of the charges he traveled,

one was in Missouri; two, the Mt. Vernon and
Kaskaskia, in Illinois; and the remaining five in
Indiana. Upon one of his circuits he received
only twelve dollars for his year's services, and on
another twenty-four dollars. He was a devoted
Christian, and most of his conversation was on
religion.

The active itinerant life of THOMAS RANDLE
was spent in the Missouri and Illinois Conferences
in alternation. Uniting with the former in 1822,
he traveled two years in the State of Missouri. In
1824 he was in the Illinois Conference, on the Kaskaskia Circuit. The next year he was transferred
to the Missouri Conference, and appointed to St.
Louis and Gasconade. Then, in 1826, he was transferred to Illinois Conference, and traveled in succession the Mississippi and Shoal Creek Circuits,
and in 1828 was granted a location. Five years
afterward, in 1833, he was readmitted in the Missouri Conference, traveled in it two years, and in
1835 was placed on the superannuated list, and the
next year located. He remained a local preacher
for thirty-one years. In 1867 he was readmitted in
the Southern Illinois Conference, and granted a superannuated relation, in which he continued until
his death, July 18, 1874. During his long location
he lived in the neighborhood of Edwardsville. He
was a man of stern appearance, but with no disposition to be harsh or tyrannical, and despite his appearance he was really full of humor and good
sense. He had a strong constitution, and in old age
was a young old man. He was pleasant without

trifling, a good, strong, old-fashioned preacher, and a warm friend of the itinerants.

This was JAMES E. JOHNSON's second year in the itinerancy. He had traveled the Spring River and White River Circuit, in Missouri, the year before; and at the close of his service this year on the Illinois Circuit, "after some deliberation concerning his peculiarities, he was, according to his own request, discontinued," by the conference.[1]

WILLIAM MEDFORD traveled in connection with the Missouri Conference in Missouri and Indiana from 1818 to 1824. At the first session of the Illinois Conference he was appointed, as stated above, to the Mississippi Circuit, to which he was returned the next year; in 1826 he was sent to the newly formed Atlas Circuit, and at the close of the year he located.

EBENEZER T. WEBSTER had traveled in the Missouri Conference, two years in Indiana and one in Missouri, before receiving his appointment this year to the Shoal Creek Circuit. In 1825 he was appointed to the Illinois Circuit, and in 1826, according to the General Minutes, was located. But the journal of the conference makes no mention of his location. It merely states that when his name was called, at the request of the presiding elder, his case was laid over, and no further mention is made of him. This is probably an unintentional omission by the secretary. Whether the difficulties in his case, resulting in his location, grew out of his connection with Masonry, we are not informed. But

---

[1] Conference Journal.

the action of the conference in his case, at its session in 1825, shows that there was at that time a strong opposition to the order in the conference, and that this *may* have been the cause of his location.

PETER CARTWRIGHT, who was this year transferred to the newly formed conference, and who remained connected with it during the remainder of his life, was born of poor parents in Amherst County, Virginia, September 1, 1785. While he was an infant his parents moved to Kentucky, settling first in Lincoln County and afterwards in Logan County. His mother was a member of the Methodist Episcopal Church, and, as soon as the family reached their new home, their cabin was opened for preaching. Young Cartwright was naturally a wild, wicked boy, and, as he grew up, delighted in horse-racing, card-playing, and dancing. His father, who, says Mrs. Johnson, "was not so much a bad as a good-for-nothing kind of man," restrained him but little, though his mother often talked to him, wept over him, and prayed for him, and often, he tells us, drew tears from his eyes; and, though he often wept under preaching, and resolved to do better and seek religion, yet he broke his vows, went with young company, rode races, played cards, and danced. Early in 1801 he was powerfully convinced of sin; and after groaning under its burden for about three months, was converted at a meeting held by a Mr. McGready, a Presbyterian minister, in the month of May. The next month he united with the Methodist Episcopal Church. In the Spring of the following year he was licensed to exhort by Jesse Walker, preacher in charge of the Red River Circuit, on which he lived; and this license to exhort, he tells us, was all the authority he ever received from the Church until he received his ordination parchment. In the Fall of that year he moved with his parents to Lewiston County, near the mouth of the Cumberland River, a new country not yet embraced in any circuit. The Church letter he received from his presiding elder, John Page, was not only a certificate of membership, but an authorization to hold meetings, organize classes, and form a circuit in this new territory, and then report to him at the last quarterly-meeting of the year. He accordingly gathered into the Church about seventy persons, organized them into classes, appointed leaders, and reported them to the preacher and presiding elder at the appointed time, and to the charge thus formed was given the name Livingston Circuit. The following year he was employed by the presiding elder on the Red River Circuit for one quarter, and then removed to the Wayne Circuit, whose preacher had been compelled by sickness to leave the work. It was on this circuit that his singular controversy occurred with the Baptists, who had attempted to proselyte his converts, and of which he gives a humorous account in his autobiography, which resulted in the breaking up of the Baptist society, and the establishment of a Methodist Church of over seventy members. At the session of the Western Conference of 1804 he was formally received into the itinerant ranks, and sent as junior preacher to Salt

River and Shelby Circuit, with Benjamin Lakin as
his senior, and William McKendree as his presiding elder. His early educational advantages had
been quite limited. He had acquired while at his
father's house some knowledge of the common English branches, but while on this circuit his presiding elder directed him to a proper course of reading and study, selecting books for him both literary
and theological, and at his quarterly visitations examining into his progress and correcting his errors.
He acknowledged himself more indebted to Bishop
McKendree for his attainments in literature and
divinity than to any other man on earth. The next
year he was sent to the Scioto Circuit in Ohio, with
James Quinn as his senior and John Sale as his
presiding elder. The impress made upon him by
his colleagues and presiding elders, Lakin and Mc-
Kendree, Quinn and Sale, during these first two
years of his ministry could not have been other than
good, and doubtless contributed much toward his
success in after years. At the close of the year he
was ordained deacon by Bishop Asbury, and in
1806 was sent to Barren Circuit, in Kentucky, and
Lewis Anderson was employed by the presiding
elder, James Ward, as his assistant. In the Summer of this year he was married to Miss Frances
Gaines, a woman worthy to rank with the noble
women of Methodism, and who exerted a more
favorable influence upon her husband during their
long pilgrimage together, than was exerted by any
or all other persons. Her character is well drawn
by Solomon in his description of the virtuous

woman: "The heart of her husband doth safely trust in her, so that he shall have no need of spoil. Strength and honor are her clothing, and she shall rejoice in time to come. She openeth her mouth with wisdom, and in her tongue is the law of kindness. She looketh well to the ways of her household, and eateth not the bread of idleness. Her children arise up and call her blessed, her husband also, and he praiseth her." One who was an inmate of her dwelling in Kentucky for some time, Mrs. Johnson, says of her: "Sister Cartwright was one of the most industrious and amiable women I ever knew. Whatever she did seemed to be done better and quicker than any body else could do it." Her death, a few years after that of her husband, was most triumphant. At a meeting for the promotion of holiness, held near her residence, she had borne testimony to the power of Christ to save to the uttermost, and then remarking, "I know not why I am permitted to linger here, but I am waiting for the chariot to come," sat down, and in a few minutes her head dropped, and the chariot came to convey her spirit to paradise.

The next year after his marriage Mr. Cartwright was appointed to Salt River Circuit; and, during the two following years, he traveled the circuit he had formed as an exhorter, the Livingston. There was not much prosperity on the charge until near the close of his first year, when a gracious revival began at a camp-meeting, which spread over the country until scores were brought to a saving knowledge of the truth. In 1811 he was sent to

Christian Circuit, with James Axley as his presiding elder. It was a year of revival, some three hundred uniting with the Church. At one of the camp-meetings, near the close of the year, he baptized one hundred and twenty-seven adults and forty-seven children, all but seven, who insisted upon being immersed, in the Scriptural mode, so beautifully representing the baptism of the Holy Ghost. In 1812 he fell into the Tennessee Conference, and was appointed as stated before, to the Wabash District in Indiana and Illinois. For the three following years he traveled the Green River District. At the conference of 1815 he was elected, for the first time, to the General Conference, to be held in Baltimore the following May. In 1816 he was again appointed to Christian Circuit, and was blessed with some glorious revivals during the year. For the two following years he traveled the Red River Circuit. These were years of great losses by the faithful administration of Discipline, and of great gains by the displays of the power of God, and the accession of multitudes to the Church.

At the conference of 1819 the election of delegates to the General Conference turned on the question of slavery. Mr. Cartwright was a very decided opponent to the institution, and though far from advocating the extreme measures of the Abolitionists, was yet bitterly opposed by the advocates of slavery, then unfortunately becoming quite numerous in the Church. He, with the whole anti-slavery ticket, was elected by a handsome majority. He was appointed that year to the Christian Circuit, and returned the following year. It was during his pastorate in that charge that he published his celebrated "Letter to the Devil." For the three following years he was on the Cumberland District as presiding elder. These were years of some religious prosperity, but at the same time of almost constant controversy with the Calvinists on decrees and unconditional final perseverance, and with the Baptists on the mode and subjects of baptism. Every preacher was expected to be always prepared to defend his own doctrines and practices, and to refute the errors and heresies of others; yet much of this controversy necessarily, from their position and experience, fell to the lot of the presiding elders; and it was often the case that the Sunday morning sermon at a quarterly-meeting was a long-drawn-out attack upon and refutation of some form of error prevalent in the neighborhood. It was not uncommon then for a quarterly-meeting sermon on some disputed doctrine to be from three to four hours long; and if the preacher was a fluent speaker the people would listen to it with apparent interest to the end. The result of this frequent and almost constant controversial preaching was the training of a race of theological stalwarts in the ministry, ardently attached to the doctrines and practices of their own Church, intolerant of every form of error, and quick to discern the slightest departure from the truth. The continuance of errorists and heretics in the ministry of the Methodist Episcopal Church then would have been an impossibility.

In 1823 Mr. Cartwright was again elected to the

General Conference; and at the session of 1824, as stated above, he was transferred to the Illinois Conference. His intention was to attend the session of the conference at Padfield's; but he was prevented from reaching it by the death of one of his daughters, who was killed by the falling of a tree upon her while the family was encamped one night on the way. This led him to move directly to the farm he had purchased the year before on the head of Richland Creek, in Sangamon County, which continued to be his home as long as he lived. The following extracts from Mrs. Johnson will give us a picture of the man at this period of his life: "He was short, thick, heavy set, with a large head and short neck, coarse and rough in his manners, and any thing else but grave. After preaching with power, and praying as few other men could—for he was unsurpassed in prayer—he would have a dozen or twenty persons, frequently some of them the roughest in the congregation, all indulging in uproarious laughter at his jests, before he was ten feet from the pulpit." "He was at times as kind and affectionate as any man, but often as abrupt as if entirely destitute of feeling." "He was, however, generally affectionate in his family. When his wife would chide him for leaving home so much when all were not well, I have seen him sit down and weep like a child; and when he came home from his round of quarterly-meetings, it was not an hour before he got up a general romp with the children." Rev. J. M. Gunn, in McFerrin's "Methodism in Tennessee," thus refers to him: "About the year 1818

Peter Cartwright traveled the Red River Circuit. His house was thirty miles from the nearest appointment, which was Gunn's society. I have known him to leave home and be at our house at eleven o'clock, preach, and hold class-meeting, and then go five miles and preach at night, carrying his saddle-bags of books for sale. I never knew him to get hoarse or to appear tired. He was death upon whisky-drinking, tobacco-chewing, and coffee-drinking. Take him altogether, he was one of the most powerful men I ever heard." The following is Dr. Redford's estimate of him: "But few men in the West have labored with more untiring energy in the ministry than Peter Cartwright. At the time he entered the conference the circuits were large and accommodations poor, and a very small pittance was all that could be expected for the support of a preacher. Whilst traveling the Cumberland District he often returned home worn and weary from his quarterly-meetings, and, in order to support his family, would work his fields by the light of the pale moon. Prompt in meeting his appointments, it was but seldom that he disappointed a congregation. Devoted to the Church of which he was a member and minister, he boldly defended its peculiarities and advocated its doctrines. He became in Kentucky, before he left the State, a 'terror to evil-doers,' administering reproofs with unsparing hand. Whether we consider the extent and severity of his labors, the privations he endured, the humble support he received from the Church, the fidelity with which he performed his duties, or his deep devotion to the cause for which he was laboring, he was not surpassed by any of his contemporaries. It is true there was much in Mr. Cartwright of which we would gladly have divested him. If we admire the boldness with which he defended the Church, we would have preferred the employment of milder epithets toward his adversaries. If we approve of his preservation of order in the house of God, we would remember his reproofs with greater pleasure if they had been administered more in the spirit of meekness. With less of the temper of resentment that so often distinguished him, he would have been more useful as a minister of Christ; nor can it be concealed that his peculiar views, as well as his manner of expressing them, on the subject of domestic slavery, not only greatly impaired his usefulness, but arrested the advancement of the Church. We have already referred to the injury Methodism sustained in Kentucky, in an earlier period of its history, by the unfortunate legislation of the Church on this question. It is equally true that at this period we find a few of the preachers, of whom Mr. Cartwright was the acknowledged leader, by their interference with slavery *as a civil institution,* guilty of embarrassing the progress of the Church in the portions of the State in which they labored, and keeping out of its communion many families of influence." That which Dr. Redford so deeply deplores in Mr. Cartwright—his opposition to human slavery—will in the North be regarded as one of his greatest excellencies. Nor will the spiritually minded, whether

in the North or South, regard the Church as suffering loss by the continued exclusion from it of
worldly-minded slaveholders, however high their
social standing, or however great their political influence.

From this time his history becomes closely iden-
tified with that of the Illinois Conference, of which
he continued to be one of the leaders until his
death. His first year on the Sangamon Circuit was
only moderately successful, the increase in the membership during the year being only nineteen.

CHAPTER II.

1825.

Wabash District—Charles Holliday, P. E.
Vermillion—James Hadley.
Carmi—Robert Delap.
Wabash—Thomas Davis.
Mt. Carmel—J. W. McReynolds.

Illinois District—Samuel H. Thompson, P. E.
Illinois—Ebenezer T. Webster.
Kaskaskia—William Moore.
Cash River—Philip Cole, Asa D. West.
Mt. Vernon—Orceneth Fisher.
Shoal Creek—Joseph Foulks.
Sangamon—Peter Cartwright (who is also Super-
     intendent of the Pottawattomie Mission),
     William Chambers.
Peoria—William See.
Mississippi—William Medford.
Brownsville—Josiah Patterson.
Jesse Walker, Missionary to the Pottawattomie
     Indians.

THE second session of the Illinois Conference
was held at Charleston, Indiana, beginning on
Thursday, August 25th, and closing on the following
Monday. Bishops McKendree and Roberts were
both present; but the journal is signed by Bishop
Roberts. Calvin W. Ruter was secretary. In addition to the usual minute business, the following items
are of interest. When the name of Ebenezer T.

Webster, a deacon of the second year, was called, some objections were made on account of his having become a Freemason, and the conference refused to elect him to elder's orders. Some days afterwards the vote was reconsidered, and he was elected. The Book Concern dividend to the conference this year was $150, and that of the Chartered Fund $80.

The conference resolved that in future a recommendation in favor of every local preacher who applies for readmission into the traveling connection should be obtained from the quarterly conference of which he is a member.

A memorial having been presented from a local preacher who had been expelled in 1823, two years before, the conference submitted to the chair the question whether his case could now legally be considered, and Bishop Roberts decided that it could not.

Jesse Walker, conference missionary among the Indians, submitted a report respecting his labors, which was accepted, and articles of agreement between him and the chiefs of the Pottawattomie Indians having been read and approved by the conference, he was clothed with proper authority to enter into such agreement, and furnished with suitable instructions as missionary amongst them. A committee was appointed to meet with the bishops to estimate the amount of money needed for the support of the mission.

Mr. Walker wrote shortly afterwards to the missionary society, giving the following sketch of his operations. His letter is dated October 25, 1825.

"In the Spring of 1824 I opened a communication with the Pottawattomie Indians, and found they were willing to receive a missionary then; but my call to the General Conference prevented me from holding a satisfactory council with them. Being reappointed the next Autumn by Bishop Roberts, I opened a school at Fort Clarke on the Illinois River, which continued through the Winter, and in which I had six Indian children, whose progress was extremely flattering for so short a period. In the Spring of 1825, with five white families, I proceeded to the mouth of Fox River, shortly after which I had a most satisfactory council with five chiefs of said tribe. We immediately built cabins for the accommodation of the families. I then opened a school into which I received fourteen Indian children. But finding that the station was not located on Indian land, I proceeded up Fox River about thirteen miles further, selected a station, and am now preparing to move into it. The place selected for the establishment is about one hundred miles above Fort Clarke, about twenty miles north of the Illinois River, and between it and Fox River. The soil is very good, timber plenty, and the spot well watered."

At this session a committee on necessitous cases seems to have been appointed for the first time. "The stewards having made a distribution of the dividend money to the claimants, a committee of three was appointed to appropriate a small balance that had been reserved to those whom they might conceive the most needy, and report their doings to the conference." Forty-five dollars was distributed by them.

The conference ordered that each preacher shall in future bring a certificate from the recording steward of the circuit or station where he has labored, stating how much he has received as quarterage, how much as traveling expenses, and how much for table expenses.

Near the close of the session a conference missionary society was formed.

Six preachers were received on trial this year:— Philip Cole, Eli P. Farmer, James Hadley, William See, Joseph Tarkington, Asa D. West.

William Chambers, Charles Holliday, and George Locke were received by transfer from the Kentucky Conference.

Joseph Foulks, John W. McReynolds, and William Shanks were readmitted.

Samuel Hull, Cornelius Ruddle, Peter Stephens, and Dennis Wiley were located.

John Fish, Jacob Varner, and James E. Johnson were discontinued.

John Dew and Thomas Randle were transferred to the Missouri Conference, Thomas Rice to the Holston Conference, and Edward Smith to the Baltimore Conference.

The following local preachers were elected to deacon's orders: John Havens, James Jaggers, Bennett Hancock, William Sterrett, Joseph Basey, William See.

And the following local deacons to elders' orders; Joseph Arnold, Isham West, James Nolan.

A change was made in the arrangement of the districts this year, all the charges on the Wabash in Illinois being united with a number in Indiana, and formed into a Wabash District, under the superintendence of Charles Holliday; the remainder of the work constituting the Illinois District, of which S. H. Thompson was presiding elder. A new circuit, the Carmi, was formed from the Mt. Carmel and Wabash Circuits; but this seems to have been only a temporary arrangement, for the next year it disappears, reunited to the original charges. Two new circuits were formed on the Illinois District, the Peoria (or Peora or Paori as it is printed in the Minutes), including the town of Peoria on the west side of the Illinois River, and the settlements previously embraced in the Sangamon Circuit north of Salt Creek; and the Brownsville Circuit formed from the northern part of the old Cash River Circuit.

The first Methodist sermon was preached this year in the town of Rushville by Rev. LEVEN GREEN, who had just moved to the neighborhood from Missouri. Mr. Green first appears as a supply on the Maramec Circuit, Missouri, in 1811, having been appointed by the presiding elder, Samuel Parker, to travel under John McFarland. Whilst on this circuit he married the belle of the settlement, which so enraged her numerous suitors, amongst whom was his colleague, that they did not rest until Green was expelled from the Church. In 1818 John Scripps, who had charge of Boonslick Circuit, found him living on the Missouri River, and received him again into the Church and gave him license to exhort. He was soon after licensed to preach, and in 1821 was sent as a supply to the Lamoine Circuit. In 1825, as stated above, he moved to Schuyler County, Illinois, and remained there five or six years. He then returned to Missouri, where he probably died. He was a great oddity. Utterly indifferent about his personal appearance, he would frequently appear in the garb in which Mr. Scripps met him as he was exploring the country—"an old round-crown felt hat, with half the rim torn or worn off, the other half slouching down behind; a coarse shirt stuck into the waistband of an almost worn out pair of deerskin breeches, reaching a little below the knee, barelegged and shoeless." He had but three books, his Bible, hymn-book, and camp-meeting songs. Yet, "his discourses were clear, comprehensive, appropriate, and to the point, delivered in good language, yet not unmixed with a plentiful sprinkling of various backwoods idioms, sayings, and witticisms, giving a startling effect and attractive raciness to his discourses, and rather adding to than detracting from their merits." "He was purely an original, no man's counterpart, an eccentric genius, an interesting and always acceptable preacher, whenever, wherever, and by whomsoever listened to. His sermonizings were at once the admiration and astonishment of all competent judges of good preaching, looking to the presence from whence they emanated. I used to denominate him 'the Lord's prodigy.'"[1]

---

[1] Rev. J. Scripps.

This year, too, the first society was organized in Lebanon. The first place of worship was a log school-house, which was afterwards replaced by a frame building. But as soon as a seminary building was erected the society worshiped in the chapel, which they continued to occupy until the erection of a brick church in 1853.

A class was also organized in Belleville this year. It consisted of Richard Randle and wife, James and Ann Mitchell, James Harrison and wife, Susan Dennis, and Caroline E. Blackwell. The class met in Dennis's school-house, with Richard Randle as the leader. A class had been formed some time before this about a mile and a half north-west, but this was the first in town.

The increase in the membership this year was only 176; the entire report being 3,859 whites and 49 colored.

CHARLES HOLLIDAY began this year his connection with the Illinois Conference. He was a native of Baltimore, born November 23, 1771. His parents were Presbyterians, and he was educated for the ministry of that Church. But his parents dying before he was of age, he abandoned the idea of entering the ministry and turned his attention to secular pursuits. In his twenty-second year he was married, and the day after his marriage, with his wife, he united with the Methodist Episcopal Church, and on the same evening commenced family devotion. Of the time or circumstances of his conversion, we have no information. He was licensed to preach in 1797, and in 1809 he united with the Western Conference, and was appointed to Danville Circuit. The two following years he traveled the Lexington Circuit. In 1812, falling into the Ohio Conference, he was sent to Shelby, and in 1813 to the Salt River District, on which he remained three years, at the expiration of which he located. The next year he was readmitted in the Tennessee Conference, and appointed to the Cumberland District, on which he traveled three years in connection with that conference, and one in the Kentucky Conference, into which the district fell in 1820. Then for the four following years, he was on the Green River District, and in 1825 was transferred to the Illinois Conference and placed on Wabash District, which he traveled for three years. When first transferred to Illinois he settled near Whitehall, but on account of sickness he changed his residence to Mt. Carmel, where he continued, until his removal to Cincinnati.

At the General Conference of 1828 he was elected agent of the Western Book Concern, and four years afterwards he was re-elected to the same position. During this period he held his membership in the Ohio Conference, but at the expiration of his service as Book Agent, he transferred again to the Illinois Conference and was appointed to Lebanon District, upon which and on Alton District he traveled until 1844. He was then assigned to the Grafton Circuit, and the following year to Carlinville, where he closed his active labors. His health having failed, he was granted a superannuated relation in 1846, in which he remained until his death,

March 8, 1850, at his residence near Chesterfield. He was five times a member of General Conference, twice from the Ohio Conference, and once each from Tennessee, Kentucky, and Illinois. From his memoir in the General Minutes, and from the statements of others who knew him, we may form a fair estimate of his character and worth. Says his memoir: "Although his sufferings in his last illness were extreme, he frequently exulted in the grace of our Lord Jesus Christ, which enabled him to bear so much suffering without complaining. He retained his reason to the last. It had been his practice for thirty years to pray three times a day in his family, and from his devotional spirit we wonder not that his sun of life set in great peace. In summing up the character of our lamented Brother Holliday, we may say that there are few traits of real excellence that he did not possess in an eminent degree. As a preacher, he was clear, sound, and practical. When he indulged in doctrinal controversy, although he was decided and expressed his views in strong language, he was always kind and loving to the person of an opponent. In all the relations of life, as a husband, a father, a pastor, a friend, a companion, he was a most lovely and interesting man, and in the sufferings and disappointments of life his conduct was characterized by that charity which ' suffereth long and is kind.'"

Mr. Beggs says of him: "He was my elder when I was on the Vincennes Circuit, and few men ever proved a greater blessing to me. The precision and directness of the appeals in his edifying, soul-stirring sermons produced effects which remained fresh and powerful for weeks. He was a great help in establishing me in the work of holiness of heart. What a man of God was he! A Methodist preacher in very truth. I am afraid I should have gone astray had he not held me to the virtue of wearing plain apparel."

"Charles Holliday," says Mrs. Johnson, "was our presiding elder (on the Green River District), and an excellent man he was. He was somewhat tall and very spare, but full of fire when roused. Few men had so shrill and musical a voice as he; and when he became animated with his subject his thin form seemed to tremble in every muscle, and his clear, ringing tones thrilled like electricity."

"For the office of presiding elder," says Dr. Redford, "he was eminently qualified. His fine executive talents, his marked ability in the pulpit, whether in defending the doctrines and peculiarities of Methodism, or enforcing its practical and experimental truths, together with the kindness and gentleness he showed toward the younger preachers in his district, rendered him a universal favorite as a presiding elder during his stay in Kentucky. No man in the West was better adapted to the training of young men for the work of the ministry than he." Says Dr. McFerrin: "He was a man of power and great circumspection, and wielded great influence in favor of religion."

JAMES HADLEY had just been received on trial in the conference. He traveled in succession the

Vermillion, Kaskaskia, Wabash, Carlisle, Petersburg, Greencastle, Washington, Fairfield, Alton, Quincy, Iowa, Mt. Carmel, Sangamon, Shawneetown, and Worcester Circuits, and in 1840 he was granted a superannuated relation, in which he continued for three years. Then he labored on the Greenville, Carlisle, Lebanon, and Waterloo Circuits until 1847, when he was again placed on the superannuated list for a year. In 1848-9 he was on Edwardsville Circuit, and in 1850 at Illinoistown. The next year his name does not appear on the minutes. In 1852 he fell into the Southern Illinois Conference, and was sent to Marion Circuit. The next year he was appointed to Collinsville Circuit as supernumerary, and in 1854 he was again on the superannuated list. In 1855 he was sent to Carlisle, the next year to Waterloo, and at the conference of 1857 he was granted a location. He died a few years afterwards at his residence near Collinsville. He was a good man, calm and equable in disposition, and uniform in his religious life, a moderate preacher, yet generally acceptable to the people, and standing fair on the circuits he traveled.

JOHN WHEELER McREYNOLDS was born in Washington County, Virginia, February 6, 1800. As stated in the sketch of his brother William, he was the child of deeply devoted Christian parents, under whose faithful instruction he not only became deeply impressed with religious truth, but well-versed in the doctrines and usages of the Church. He was converted in 1819, and the following year was sent by the presiding elder, Charles Holliday, as a supply to the Somerset Circuit, with G. W. Taylor as his colleague. At the session of the Tennessee Conference, in 1820, he was received on trial, and assigned to Little Sandy Circuit, in the Kentucky Conference, and the next year to Goose Creek. In 1822, after having been admitted into full connection and ordained deacon, owing to feeble health, he located. The same Fall he removed to Illinois, and settled near his brother-in-law, Colonel Mayo, in Edgar County. In 1825 he was readmitted in the Illinois Conference, as already stated, and assigned to the Mt. Carmel Circuit, which he traveled for two years. From 1827 until 1834 he traveled in Indiana, becoming a member of the Indiana Conference at its formation, in 1832, and in 1835 he was placed on the superannuated list. The next year he was transferred to the Illinois Conference, and continued in a superannuated relation until 1841, when, owing to the protracted affliction, mental and bodily, of his wife, which rendered his return to the active work of the itinerancy highly improbable, he asked and received a location. Eight days after the death of his afflicted companion, he died, filled with joy, on the 15th of October, 1846.

Philip Cole traveled only this year. At its close he was discontinued at his own request.

Asa D. West was assigned to the Cash River Circuit this year, in 1826 to Patoka, and at the conference of 1827 he was received into full connection, ordained deacon, and, at his own request, granted a location. The next year he was readmitted and assigned to the Atlas Circuit, and in

1829 to the Spoon River Circuit, and again located in 1830. Six years afterwards he was readmitted and assigned to Rock Island, in 1837 to Mt. Pleasant, and in 1838 to Knoxville; in 1839 he again retired from the itinerant to the local ranks. In 1855 he was readmitted in the Missouri Conference, traveled until 1860, when, for the fourth time, he located, and the Minutes give no further account of him.

Of JOSEPH FOULKS, who was this year readmitted into the itinerant work, we have an interesting account in Redford's Methodism in Kentucky, from which the following sketch is in part condensed.

He was born in Monmouth County, New Jersey, August 30, 1786. His parents were from Wales and were members of the Moravian Church. His mother, however, became a Methodist, and two of his sons afterwards became Methodist preachers. Before Joseph was seventeen he was converted and united with the Methodist Episcopal Church. In 1811 he was licensed to preach, and in the Fall of the same year united with the Western Conference. After traveling four years in Tennessee and Kentucky, he located in 1815 and settled in Logan County, Kentucky. In 1820 he removed to Illinois, laboring with energy as a local preacher; and by his labors in the pulpit and the piety of his life, contributing much to the prosperity of the Church. In 1825, as already stated, he was readmitted to the Illinois Conference and appointed to Shoal Creek Circuit. Whilst on this charge, he killed a man in self-defense. He had said something in a sermon that displeased the man, a drunken half Indian, half negro, who swore that he would take the preacher's life. The fears of the family with whom he was staying being aroused by seeing the man whet his knife, they urged Mr. Foulks to be on his guard. Accordingly, upon retiring, he took with him a gun and remained awake to watch. In the night the Indian crept stealthily up the stairway with his knife and gun in his hand, and just as he appeared above, Mr. Foulks fired; the ball struck the man in the breast, killing him instantly. At the ensuing conference his conduct was " fully approved." At the close of his second year on this charge he again located. In 1835 he was again readmitted and appointed to Alton City, but with impaired health he was compelled to locate at the close of the year, and never re-entered the traveling connection. In 1837 he returned to Kentucky and settled in Logan County, where he spent the remainder of his life. In this community he lived for a quarter of a century, a laborious and successful local preacher, and where his name and memory will long be fragrant. One who knew him well says: " His call to the ministry was fully established by the success that crowned his efforts in the various departments of ministerial labor. His talents were above mediocrity. He spoke with fluency; and, although his preaching was generally of a practical and experimental character, yet he was perfectly familiar with the doctrines of the Bible. His literary attainments were not such as to entitle him, in modern parlance, to the name of a learned man, yet his mind was well stored with useful knowledge. He was uncompromising in his fidelity to his own branch of the Church, and deprecated every departure from the old paths." On the 3d of May, 1863, he slept with his fathers. His last illness, though not protracted, was attended with severe suffering; but his mind was kept in perfect peace. His last moments were full of triumph.

William Chambers was born in Calvert County, Maryland, in 1796. He was brought up in the Protestant Episcopal Church, but in early life professed religion and united with the Methodists in Baltimore. When a young man he served two years in the War of 1812. In 1820 he was received on trial in the Kentucky Conference, and after traveling in it four years was transferred to the Illinois Conference and appointed to the Sangamon Circuit as junior preacher, with Peter Cartwright as his senior. At the close of the year he asked and was granted a location. Two years afterwards he was readmitted, and traveled first the Illinois, and then the Shoal Creek Circuit, and at the end of the year again located. In 1838 he was readmitted, and, after traveling Apple Creek and Carlinville Circuits, again located. The next year he was readmitted once more, and appointed successively to the American Bottom, Manchester, Carlinville, and Sharon charges. Refusing to go to his last appointment, his place was supplied by the presiding elder, and, at the ensuing session of conference one of his friends asked for him a location, which the conference granted. He continued in the local ranks until his death in 1859, at his residence near Taylorville. Brother Chambers was a little below medium size, spare and delicate in appearance. He was an acceptable preacher, and an active, energetic man.

WILLIAM SEE traveled only two years—both on the newly formed Peoria Circuit, and at the expiration of his term was discontinued at his own request. During these two years he was active in carrying the Gospel to the newly formed settlements, and organizing the scattering Methodists into societies. He formed the first class in Schuyler County, in the cabin of the first settler, Calvin Hobart. After he ceased traveling, he became government blacksmith for the Indians. He lived in Chicago, where Mr. Beggs, the pastor, appointed him the first class-leader.

CHAPTER III.

1826.

WABASH DISTRICT—Charles Holliday, P. E.
Vermillion—Eli P. Farmer.
Wabash—Robert Delap.
Mt. Vernon—Thomas H. Files.
Mt. Carmel—John W. McReynolds.
Cash River—William Evans.

ILLINOIS DISTRICT—Peter Cartwright, P. E. and
    Superintendent of the Pottawattomie Mission.
Illinois—Samuel H. Thompson, Sup., John Miller.
Kaskaskia—Josiah Patterson, sup., James Hadley.
Shoal Creek—Joseph Foulks.
Sangamon—Richard Hargrave, Joseph Tarkington.
Peoria—William See.
Mississippi—Thomas Randle, Isaac S. House.
Atlas—William Medford.
Pottawattomie Mission—Jesse Walker.

THE conference held its third session at Bloomington, Indiana, commencing on Thursday, September 28th, and closing on the following Tuesday. Bishops Roberts and Soule were both in attendance, presiding alternately, and the journal is signed by both. The attendance seems to have been small, only eleven answering to their names at the opening session. Calvin Ruter was elected secretary, and Charles Holliday assistant secretary. The journal was written by Mr. Holliday, and is a model of chirographical neatness and clearness. At this session a committee was appointed to draw up rules for the government of the conference, with instructions to report as soon as convenient. The report was not presented until the next session. Drafts were ordered on the Book Concern for $150, and on the Chartered Fund for $190.

Some complaints were made against Peter Cartwright through a member of this conference by John Schrader, a local preacher, relative to the proceedings of Brother Cartwright when acting as president of the board of trustees of Hopkinsville meeting-house in Kentucky. After some discussion, Brother Cartwright was exonerated from any censure in the case, and his character was approved.

The conference voted unanimously to concur with the Mississippi Annual Conference in recommending to the General Conference at its next session to alter the Restrictive Rule so that it would read: "They shall not allow of more than one representative for every seven members of the annual conference, nor allow of a less number than one for every twenty-one." Votes were carried to patronize the *Christian Advocate*, published by the agents of the Methodist Book Concern at New York, and also to patronize Augusta College.

A committee was appointed to address a letter to the Rev. John T. Hamilton, a member of the committee on correspondence of the General Assembly of the Presbyterian Church, in answer to a communication which this conference had received from him. The subject of the communication is not stated.

The Sabbath collection was placed in the hands of the four presiding elders to be distributed to the most needy; and a surplus of $14.37½ in the hands of the stewards was ordered to be given to the preacher who may be appointed to the Atlas Circuit.

It was ordered that the Pottawattomic Mission be continued, and that every preacher of the conference exert himself to procure funds and means for the support of said mission, and that St. Louis and Fort Clarke be the places of deposit of those articles conveyed by water, and Springfield, Sangamon County, for those articles and moneys by land. It was estimated that one thousand dollars would be necessary and amply sufficient for the support of the mission.

On the 25th of December of this year, the superintendent of the mission wrote to John Emory, the corresponding secretary of the Missionary Society, as follows: "The Pottawattomic Mission was established on Fox River, twenty miles from its entrance into the Illinois River. We have prepared a building, thirty by fifty, with five rooms, two stories high, and some other buildings. We have opened forty acres of a farm. We have a school in operation, with about twenty Indian children, who promise to learn rapidly. The mission family consists of the missionary and wife, one teacher, two laboring men, and two women. I think this nation will receive the Gospel."

The following mysterious item appears among the closing proceedings of the session: "Samuel H. Thompson was by the president appointed to obtain a copy of the report of the committee of safety that it may be entered on the journals of this conference."

The following class was received on trial: Henry Buell, Robert Burns, Abner H. Cheever, William Evans, Thomas H. Files, John Hogan, Isaac S. House, John T. Johnson, Daniel Newton, Stith M. Otwell, Smith L. Robinson.

James Scott was readmitted.

Seven located, viz.: Thomas Hewson, George K. Hester, William Chambers, Hackaliah Vredenburg, Samuel Bassett, James Jones, Ebenezer T. Webster.

One local deacon was elected to elder's orders; viz., Robert Burns. And Samuel Bellamy, Levi Poston, Samuel Morrison, Gamaliel Taylor, Thomas Lowry, Thomas C. Collins, Reuben Clearwater, Humphrey Finch, and Samuel Lyon were elected to deacon's orders.

Some changes were made in the plan of the work in Illinois. The Carmi and Brownsville Circuits were merged in the circuits from which they had been taken. The Cash River and Mt. Vernon Circuits were transferred from the Illinois to the Wabash District. Perhaps this was done to conciliate Peter Cartwright, who was appointed presiding elder of the Illinois District. He once said of Cash River in the cabinet: "I have known that country for many years. The raccoons get half the corn, and the people have none to sell, and I won't have it in my district." A new circuit, the Atlas, was formed of the southern portion of the Territory between the Illinois and Mississippi Rivers, known familiarly as "the Military Tract," extending from the mouth of the Illinois River to Canton, in Fulton County.

There were extensive revivals on several of the charges both during the Winter and at the camp-meetings. On Big Creek, Vermillion Circuit, under the labors of Eli P. Farmer, was a good work of grace, and many were gathered into the Church. Under the labors of William Blackwell, a local preacher, there was a good revival in Bellevelle, and about forty united with the Church. On the Sangamon Circuit a change was made in the pastorate. The health of Mr. Hargrave, the preacher in charge, having failed, he left the circuit in the Spring for his home in Indiana, and the junior preacher, Joseph Tarkington, was put in charge, and James Johnson employed as his assistant to the end of the year. Two camp-meetings were held on the circuit; one at Walter's camp-ground, on Spring Creek, and another near Jacksonville, at Hendershott's, at both of which were good revivals. Towards the close of the conference year a camp-meeting was held in Pike County, of which Peter Cartwright gives an account: "We had but one tent on the ground, and that was called 'the preacher's tent.' The people rolled on to the ground in their wagons. We held this meeting several days and nights in this way, and we had a prosperous meeting. We held one in Schuyler County the same season, and many souls were blessed."

Among the laymen who this year became identi-tified with Methodism in Illinois was DR. JOHN

LOGAN, who afterwards occupied a prominent position in the State as well as in the Church. He was born in Hamilton County, Ohio, December 30, 1809. When but a child he removed with his parents to Perry County, Missouri, and in 1826 to Jackson County, Illinois. He was converted this year, and united with the Methodist Episcopal Church. When only twenty-two he was elected major of the Ninth Regiment of Illinois Militia, and the next year served in the Black Hawk war. In 1833 he settled at Carlinville, and soon after engaged in the practice of medicine. At the beginning of the war of the rebellion, in 1861, he was elected colonel of the Thirty-second Regiment of Illinois Volunteers, and served until 1865. The next year he was appointed United States marshal for Southern Illinois, and held the office until 1870. He was one of the original abolitionists who voted for Birney, in 1844. Dr. Logan has been an active member of the Church for over fifty years, and has filled most of the offices to which a layman is eligible.

ISAAC LANDIS, a local preacher, moved from Missouri to Indiana, and thence to Greene County, Illinois, in 1827, and settled in the neighborhood of Carrollton. He was elected to deacon's orders in 1832, and to elder's in 1840. His house was for a long time a preaching-place on the Grafton Circuit. He was a man of moderate ability as a preacher, but of deep piety. He died in 1857, aged seventy-nine.

In November of this year, RICHARD GAINES, a brother-in-law of Peter Cartwright, moved from

Kentucky and settled in the neighborhood of Pleasant Plains, in Sangamon County. He was born November 8, 1777, in Charlotte County, Virginia, and died January 7, 1845. He was a useful and faithful local preacher.

The membership reported at the close of the year was 4,412 whites, 53 colored, and 1 Indian, an increase during the year of 558. The largest increase was on the Vermillion Circuit, being 197. Sangamon Circuit had an increase of 125, and in several other charges there was an increase of from 40 to 60 each. In the Shoal Creek and Cash River Circuits there was a slight decrease.

The following brethren appear for the first time in connection with the work in Illinois:

ELI P. FARMER was born in Virginia, January 27, 1794. He removed to Indiana in 1822, and three years afterwards was received on trial in the Illinois Conference and appointed to Bloomfield. In 1826 he was sent to Vermillion Circuit. This was the only year in which he labored in Illinois. He continued in the conference, however, until 1832, when he fell into the Indiana Conference, in which he traveled a year and then located. In 1837 he was readmitted, traveled two years and located again in 1839. His died at his residence near Bloomington, Indiana, February 6, 1881. Mr. Farmer was a man of marked peculiarities. He believed in muscular Christianity. Regarded as one of the strongest and most active men in the State, he did not hesitate to use his strength in the maintenance of order at the meetings he held; and

it was not infrequently the case that he would leave
the pulpit to administer personal chastisement to
the rowdies who attempted to disturb the peace of
his meetings. Though of moderate education, and
not excelling as a preacher, he was yet a man of
great power in the pulpit, and many were won to
Christ through his instrumentality. He was a soldier in the war of 1812, and took part in the battle
of New Orleans. When the war of the rebellion
broke out, though he had previously been a Demo-
crat, he at once espoused the cause of his country,
making many strong speeches in favor of the preservation of the Union, and bitterly denouncing
those with whom he had formerly acted. Though
then nearly seventy years of age, he entered the
army as a chaplain, and not only did his duty as
such faithfully, but refused to receive compensation
for his services. Indeed, this was one of his peculiarities. A writer in the Indianapolis *Journal* says
of him: " His profession was that of the ministry,
but his means of support were derived from the
farm. In his ministerial career he introduced the
novel practice of giving the people a free Gospel;
and in all his experience, extending over a long
life, he was never known to ask any congregation
or Church for a contribution on his own behalf."

After his location he became an active partisan
politician, and represented his county in the State
legislature. While there, he became involved in a
quarrel with the speaker of the house, and administered to him a severe thrashing. He also studied
law and was admitted to the bar. " He passed

through many storms in his day, but his sun came to a golden setting. For several years he gave himself to seek holiness and walk with God alone. At the last he rejoiced greatly, and was eager to depart and go home."[1]

This was the first year of the itinerant life of THOMAS H. FILES. He traveled in succession the Mt. Vernon, Cash River, Golconda, Wabash, McLeansboro, Frankfort, and Paris Circuits, and in 1835 was granted a superannuated relation, in which he remained until his death, in 1849. His memoir is not published in the General Minutes, but Mr. Beggs says he was "of great service to the Church."

WILLIAM EVANS was also received on trial this year. He traveled only two circuits in Illinois—the Cash River in 1826, and the Golconda in 1831. The rest of his charges were in Indiana, and in 1832 he was transferred to the Indiana Conference, and located at its first session.

RICHARD HARGRAVE was a native of North Carolina, born December 5, 1803. In youth he removed with his parents to Indiana, and when he was nineteen he was converted and joined the so-called "O'Kelly Christian Church." He remained in it but for a short time, and then united with the Methodist Episcopal Church, in which he was licensed to preach in 1823. He traveled some months under the presiding elder, William Beauchamp, during the Summer of 1824, and in the Fall united with the Illinois Conference at its first session and was appointed to Salem Circuit. In 1825

---

[1] Rev. J. W. Webb.

his appointment. was Honey Creek, and in 1826 Sangamon. Here his health failed, and he was compelled to retire from the work in the Spring, but was so far restored as to receive an appointment at the next session of conference. This was the only year he traveled in Illinois, all the rest of his itinerant life being spent in Indiana. He belonged successively to the Illinois, Indiana, North Indiana, and North-west Indiana Conferences, occupying many of their most important charges. He was. seventeen years in the presiding eldership, twenty-four years in circuits and stations, and fourteen on the superannuated list. He died near Attica, Indiana, June 23, 1879. Mr. Hargrave was one of the strongest preachers in the West. He delighted to dwell on the doctrines of the Bible. " With a voice full of melody, and forceful enough for greater audiences than ever assemble; with a sharp, clear, articulation, and a phraseology so unique as to charm the ear strangely, he uttered great doctrinal sermons, which in other hands might have been dry and stale, but from him possessed all the enchantment of tales of the heroic. This was not all. He drew argument and illustration from the common scenes observed by common sense men, and convinced the mind. Then, so rapidly as to startle the sinner, he made him conscious of his guilt, and left the soul with a loving Savior. On many occasions members fell around him as if dead, and remained so in some cases for hours, coming to consciousness with the song of salvation on their lips."[2]   An ex-

---

[2] *Western Christian Advocate.*

hortation delivered during his year on the Sangamon Circuit was long remembered. Standing on the roof of the jail at Springfield, he addressed the thousands who had come to witness an execution in such burning and eloquent words that twenty years afterwards the writer heard many who listened to it declare it the most powerful address they had ever heard from human lips. Perhaps the most marked traits in Mr. Hargrave's character were his deep reverence and strong trust in God, and his earnest and hearty sympathy with suffering humanity. In labors he was more abundant. Even when superannuated he preached above two hundred sermons a year, and in the last year of his life, during the seven months in which he was able to get about, he preached one hundred and four times. He was, during his whole life, a great sufferer from disease. His last illness of over two months was attended with the most acute suffering. But over all he triumphed through grace, desiring to depart and be with Christ. He was a member of the General Conferences of 1848 and 1860.

JOSEPH TARKINGTON was born at Nashville, Tennessee, October 30, 1800. In his twentieth year he was converted at a camp-meeting near Bloomington, Indiana, and in 1825 was received into the Illinois Conference and appointed to Patoka Circuit. For the two following years he traveled the Sangamon Circuit. The remainder of his itinerant life has been spent in Indiana. He is still living at Greensburg, Indiana, and is a superannuated member of the South-east Indiana Conference.

He was presiding elder eight years and agent for
Asbury University two years. He has filled several
leading stations in the conferences of which he has
been a member.

Isaac S. House was born at Brookfield, New
York, April 7, 1806. His parents were among the
first Methodists in that section of the country and
early instructed their son in the principles of our
holy religion. At the age of twelve he became a subject of converting grace and united with the Church.
For several years he remained faithful; but, having
removed to the West, where he was deprived of
the care of Christian friends and of many of the
privileges of the Church which he had previously
enjoyed, he backslid, sought enjoyment in the pleas-
ures of the world, and became very wicked. In
1821, at a camp-meeting at Gilham's camp-ground,
between Alton and Edwardsville, he was reclaimed,
and the next year received license to preach, and
united with the Illinois Conference. His first appointment was the Mississippi Circuit, with Thomas
Randle as his senior. The next year he was junior
preacher on the Sangamon Circuit; and at the conference of 1828, after being received into full connection and ordained deacon, his health being poor,
he was placed on the superannuated list. At the
next session he located. In this relation he continued for fifteen years, preaching and laboring for the
cause of Christ as his health would permit. In
1844 he was readmitted in the Providence Conference, and stationed at Fourth Street, New Bedford,
to which he was returned the next year. Then, his

health again failing, he was granted a superannuated relation, in which he remained until his death, July 7, 1847. " Brother House was a good man, was distinguished for his social qualities, and was a kind and affectionate father and husband. He often spoke of his parents with strong filial affection, and of the gratitude he owed them for early religious instruction. He was more than an ordinary preacher, sound in doctrine, fervent, affectionate, and powerful. He united many excellencies as a man, a Christian, and a minister, and was respected and beloved by those who knew him. His sickness was painful and protracted, but he was patient and resigned, and died in peace and full assurance of a blissful immortality."[3]   One of his early colleagues says, " He was a sweet-spirited young man, who labored earnestly and was much beloved."

[3] General Minutes.

CHAPTER IV.

1827.

Wabash District—Charles Holliday, P. E.
Vermillion—John Fox.
Wabash—James Hadley.
Mt. Vernon—Thomas H. Files.
Mt. Carmel—Aaron Wood.
Cash River—Samuel C. Cooper.

Illinois District—Peter Cartwright, P. E.
Illinois—Samuel H. Thompson, John Hogan.
Kaskaskia—William Echols.
Shoal Creek—John Kerns.
Sangamon—Joseph Tarkington, Isaac S. House.
Peoria—Smith L. Robinson.
Apple Creek—Isaac Scarritt, John T. Johnson.
Atlas—Samuel Bogart.
Pottawattomie Mission at Salem—John Dew, super-
    intendent and collector for the mission.
    Jesse Walker, missionary.

THE session of 1827 was held at Mt. Carmel, Illinois, in an upper room of the house of T. S. Hinde, beginning on Thursday, September 20th, and closing on the following Wednesday. Bishop Roberts presided, and Calvin W. Ruter was elected secretary. The attendance was much larger than at any previous session, twenty-seven answering to their names at the first calling of the roll. Then the probationers of the first year did not attend conference, but remained on their circuits.

The session was an important one on account of the amount and variety of the business transacted.

Eleven persons were received on trial; viz., John Hardy, Constant B. Jones, Enoch G. Wood, Asahel L. Risley, Benjamin Stephenson, Samuel Bogart, John Kerns, William Mavity, William Echols, Samuel C. Cooper, James McKean.

John Fox, Isaac Scarritt, and Charles Slocumb were readmitted.

Asa D. West, Joseph Foulks, George Randle, and William Medford were granted a location.

William See was discontinued. Two had died, William Cravens, and John Cord.

Three local deacons were elected to elder's orders; viz., Robert Ray, Hezekiah Holland, and Ebenezer Jones.

And eight local preachers were elected to deacon's order. Charles W. Morrow, Elijah McDaniel, Alfred J. Colton, Daniel Dillings, John Givens, Thornton Peeples, William Meldrum, Lorenzo Edwards.

The rule adopted by the conference at its session in 1825, requiring of located preachers applying for readmission into the traveling connection a recommendation from the quarterly conference, was rescinded.

Much has been said and written about the ignorance of the early Methodist preachers, their lack of culture, and general inferiority in scholastic attainments to the preachers of the present day. The following course of reading and study, to be pursued by the candidates for the ministry, which was presented by Bishop Roberts and ordered to be spread on the conference journal, shows that our fathers were not inattentive to the work of ministerial education. And while our modern caurses of study may be more extensive than this, running through a longer period and embracing a wider range, with vastly improved text-books, the mastering of this course by a candidate would secure for him a qualification for the work of the ministry not greatly inferior to that demanded of candidates at the present day.

"The Holy Ghost saith: 'Study to show thyself approved unto God, a workman that needeth not to be ashamed, rightly dividing the word of truth. Hold fast the form of sound words which thou hast heard from me, in faith and love which is in Christ Jesus. Give attendance to reading, to exhortation, to doctrine.'

"It is therefore recommended to candidates for the ministry to study and make themselves acquainted with the following important points of doctrine: The general depravity and corruption of the human heart, redemption by Christ, repentance toward God, justification by faith, the direct witness of the Holy Spirit, holiness of heart and life, including regeneration and sanctification, the divinity of our Lord Jesus Christ, the perseverance of those who have been justified, baptism, the resurrection of the dead, and future rewards and punishments.

"It is recommended to them to study the nature and principles of Church government, especially our own; the philosophy or grammar of the English language, geography, ancient history, ecclesiastical history, moral and natural philosophy, and logic.	.

"To aid the student in the acquisition of these important branches of knowledge, the reading of the following books, or as many of them as can be obtained, is recommended: The Holy Scriptures, Wesley's Notes, Benson's, Coke's, and Clarke's Commentaries, Wesley's Sermons, Answer to Taylor, Saints' Rest, Benson's Sermons, Fletcher's Checks and Appeal, Portrait of St. Paul, Watson's Theological Institutes, Wood's or Martindale's Dictionary, the Methodist Discipline, Murray's Grammar, Morse's Geography, Rollin's Ancient History, Mosheim's Ecclesiastical History, Locke on the Understanding, Paley's Philosophy, Duncan's or Watts' Logic, the *Methodist Magazine*."

The committee appointed at the last session to draft rules for the government of the conference presented a report, which, after amendment, was adopted. The rules, twelve in number, are those by which deliberative bodies are usually governed. The eleventh and twelfth, however, are especially appropriate to a body of Christian ministers: "Every member of this conference, in his debates, shall have due regard to the feelings of his brethren, and avoid all personality." "No member shall prefer a complaint against another member of this conference, unless he has spoken to him on the subject first out of conference."

At this session the question of a conference seminary was introduced. A petition on the subject was presented by Peter Cartwright from certain citizens of Greene County, which was referred to a committee, with instructions to report at this session. Their report, which was adopted, recommended the appointment of a committee of five to obtain all the information they could on the subject during the ensuing year, and report the result of their inquiries to the next conference. And John Strange, James Armstrong, Charles Holliday, Peter Cartwright, and William Shanks were appointed that committee.

The Pottawattomie Mission at Salem, on Fox River, occupied much of the attention of the conference. When the superintendent and missionary made their reports, a committee of five was appointed to take into consideration the state of the mission, and the expediency of continuing it. That committee reported as follows: "At the Illinois Conference held in Charleston, 1825, an allowance of one thousand dollars was made for the support of the mission, and put into the hands of the missionary. From our recollection of the missionary report to the conference of 1826, that money was laid out for the mission, and a debt contracted of $1,208.80; cash on hand to meet the debt, $150; which leaves the mission in debt, $1,058.80. At the conference of 1826 an allowance was made for the support of the mission of one thousand dollars, and put in the hands of the superintendent of the mission. From the report to this conference it appears that the money has been laid out for the mission. No debts have been contracted the past year.

" According to the report to this conference, the mission property amounts to $303.25. The crop, as valued in the report, amounts to $502. The property offered in the report, which we advise the conference to accept and make mission property, amounts to $250. If the conference accept this property, then the property and crop belonging to the mission will amount to $1,055.25.

" But little has been effected, as yet, by the mission when compared to the expense, labor, and sufferings of the missionary and his family; but, when we consider what it has cost, and the probability of its being less expensive in future, we can not advise its discontinuance until further trial is given it.

" As it respects the debt now against the mission, it is our opinion that a man had better be appointed, whose duty it shall be to make collections in the bounds of the conference and elsewhere to pay that debt." The person appointed in accordance with this report to make collections for the mission, John Dew, was styled the superintendent, and the collections made during the past year, in money and property, were ordered to be placed in his hands.

A case of supposed heresy was before the conference, and excited considerable interest. When the name of James Scott, an elder, was called, objections were made to the passage of his character, on the ground that he had advanced certain ideas believed to be heterodox. A committee was appointed to wait on Brother Scott and obtain his views on certain

doctrines by him advanced, and report to the conference. When two days afterwards, the committee
presented their report, after considerable discussion
the further consideration of it was postponed until
the next annual session, the conference ordering
that he be admonished by the president not to dis-
seminate his peculiar views on the points of doctrine
referred to in the report of the committee. His
character was then passed. Dr. Aaron Wood gives
the following statement of the case: "At the re-
bound from the Augustinian doctrine and Edward-
ean philosophy which affected the three churches in
the West, viz.: Methodist, Baptist, and Presbyterian,
the three errors of the ancient Church were broached
afresh in Kentucky, and many of the members and
some preachers were Pelagians, Arians, or Socinians,
and though most of them went with the New Lights,
yet some remained with the Methodists. Holliday,
Cartwright, S. H. Thompson, and George Locke
had all contended with these errors in Kentucky,
and knew the men. One of them was the father-
in-law, and three others the friends, of Scott, located and living in Indiana. Scott was arrested on
certain expressions in a sermon preached at the conference, and was called before a committee. Scott
was a hypercritical, sharp Jerseyman, who, instead
of a frank statement of his views, did what he could
to puzzle the committee, and they reported as pun-
ishment that he be kept from charge of a circuit,
which was indefinitely postponed. At the next conference, I remember that when, on the motion of
his presiding elder, he was asked " Do you believe

in the generation, or traduction, or impartation of depravity?" he replied, "I do n't *believe* either, for it is a matter of opinion, and can not be faith, as there is no testimony."

Mr. Scott, after traveling a number of years in the conferences in Indiana, was finally deposed from the ministry in 1860.

The conference at this session elected its first delegates to the General Conference to meet the next year. They were John Strange, Peter Cartwright, James Armstrong, Charles Holliday, Samuel H. Thompson, and John Dew.

A resolution was adopted, which, if carried out, would have greatly aided the historian of the Illinois Conference; but, like too many conference resolutions, it was adopted, and then forgotten. It was a request that each preacher belonging to the conference present in writing to the next conference a succinct account of the time and place of his birth, the most important incidents of his life, when and by what means he was brought to the knowledge of salvation, with any other important matter that may concern him, and that the same be kept on file among the papers of the conference.

This was a year of prosperity. All the charges in Illinois, save two, report an increase in the number of members. The Wabash, Mt. Vernon, Illinois, Shoal Creek, Mississippi, and Atlas Circuits, each reported an increase of over one hundred, the increase for the State being 920, or more than twenty-five per cent. The entire membership was 5,335 whites and fifty-two colored.

Several interesting camp-meetings were held this year; among them were two on the Sangamon Circuit, one east of Springfield, and the other at Hussey's, on Fancy Creek. This was a very successful meeting, and many were born into the kingdom. A meeting described by Mr. Beggs was held on Farm Creek, on the Peoria Circuit, of which S. L. Robinson was preacher in charge, Jesse Walker and William See assisted at the meeting, which was conducted by the presiding elder. Governor Edwards, the first governor of the State, was also present. They had a gracious time, yet even in that early day they were not free from disturbance. A certain individual was sent after whisky, and who, in going for it, had to pass the camp-ground. He stopped to hear the presiding elder's sermon. After its close a collection was taken up, and the money designed for the whisky (fifty cents), was thrown into the hat. When he returned, and was asked where his money was gone to, he replied, " O, I thought the preachers needed it more than you did the whisky."

Some new societies were formed this year. Rev. J. Mayo, a local preacher, preached the first sermon in Brouillett Township, Edgar County, this year. The first society was also formed in Pekin by Smith L. Robinson. It consisted of eight or ten members. A class was also organized on Robinson's Creek, in Shelby County, by Thomas Randle, who traveled the Shoal Creek Circuit. Preaching was introduced and societies formed at Lawrenceville and Palestine, on the Mt. Carmel Circuit. At the former of these places was a great revival. Under the labors of John Fox on the Vermillion Circuit, there was a good work of grace.

Among the removals to the State and accessions to the Church this year was ABEL L. WILLIAMS, who settled in Vermillion County. He was a native of North Carolina, and was born January 30, 1786. When a child, he moved with his parents to Tennessee. In 1811, with his wife, he united with the Methodist Episcopal Church, and after coming to their new home in Illinois, such were his faith and zeal, that he took his ax, went to the timber, and upon his own responsibility, began cutting the timber for the erection of a church. Witnessing his determination, his neighbors came to his assistance, and soon the old Lebanon Church took the place of the private house as a place of worship. This became and was for many years a center of Methodism in Eastern Illinois. He became superintendent of the Sunday-school, and served as such for twenty-five years. While listening to the fireside conversation of the old preachers in his boyhood home, a desire for the attainment of knowledge was excited, and though unable to reach a collegiate or even academic education, yet such was his thirst for knowledge, that, availing himself of the opportunities in his reach, he became a proficient in ancient and modern history, and well acquainted with the literature of the Church. He had a well-selected library, embracing the complete works of Wesley, Fletcher, Watson, and Clarke, besides many works on philosophy and science. He

was much interested in the educational interests of
the Church. To the first conference academy built
in Eastern Illinois, the Georgetown, he was the
most liberal contributor, and of all the institutions
of the Church he was a liberal supporter. He died
full of years at the house of his son, Rev. James
Williams, near Newman, Douglas County, February
15, 1881, in his ninety-sixth year.[1]

REV. MILES HART, a local preacher from Kentucky, settled this year at Wabash Point, in Coles
County. He was the first permanent settler there.
Finding a cabin that had been erected by a Mr.
Sawyer, who, after building it, had gone after his
family, Mr. Hart took possession of it, and, by the
time the owner returned with his household, had
put up one for himself, into which he removed.
He was a good preacher, rather above the average,
very pleasant and smooth in his address, even and
uniform in his whole course, and so agreeable in his
manners that he acquired the sobriquet of "Old
Jolly." He was about six feet high and very slender. He died highly respected about twenty years ago.

The plan of the work remained the same as it
had been the year before, the only change being the
substitution of Apple Creek for Mississippi as the
name of one of the circuits.

Ten new preachers labored this year in Illinois.

JOHN FOX was a native of New Jersey, born in
1774. In 1809 he united with the Philadelphia
Conference, and traveled in it until 1820, when he
located. He then moved to Illinois, and settled on

[1] Rev. W. S. Calhoun.

a farm a few miles from Palestine. Here he accumulated a handsome property. In 1827 he was readmitted in the Illinois Conference, and traveled in succession the Vermillion, Mt. Vernon, Wabash, Mt. Carmel, Paris, Eugene, Shawneetown, Wabash, Eugene, Mt. Carmel, Maysville, Charleston, Carlisle, McLeansboro, Richland, Crooked Creek, and Urbana Circuits. He died at Homer, Champaign County, Illinois, August 26, 1846. His memoir says of him: "As a man, Brother Fox was a pattern of neatness and industry; as a Christian, uniform and consistent; as a preacher, plain, practical, and pointed; and as a pastor, faithful and affectionate." One of his parishioners on the Vermillion Circuit describes him as "a nice man and a good singer. He was a rigid disciplinarian, excluding from the Church many of those who had been received by his predecessor."[2] As a preacher he was moderate, and was accustomed to relate many anecdotes in his preaching. One who listened to him heard him tell thirty-two anecdotes in one sermon. He had a thorough knowledge of Methodism as a system of Church polity, and insisted strongly upon the observance of all its peculiarities. Mr. Beggs speaks of "John Fox, of precious memory—neat in person and attire, correct in his preaching, diligent in pastoral visitation, strict in administration of discipline, and powerful in prayer—his labors never failing to result in the salvation of souls." He died in holy triumph. The last words he uttered, just as the soul left the body, were "Jesus, Jesus."

----

[2] Col. Mayo.

AARON WOOD was born in Pendleton County, Virginia, October 15, 1802. He was the first-born of praying parents. His father's house was occasionally visited by Bishop Asbury, whose horse Aaron would care for, and who always spoke to the boy about his soul, urging him to give himself to the Savior, that he might grow up to be a good and useful man. In 1815 he was converted, and in 1822 united with the Ohio Conference, in which he traveled two years, and then fell into the Illinois Conference, of which he remained a member until 1831, when he located. His only appointment in Illinois was Mt. Carmel Circuit, which he traveled two years. They were years of great spiritual prosperity. In the Fall of 1827 he had married the daughter of Rev. William Beauchamp, with whom he lived until 1838 when she died. The years in which he was located he spent in Mt. Carmel, where he engaged in teaching school, laboring faithfully meanwhile as a local preacher. In 1834 he was re-admitted in the Indiana Conference, and has been connected ever since with the conferences in that State, being now (1883) an honored member of the North-west Indiana Conference. During his itinerant life he has spent thirteen years on districts, thirteen years in agencies for Asbury University, the American Bible Society, and the Preachers' Aid Society, six years as chaplain to the Penitentiary and Orphans' Home, and twenty-four years on circuits and stations. He was a member of the General Conferences of 1840, 1844, 1864, 1868, and 1876. Mr. Beggs says of him, "A. Wood, D. D., and myself were both young men when we became acquainted. He bid fair, at an early age, to become a useful man. He had a sound mind, a most felicitous elocution, and a zeal without bound. He preached always with all his power, frequently becoming so exhausted as to fall helpless into the arms of those near him." "The fields of his labor have been as wide as his eventful experience, for he began his ministry in the days when a circuit was as large as a modern conference, a district as extensive as a State, and a conference was bounded almost alone by the possibility of the itinerant's return in time for the next session. These fields embraced Western Ohio, all of Indiana, Eastern Illinois, and Southern Michigan. All this labor has been unrelieved by one hour of superannuation, and all his life untarnished by a moment of moral reproach."[3]

SAMUEL C. COOPER traveled two circuits in Illinois, the Cash River this year, and the Jonesboro, a part of the same circuit, two years afterwards. He was born of Methodist parents in the city of Baltimore, May 17, 1799. In 1818 he was converted in the State of Ohio, and was soon after licensed to exhort. He felt that God had called him to preach, but resisted the impression and engaged in worldly business. He prospered for a time, but the hand of God was then laid upon him—his wife died, he was compelled to close his business, and at length, after a severe mental conflict, he yielded to his convictions of duty. After serving as a supply on the Vincennes Circuit, he was received in the Illinois

---

[3] Dr. A. Edwards.

Conference in 1827, but all his itinerant life, with the exceptions above named, was spent in Indiana. He died, a member of the North Indiana Conference, July 19, 1856. He was eleven years on districts, seven years agent for Asbury University, one year agent for the Fort Wayne Female College, and ten years in circuits and stations. He was twice a member of the General Conference, and performed his last service for the Church at its session in Indianapolis a few weeks before his death. In his early ministry he experienced much of the hardships and privations of the itinerancy. During his first year in the conference, on Cash River Circuit, he received but fifteen dollars in money for his services, and of that five dollars was given by one man. "He was a good preacher, always systematic and clear. He had great business capacities and was a safe counselor to his younger brethren."[4]

The life of JOHN HOGAN belongs to civil rather than ecclesiastical history. He traveled only four years as a preacher, and then engaged in secular business. He came to the Illinois Conference with a recommendation from the quarterly conference of Baltimore city station, and was received at the session of 1826 and appointed to Salem Circuit, and in 1829 transferred to the Missouri Conference and stationed in St. Louis. At the close of the year he located. He settled at first in Alton, and engaged actively in politics. In 1836 and 1837 he represented his county in the State Legislature. Mr. Linder says of him that he was a fluent and inter-

---

[4] General Minutes.

esting speaker. In 1838 he was a candidate for Congress in opposition to Governor John Reynolds, and was defeated. He soon after removed to St. Louis, where he is still (1883) living. Whilst in the itinerancy he was an effective, useful, and popular preacher.

Of WILLIAM ECHOLS we know but little. From the journal of conference and General Minutes we learn that he was received on trial in 1827, appointed to the Kaskaskia Circuit, and at the close of the year was discontinued at his own request. One who knew him well says, "He was a young man of a good deal of vivacity and a fair preacher. He was gentlemanly in his manners, and had been accustomed to good society." [5]

JOHN KERNS is now (1883), and has been for the last ten years, a superannuate of the Minnesota Conference. After his year on Shoal Creek Circuit he traveled in Indiana until 1853, when he was transferred to the Wisconsin Conference, and in 1856 fell into the Minnesota Conference. He served several years in the presiding eldership, and has filled many of the most important circuits and stations in the conferences to which he has belonged.

SMITH L. ROBINSON was born in the State of Kentucky, in 1806. His parents were Presbyterians. While he was a child they emigrated to Illinois, and settled in the neighborhood of Shawneetown. In his nineteenth year he was powerfully converted at a camp-meeting in Madison County,

---

[2] Dr. John Logan.

at which Isaac S. House and Stith M. Otwell were also converted. His conversion is thus described by Rev. N. P. Heath : "He had been at the altar as a seeker of religion, and was apparently in great agony of mind. All at once he became perfectly calm, and remained in that condition for about an hour and a half, lying on his back and not moving a muscle. His eyes were closed, and he was seemingly unconscious. Suddenly he sprang to his feet, caught hold of a small tree, and sprang up it about ten feet, crying in a loud voice, 'Hello, Jesus!' Then he fell back in the altar, where he lay some time, apparently dead, and as cold as a corpse. Finally he sprang to his feet and praised God for pardoning mercy." He was received in the Illinois Conference in 1826, and assigned to the Paoli Circuit, in Indiana. He then traveled in succession the Peoria, Kaskaskia, Sangamon, Galena, and Lebanon Circuits. In 1833 he was agent for the newly established Lebanon Seminary. The next year he was in the Jacksonville Station, and at the close of the year was transferred to the Indiana Conference, and stationed at Terre Haute. At the session of 1836, being then sick, he was placed on the superannuated list, and died a few days after the close of the session.

ISAAC SCARRITT was born in the State of Connecticut, in 1775. After he reached the age of manhood, he was alone, engaged in his work, when ·there came upon him an overwhelming sense of sin and guilt before God. He knew nothing of conversion as now taught and understood, but with a depth of sorrow and anguish which almost crushed him, he dropped upon his knees, and immediately his sorrow was gone, and joy and peace filled his whole soul. His love to God was such as he could not express, and he praised him constantly as he went on with the work of the day where he was then engaged. He was alone in the woods, and his business detained him there for several days. During all this time he was happy, and praise to God was the abiding sentiment of his heart. He had heard a Baptist preacher several times, and although he could not recollect any thing by way of impression made on his mind before this great change was wrought, yet now some things he had heard came to his remembrance, and he began to think this was the new heart he had heard about; and, feeling a love for the preacher he had never felt before, and for those who were members of his Church, he resolved to see and converse with the preacher, and, if worthy, to offer himself to the Church. But, after a walk of ten miles, he failed to meet him, and shortly after he met with Rev. E. R. Sabin, a Methodist preacher and presiding elder. He heard him preach, and the doctrine and spirit of the sermon were in such complete harmony with his views and feelings at the time, that he invited him to his father's house. They conversed together, and as a result which shortly followed, he united with the Methodist Church, and after a hasty preparation he accompanied him on his district, and under his instructions and by his advice began to preach the Gospel. He was received on trial in the New

England Conference, in 1807, and appointed to Needham, the next year to Durham, and in 1809 to Portsmouth. His health having failed, he located. In 1818 he removed to Edwardsville, Illinois, and nine years afterwards he was readmitted in the Illinois Conference, and appointed to Apple Creek. In 1828 he was appointed missionary to the Pottawattomies, on Fox River; in 1829 he was sent to the Kaskaskia Circuit, and in 1830 to Fort Clark. At the close of the year he located and settled on the Dupage, in Will County. In 1860 he was readmitted in the Rock River Conference and placed on the superannuated list; and, on the 15th of May following, at the residence of his son-in-law, at Joliet, he closed his life with unwavering faith in Jesus Christ, and a firm hope of a glorious immortality. He was courageous in difficulties, patient under suffering, strong in faith. He cheerfully performed every duty required of him to the full extent of his ability. He was sound in doctrine, pure in motive, and correct in life, and possessed the confidence of all who knew him.[6] Mr. Heath, who knew him well, says of him : " He was a real, live Yankee, sharp, far-seeing, and when he spoke it was evident that he had something to say. He was a strong and smooth preacher, easy in manner and forcible in style, very logical and convincing in argument, often completely overwhelming his opponents, and yet using so keen a sword that they would hardly be conscious of the wound until they attempted to defend themselves, when they would

---

[6] General Minutes.

discover that they were mortally wounded. He was particularly strong on the Calvinistic controversy."

JOHN T. JOHNSON was received on trial in the Illinois Conference in 1826, and appointed to the Whitewater Circuit. In 1827 he was junior preacher on the Apple Creek Circuit with Isaac Scarritt, and the three following years he traveled in Indiana. In 1832 he fell into the Indiana Conference, in which he remained until 1836, when he located. Twelve years afterwards he was readmitted in the Illinois Conference, and traveled in succession Mc-Leansboro, Wabash, Palestine, and Lawrenceville Circuits. In 1852 he fell into the Southern Illinois Conference, and filled the Olney, Mt. Carmel, Benton, Richview, Tamaroa, Spring Garden, and Hickory Hill Circuits until 1862, when he again located. He was readmitted in 1871, and appointed to Ramsey, but at the close of the year was granted a superannuated relation, in which he still continues. He resides on his farm a few miles from Mt. Vernon, Illinois.

SAMUEL BOGART was received on trial in the conference this year, and appointed to Atlas Circuit. In 1828 his appointment was Apple Creek, from which he had been recommended to the conference. The next year he was sent again to Atlas, and at the session of 1830 he received a location at his own request. "He was a man of fine appearance, six feet high and well proportioned, and of good address. He was rather illiterate, but was quite popular as a preacher. After he ceased traveling he settled at Rushville, and his house was for a time the preaching-place. He afterwards moved to Macomb, and during the Black Hawk War raised a battalion, whence he obtained the title of colonel. He subsequently moved to Missouri, where, having been set upon by ruffians he killed one of them in self-defense; but such was the combination against him that he fled to Texas, after which we have no account of him."[7]

[7] Dr. A. Dunlap.

CHAPTER V.

1828.

WABASH DISTRICT—George Locke, P. E.
Vermillion—Henry Buell, Asahel L. Risley.
Wabash—William Mavity.
Mt. Vernon—John Fox.
Mt. Carmel—Aaron Wood.
Cash River—Thomas H. Files, Miles Huffaker.

ILLINOIS DISTRICT—Peter Cartwright, P. E.
Illinois—William Chambers.
Kaskaskia—Smith L. Robinson, Asahel E. Phelps.
Shoal Creek—Samuel H. Thompson, William L. Deneen.
Sangamon—James McKean, John H. Benson.
Peoria—Jesse Walker, Hardin A. Tarkington.
Apple Creek—Samuel Bogart, J. French.
Atlas—Asa D. West.
Galena—John Dew.
Pottawattomie Mission at Salem, Isaac Scarritt.

THE Illinois Conference held its fifth session in
the Masonic Hall, Madison, Indiana, beginning on Thursday, October 9, 1828, and continuing
until Wednesday, the 15th. Bishop Roberts was
the presiding officer, and Calvin W. Ruter was secretary. Twenty-five members were present at the
opening session.

Twelve preachers were admitted on trial; viz.,
Asa Beck, John H. Benson, Charles Bonner, David
Bruner, William L. Deneen, John E. French, Miles
Huffaker, Asahel E. Phelps, Cornelius Ruddle,

Hardin A. Tarkington, George W. Teas, John Van Cleve.

Asa D. West and William Chambers were re-admitted.

Two located, Charles Slocumb and Thos. Randle.

And three, John Hardy, William Echols, and Daniel Newton were discontinued, the two latter at their own request.

None had died, and none were transferred to or from the conference.

Six local deacons were elected to elder's orders: Thomas Silvey, John Mercer, George A. Colbert, Zadoc Casey, Anthony W. Casad, and John Burns.

And fifteen local preachers were elected deacons: Samuel Barrett, James Lunaville, Philip Connor, Isaac N. Ellsbury, George Swartz, Henry Summers, Benjamin Davis, Jacob Swartz, Braxton Parrish, Richard Wheeler, John Dallihan, Robert Parritt, Little Page Proctor, David B. Carter, William Mills.

Two of the preachers, William Shanks and James Garner, were, at their own request, left without appointments.

The conference received from the Book Concern $150, and from the Chartered Fund $90.

A communication was received from a society denominated "The Female Domestic Missionary Society of Madison," accompanied with a donation of $6.46¼. The conference gave a vote of thanks to the society for "their laudable zeal in support of the Gospel," and appointed a committee of four to appropriate it to the most needy.

Thomas Biggs, a local preacher, who had been expelled by the quarterly conference of Whitewater Circuit, appealed from their decision to the annual conference. The case was sent back for a new trial.

The Pottawattomie Mission, as usual, received attention from the conference. The superintendent presented a report, and a committee was appointed upon the mission, who also made a report, which was read and accepted, but the journal does not show what the report recommended, or whether the conference took any further action upon it. Indeed, the journal of this year is so brief as to show but little of the action of conference beyond the regular minute business.

"The book agent from Cincinnati made a verbal communication relative to the books on hand in the bounds of the conference." This item to one not acquainted with the former mode of operations by the Book Concern, would be unintelligible; but to those who are aware that for some years books were deposited with the presiding elders, who were to supply the preachers and people, and that serious losses were incurred by the conference from this mode of doing business, the item will be plain enough.

Upon the subject of a conference seminary the following action was had: The vacancy in the committee appointed at the previous session, occasioned by the absence of Peter Cartwright, was filled by the appointment of Samuel H. Thompson. A memorial with accompanying documents in his hands, concerning a seminary at Lebanon, Illinois, was read and referred to a committee of three to consider and report on. They presented a report, which was read and accepted. Then the vote by which it was accepted was reconsidered, and it was resolved that the report be amended by striking out that portion of it which recommends the conference at its present session to appoint trustees to said seminary, and then the report was accepted. Then it was resolved that the conference unite in requesting the stockholders of the seminary at Lebanon[1] to meet as soon as convenient, and so alter and amend their constitution as to designate the number of trustees for said institution, and the manner of their appointment more definitely; and the secretary was instructed to furnish the committee of the Illinois Circuit with a copy of the resolution of the conference. We are thus particular in detailing the action of the conference, as this was the first literary institution under the patronage of the Methodist Episcopal Church in the great North-west Territory, and also because it was the beginning of an institution (McKendree College) that has done as much by its numerous graduates who have entered into political life, and by the many ministers it has educated, to shape the policy of the State, and give character to the Church, as any institution in the State.

Resolutions were adopted requiring each preacher

---

[1] The seminary was already in operation. Its first teacher was a Miss McMurphy. Afterward Edward R. Ames was called to the principalship.

to use his best efforts to form a missionary society within his charge, to sustain the relation of a branch society to the conference society, and also to do what he could in the formation of Sunday-schools auxiliary to the Sunday-school Society of the Methodist Episcopal Church.

This session was held while the so-called Radical controversy that resulted in the formation of the Methodist Protestant Church was raging. A number of persons had been expelled from the Church in Cincinnati, Pittsburg, and elsewhere for agitating the question of lay representation and kindred topics. Many believed these expulsions unwise; some thought them illegal.

While presiding at this session of the conference, Bishop Roberts was asked, "Whether the persons who composed the quarterly conference, after having sat on a trial below, could sit as jurors in the quarterly conference?" The bishop replied: "If the same persons were to try the case again, what would be the advantage of an appeal?" The questioner then observed that the Discipline was in favor of it. The bishop said, "The Discipline gives them a seat in the conference, and though it does not say they should not act, yet delicacy and a sense of propriety would dictate that they should not act in such case."[2]

The only change in the plan of the work this year was the establishment of the Galena Mission in the lead mining region in the north-western portion of the State.

---

[2] Bassett's History of the M. P. Church.

Charles Holliday, having been elected book agent at Cincinnati, was succeeded on the Wabash District by George Locke; and John Dew, who had been superintendent of and collector for the Indian Mission the year before, was now sent to the newly formed Galena Mission.

This year witnessed the first organization of the Methodist Protestant Church in Illinois. It took place in Morgan County, on the Sangamon Circuit, February 13, 1829. Two local elders, Reddick H. Horne and James Sims, united in the movement with thirteen laymen. Mr. Horne had been twice suspended for his views on Church polity. After his trial and deposition, he and those who sympathized with him as the victim of oppression withdrew from the Methodist Episcopal Church, and united with the new organization. Mr. Horne afterwards became president of one of the conferences of that Church.

But despite this agitation and secession, the year was one of great prosperity to the Church. There was an increase in the membership of 1,719, the whole number reported at the close of the year being 7,042 whites, and 64 colored. The largest increase was on the Vermillion Circuit, which, under the labors of Henry Buell and A. L. Risley, gained 336 members. Shoal Creek gained 297; Kaskaskia, 208; Apple Creek, 184, and several others over 100 each. Illinois Circuit was the only charge reporting a decrease, and that of only one member.

Amongst the many new preaching places established this year was one on the Apple Creek Circuit, four miles west of Winchester, at the house of JACOB BAKER, of whom honorable mention deserves to be made. He was a native of Pennsylvania, born in 1791. He was a soldier in the War of 1812 under General Harrison, and saw the death of Tecumseh at the battle of the Thames. In 1820 he emigrated to Illinois; and in 1828, having married Elizabeth Slagel, he erected a log-cabin, and even before a floor was laid in it, offered it to the Church as a preaching place. For thirty years circuit preaching continued to be held in his house, until a comfortable church, Rutledge Chapel, was erected in the neighborhood. He died in 1879.[3]

The following appear as laborers in Illinois for the first time:

GEORGE LOCKE was born at Cannonstown, Pennsylvania, June 8, 1797. His grandfather and great-grandfather were clergymen of the Church of England. When but an infant, his parents emigrated to Kentucky, settling first in Mason County, and afterwards at Shelbyville. His early school advantages were limited; but his father had a good library, and in boyhood he acquired a great love of books, spending most of his leisure hours in reading. When about seventeen he was converted and united with the Church in a great revival that occurred in Shelbyville under the labors of a local preacher, Edward Talbot. In his twentieth year he received license to exhort, and was employed by the presiding elder, Marcus Lindsey, to travel a circuit. The next year,

____

[3] Rev. H. Miller.

1818, he was received in the Tennessee Conference, traveling in it two years, and one in the Kentucky Conference, into which he had fallen at its formation in 1820. At the conference of 1821, having married Miss Elizabeth B. McReynolds, he located and settled in Shelbyville. The following year he was readmitted, and labored in the Kentucky Conference until 1825, when, on account of his dislike to slavery, with his brother-in-law, William Chambers, and Charles Holliday, he was transferred to the Illinois Conference. He traveled for three years on circuits in Indiana, and in 1828 was appointed to the Wabash District, on which he remained four years. Here his labors and exposure were so severe as seriously to affect his health. His constitution, never strong, received a shock in the last year of his labors on the district from which he never recovered. "Some time in the Winter of 1831 and 1832, one of the severest Winters ever known in the West, Mr. Locke was returning home after an absence of several weeks. When he reached the Wabash River he found it gorged with ice. He and another traveler waited at the house of the ferryman three or four days for a change in the weather, or in the condition of the ice; but as no change came, and as they were impatient to proceed on their journey, they resolved on breaking a channel through the ice for the ferry-boat. Accordingly, the next morning they addressed themselves to the work with all diligence, and at sunset found themselves within a rod or two of the opposite shore. Mr. Locke was standing on the bow of the boat, fatigued and tremulous, breaking the ice with a rail. Striking a piece of it with all the force he could command, it suddenly gave way, not making the resistance he had anticipated, and precipitated him into the river. As he rose and was just drifting under the ice, his companions rescued him. Though the shock was a fearful one, and he was not only thoroughly drenched, but thoroughly chilled also, he resolved to persevere in his work, and actually did persevere till the shore was reached. He then mounted his horse and rode ten miles to the next house, but when he reached there he was frozen to the saddle and speechless. The horse stopped of his own accord, and the family coming to the door and perceiving his condition, lifted him from his horse and cared for him very kindly, until after a day or two he was able to resume his journey."[1]

Whilst on this district his pay was so meager as often barely to meet his traveling expenses, so that it became necessary for his wife to engage in teaching to support the family. In 1832, falling into the newly formed Indiana Conference, he was appointed to the Corydon Circuit; but at the next session, his health having failed, he was granted a superannuated relation, and removed to New Albany, where, with his wife, he engaged in teaching. After a few months, however, he was compelled to yield to the disease which had fastened on him, consumption, and on July 15, 1834, he died in full prospect of heaven, crying with his last breath, " Glory, glory, glory!" Mr. Locke was a man of

____

[1] Sprague's Annals.

more than ordinary ability. He was a hard student during his whole life. "Amidst all his manifold and self-denying labors he never abated his habits of study. He redeemed time, not only for the study of systematic theology, but for general reading. He acquired some knowledge of Greek and Latin, and made considerable proficiency in the higher branches of mathematics. He continued his studies till a few weeks before his death, and had his books brought to him even after he was confined to his bed."

During his entire ministry he was blessed with extensive revivals of religion. He was a superior preacher. His sermons were clear, forcible, and logical. He was well versed in all the doctrines of the Church, and was faithful and earnest in defending them against opposers. He was a man of strong convictions and of remarkable firmness. He allowed nothing to turn him aside from what he believed to be the path of duty. He was very decided in his opposition to slavery and to the use of tobacco. So strong was his opposition to the latter, that when in his last illness smoking was recommended to him as a means of relief, he utterly refused it, preferring to suffer rather than violate his convictions of right. His social qualities were fine; he was a true Christian gentleman. His piety was deep and ardent. So faithful was he in secret prayer that even in his journeys it was never neglected. Although traveling in company with others, when his hour for prayer arrived, he would dismount from his horse, and retiring into some secret place, would hold his accustomed communion with God. He is still re-

membered by some of the old settlers in the Wabash
valley as one of the best of men, and one of the
ablest of the preachers of his day.

Of the early history of HENRY BUELL we know
nothing. He was received on trial in 1826, and
for two years assigned to appointments in Indiana.
Whilst on the Vermillion Circuit this year, he was
charged with improper conduct, and at the ensuing
annual conference, "some objections being made to
his moral character, he received a location at his
own request, and the presiding elder of the district
was instructed to withhold the certificate of his location until his case should be legally investigated."[4]

ASAHEL L. RISLEY was a native of Kentucky,
born in Bullitt County, February 14, 1804. In
1825 he united with the Church as a seeker of religion, and was soon after happily converted at a
camp-meeting near Shelbyville. Two years afterwards, having removed to Indiana, he was licensed
to preach, and united with the Illinois Conference
in 1827. He traveled in succession the Vincennes,
Vermillion, Brownsville, Sullivan, and Eugene Circuits, the latter for two years, when, his health having failed, he was in 1833 granted a superannuated
relation. The next year he was on the supernumerary list, and in 1835 he was appointed to Alton.
At the close of the year he located. The next year
he was readmitted and assigned to Mt. Carmel, and
the following year to Danville, at the close of which
he again located. In 1842 he was readmitted and
appointed to Bloomington; for the two following

---

[4] Illinois Conference Journal.

years he was at Pittsfield, and then for three years he presided over the Quincy District. In 1848 he was transferred to Rock River Conference and appointed to Chicago District, upon which he labored two years, when he was retransferred to the Illinois Conference and appointed agent for McKendree College. The next year he fell into the Southern Illinois Conference, of which he remained a member till death. His appointments in it were Brighton, Jerseyville, Jerseyville Circuit, Collinsville two years, Pocahontas, Trenton two years, Mascoutah two years, and Centralia and Richview two years. In 1864 he was placed on the superannuated list, on which he remained until his death, August 24, 1874. "Brother Risley possessed a very amiable, loving spirit. He was a devoted lover of God and his Church. He was a good preacher, of sound doctrines, and exemplary practice in good works. He was kind to his family and beloved by his friends. Few men have traveled more extensively, or labored more faithfully, and his memory is precious in numerous places. He was a good man who passed unspotted through this world."[5]

WILLIAM MAVITY was born in Franklin County, Virginia, in the year 1780. In 1804 he removed to Tennessee, where he was converted four years afterwards, and the following year received license to preach. He labored as a local preacher in Tennessee, Kentucky, and Indiana until 1827, when he was received as an itinerant in the Illinois Conference. His first appointment was Booneville Cir-

---

[5] General Minutes.

cuit. In 1828 he was sent to Wabash Circuit, and the next year to Rockville, where he labored two years. In 1831 he was appointed to Iroquois Circuit. The following year he was on the superannuated list. From the conference of 1833 he was sent again to the Wabash Circuit, but died before completing the year, in August, 1834. "He labored with acceptance and usefulness as a minister of Christ. He lived a pious life, and died a happy death."[6]

MILES HUFFAKER was born in Wayne County, Kentucky, in the year 1806. He was converted when nine years old, and licensed to preach when twenty-one. In 1828 he was received on trial in the Illinois Conference, and traveled in succession the Cash River, Mt. Vernon, and Shelbyville Circuits in Illinois, and Frankfort, in Indiana. He then fell into the Indiana Conference, in which he traveled until 1844, when the conference was divided; and, with the exception of one year, in which he was local, he retained his connection with the North Indiana Conference until his death, July 27, 1852. "His abilities for preaching were but moderate, but he was a good man and a laborious minister. He was firmly attached to the doctrines and usages of Methodism. He was fully sustained in his last moments by the power of that Gospel he preached to others."[7]

The name of ASAHEL E. PHELPS will be long remembered in the charges in which he labored. Though his itinerant career continued only for

[6] General Minutes.   [7] General Minutes.

twenty-five years, he accomplished in it as much as many have done in a much longer period. Received on trial this year, he traveled successively the Kaskaskia, Lebanon, Salt Creek, Sangamon, Alton, Carrollton, Carlisle, and Pekin Circuits, the latter two years. In 1837 he was sent to Peoria Mission Station. Here, says Mr. Beggs, " he sustained himself well. The court-house (in which he preached) was occupied by a Unitarian preacher as well as himself. One day the former, in preaching on the divinity of Christ, ran across the track of A. E. Phelps, and so he pitched into the Unitarian champion, rough-shod, and so completely showed the fallacy of his doctrine that he had to leave, and A. E. Phelps had the house to himself. By this he rose fifty per cent in the estimation of his hearers. Here commenced his brilliant career as a successful champion against Unitarianism, Universalism, Deism, and exclusive immersionists, as practicing the only mode of baptism. I do not think any one of his antagonists ever got the better of him. He excelled as a historian, and was truly an able defender of Methodism. He increased in usefulness till he was called from his labors to his long rest." In 1838 he was appointed to the Mt. Vernon District, which he traveled four years. Of his early experience on this district we give an item or two from a letter from Rev. J. H. Dickens, who was then traveling the Nashville Circuit: " My presiding elder, Brother Phelps, was a man of fine taste, not only as to all the proprieties of life, but in his person and dress he was always neat, trim, and cleanly. He went with me to my first quarterly-meeting at the house of a Brother P. On arrival we found a little, black, round-poled cabin, twelve by sixteen, in two rooms, the front one for meeting, the other with two beds or bunks in it. The wind was high, and the front door closed, while the wooden chimney smoked terribly. To get in at the back door with our saddlebags, we had to press in sideways. The cabin was full of smoke, but the sister said, 'Sit down.' I obeyed, but the elder beat a retreat. Very soon I had to follow. I found him perched on the top of a huge pile of wood, surveying the scene. The sides of the cabin were mostly covered with deerskins, 'coon skins, and all sorts of wild game skins. The top of it (it was a very low, one-story building) was laden with horns and various bones of the animals whose hides covered the sides. When I spoke to the elder and told him it was about time for service, he, utterly discouraged at the prospect, asked me if we had not better go home. I cheered him as well as I could, and told him it would be better further on. A dozen or so of hearers were soon gathered, but the eleven o'clock service was enough for all in the house. We concluded to hold the remaining services of the meeting in a log shed the brother had erected near the house. It had no floor, the sides were open, and it was late in the Fall, but this was the best we could do. With a pile of rough boards we covered about half the floor for the ladies, raising it more than two feet from the ground, and leaving the bare earth for the men. On Sunday night we had a time of power.

The mourners were invited to the board floor, and a number came. The space was so limited, and the male mourners so crowded, that some were lying rather across the others. Soon one of the men was converted. He was a very stout man and had been at the bottom of the pile. As he felt the power he sprang up and kicked at once. Two or three others were pushed over the edge of the floor; for a few moments arms and legs seemed to be flying in all directions, and the scene was so ludicrous that, despite the surroundings, there was general laughter. A number were converted, however, that night, and united with the Church. And, amid the general joy, in which the elder shared with the rest of us, the smoke, skins, and bones were all forgotten. It was a glorious quarterly-meeting.

"In the Summer of 1839 three Mormon elders made a raid into the region south of the Nashville Circuit, and soon began their proselyting. Mr. Phelps, who was living at Mt. Vernon, heard of it, and sent a challenge to them to debate with him. Passing through Nashville, he would have me go with him. He debated with the three, one at a time, at a large, private house, until noon; when the crowd becoming too great, they adjourned to a large barn in the neighborhood. The discussion continued during the afternoon until about five o'clock, when one of the Mormons, completely discomfited, broke down, and left the field. About an hour later, a second of the champions quit, amid the derision of the crowd. The third was soon silenced, and as he started to run, Brother Phelps kept hurling at him hot, blazing missiles, while the shouts and hootings of the crowd rent the air. The next morning a committee of the citizens waited on the Mormons, giving them three hours in which to leave the country. They left."

Mr. Phelps's next appointment was Peoria District, on which he labored two years, when, falling into the Rock River Conference, he was assigned to the Washington District, on which he also continued two years. Then for three years he was agent for Rock River Seminary. In 1849–50 he was in Galena Station. In 1851 he was appointed to Rock Island District, on which he labored until his death, in 1853.

WILLIAM L. DENEEN was a native of Pennsylvania, born at Bedford, Mifflin County, October 30, 1798. He was converted at Charleston, Indiana, in 1827, under the ministry of Rev. George Locke, mentioned above. He was soon licensed to preach, and in 1828 united with the Illinois Conference. He received sixteen appointments; viz., Shoal Creek, Salt Creek, Lebanon three times, Kaskaskia, Brownsville, Carlisle, Waterloo twice, Edwardsville, Belleville twice, Upper Alton, Alton, and Staunton. During the remainder of his connection with the conferences, at first the Illinois, and after 1852 the Southern Illinois, he was on the superannuated list. "For more than thirty years he lived in Lebanon, and all concede him to have been an honest, faithful, pure, and strictly conscientious man. As a preacher he was able, searching, and very instructive. He loved all the doctrines of the Bible, and for many years was a living witness to the cleansing power of the atoning blood of Christ. For near six months prior to his decease he was mostly confined to his room; yet he never became impatient, nor did a repining word escape his lips. In visiting him his pastor always found him deeply interested in the advancement of every good and noble cause, but especially with regard to the welfare of our own Zion; and in their last interview he stated that he had no fear, no anxiety, no cloud, and that no thought nor will of his conflicted with the will of his heavenly Father."[8] For many years of his superannuation he was surveyor or deputy-surveyor for the county, a position in which he had but few equals and no superiors. It was while surveying that he took the cold that caused his last illness. He died July 1, 1879, in his eighty-first year.

Of the parentage or birthplace of JAMES Mc-KEAN we have no information. He was born in 1795, and converted in 1824. His conviction was deep and pungent, and his conversion clear and powerful. Having been licensed first to exhort and then to preach, he was received on trial in the Illinois Conference in 1827, and appointed to Paoli, Indiana. In 1828 he traveled the Sangamon Circuit, and the next two years the Vermillion Circuit. Then he spent one year each on Mt. Carmel, Wabash, Paris, and Embarrass River Circuits. In 1835 his name does not appear on the Minutes. In 1836 he was sent to Buffalo Grove; the next year

---

[8] General Minutes.

to Picatolica; in 1838 to Freeport, and in 1839 to Walworth, Wisconsin. In 1840, falling into the newly formed Rock River Conference, he was appointed to Troy, Wisconsin. During the next four years he was at Roscoe, Freeport, and Apple River, remaining on this charge two years. In 1845 he was superannuated. In 1846 and 1847 he was at Union Grove, in 1848 at Prophetstown, and at the close of the year was again placed on the superannuated list, on which he remained until his death at his own residence in Carroll County, Illinois, May, 28, 1856. " Brother McKean was not regarded as a great preacher, but he was a good preacher and useful wherever he went. He was faithful in attending to his appointments; visited from house to house, held prayer-meetings, met his classes, and instructed the children in every place. He was a most excellent pastor, and did all he could to get men converted to God and build up the Church. He was a devoted Christian, and so consistent that none doubted his piety or the purity of his motives. He was an affectionate, kind, and devoted husband. In the discharge of his duty as a father, he labored to bring up his children in the fear and favor of God. As a neighbor, he was peaceable, kind, and obliging in all his intercourse with society. He was emphatically given to hospitality. The preachers and their families were especially welcome to the best he had to give. None called who were not affectionately received; none departed who did not carry away with him a deep impression that Christianity ruled in that family. He, although superannuated, continued to preach as much as his health would allow in different neighborhoods in the country around his residence, and always with acceptance to those who heard him. His sickness, though severe, was endured with patience and Christian submission; he often expressed confidence in a living Redeemer, and an entire trust in the sufficiency of his grace. A little before his death he took his wife by the hand, and in a most touching manner, alluded to their toils and travels in the vineyard of the Lord, through the frontiers of the West; and then said, ' This is our last interview, now we must part.' Calling for his children, he spoke to each in an appropriate manner, exhorting them all to devote their hearts and lives to God. Thus finishing his work, he fell asleep in Jesus."[9]

JOHN H. BENSON was born in Boston, Massachusetts, August 10, 1797, and lived in that place and New York City until the age of twenty-three, when he came to the West. He embraced religion at the Union Grove Camp-meeting, near Lebanon, Illinois, in August, 1825, and united with the Methodist Episcopal Church. He was licensed to exhort and to preach in 1826. In 1828 he was admitted on trial in the traveling connection, and appointed to the Sangamon Circuit. In 1829 and 1830 he was at Mt. Vernon, in 1831 at Shoal Creek, in 1832 at Carlinville, and the next year he was sent the second time to Sangamon. His next appointment was Alton Circuit. In 1835 and 1836 he was at Lebanon, in 1837 in Upper and Middle Alton, and

---

[9] General Minutes.

in 1838 at Lebanon again. The next year he was sent to Carlisle, in 1840 to Waterloo, and in 1841 to Edwardsville. His last appointment was Greenville, but his health, which had for some time been very poor, growing worse, he got round his circuit but once.

On January 1, 1843, his affliction became very great (it was bronchitis), and on Sunday morning, February 5th, in great peace and composure, he fell asleep in Jesus. Brother Benson was a spare, slender man, of medium height, straight black hair, and a well-developed forehead. He was a dignified, Christian gentleman, very urbane, and an able, impressive, and interesting preacher. " Enjoying the fullness of the blessing of Christ's life and death in himself, the great trait in his preaching was Christ crucified. To 'the cross all stained with hallowed blood,' he continually pointed his weeping congregations. His leading characteristic was a grave dignity. Though very social, he was never known to jest. He was very useful; he had many powerful revivals in different portions of the fields assigned him, many souls were convicted and converted under his ministry; many wanderers were called back, many were stirred up to increased faith in the Lord."[10] His frequent reappointment to the same charge, uncommon in those days, indicated his popularity, as well as his ability as a preacher. Of the fifteen appointments he received, there were only three, exclusive of his last, to which he was not sent a second time, and on one, Lebanon, he labored three years.

---

[10] General Minutes.

HARDIN A. TARKINGTON, received on trial this year, traveled in succession the Peoria, Rockville, and Logansport Circuits, and in 1831 received a location at his own request. When admitted to conference he was quite young, and had had but few advantages.

JOHN E. FRENCH was an Englishman, born in Dorsetshire, September 29, 1805. In his thirteenth year, with his parents he emigrated to America, and settled in Cincinnati. While living there he was converted and united with the Church. In 1828 he commenced his itinerant life in the Illinois Conference on the Apple Creek Circuit. His next appointment was Bloomington, to which he was appointed again in 1833. In 1830 he was assigned to Vermillion, the next year to Brownsville, and the next to Jonesboro. In 1834 he was sent to Flat Branch, 1835 to Marion, the next year to Mt. Carmel Circuit, and in 1837 to Eugene, on which he labored two years. At the conference of 1839 he was granted a superannuated relation, in which he remained until his death, February 2, 1841. He was a man of fine appearance, large and portly, and possessed of great energy. "Brother French, as a preacher, did not excel, unless it was in usefulness. His talents were of the ordinary class, his literary attainments but moderate; but such was his deep piety, that in usefulness he excelled most of the brethren of his age."[11]

---

[11] General Minutes.

CHAPTER VI.

1829.

WABASH DISTRICT—George Locke, P. E.
Vermillion—James McKean.
Paris—Robert Delap, John Decker.
Wabash—John Fox, Alfred Arrington.
Mt. Carmel—John Miller, A. F. Thompson.

KASKASKIA DISTRICT—Samuel H. Thompson, P. E.
Kaskaskia—Isaac Scarritt.
Brownsville—Asahel Risley, Orceneth Fisher.
Jonesboro—Samuel C. Cooper.
Golconda—Thomas H. Files.
Mt. Vernon—John H. Benson, Miles Huffaker.
Shoal Creek—William Chambers, Wilson Pitner.
Shelbyville—Lorenzo Edwards.

SANGAMON DISTRICT—Peter Cartwright, P. E.
Lebanon—John Dew, Asahel E. Phelps.
Apple Creek—James Bankson.
Atlas—Samuel Bogart.
Spoon River—Asa D. West.
Sangamon—Smith L. Robinson, David B. Carter.
Salt Creek—William L. Deneen.
Peoria—James Latta.
Fox River Mission—Jesse Walker.
Galena Mission—Benjamin C. Stephenson.

THE session of 1829 was held at Edwardsville, Illinois, Bishop Soule presiding, and Calvin W. Ruter being elected secretary. It commenced on Friday, September 18th, and closed on the evening of the following Friday. At the first calling of the roll, twenty-eight responded to their names. As usual, a camp-meeting was held in connection with the conference, at which about one hundred and eighty souls were converted.

Thirteen preachers were received on trial, viz.: Richard S. Robinson, Boyd Phelps, Lorenzo D. Smith, Anthony F. Thompson, Wilson Pitner, Alfred Arrington, James Latta, John Decker, David B. Carter, Isaac N. Ellsbury, George West, Samuel Brenton, Lorenzo Edwards.

Cornelius Ruddle and David Bruner were discontinued at their own request. Abner H. Cheever was discontinued in consequence of inability, from affliction, to perform the duties of a preacher, and Constant B. Jones on account of some objections that were made.

James Garner, Henry Buell, Samuel Lowe, and Isaac S. House were at their own request granted a location.

Jesse Haile and James Bankson were transferred from the Missouri Conference to this; and also Amos Sparks and Wesley Wood, who had just been received on probation in the Ohio Conference.

William Crain, John Hogan, Robert H. Jordan, and George W. Teas were transferred from this to the Missouri Conference.

The following local preachers were elected to deacon's orders: Enoch Moore, Henry Davidson, Clarke Banning, James Bristoe, William Johnson, Thomas Depoysture, Joseph Curtis, Thomas Cottingham, Charles Robinson, John Arrington, Francis A. Brown, John Byrnes, Joseph Springer, Benjamin Blackstone, Jacob Lopp, Ebenezer Patrick, Reuben Claypool, Jonathan Shaw, James McLane, John C. Archer.

And the following local deacons were elected elders: John Kirkpatrick, James Stringfield, Parham Randle, William Hunter, Moses Osburn, Lawrence Killibrew, Thomas Upjohn, John W. Jones, David Gunn.

A draft was ordered on the Book Concern for $150, and on the Chartered Fund for $90.

A proposition made on the first day that the conference sit with *open* doors was rejected.

A resolution was adopted that in the examination of character it shall be inquired concerning each presiding elder, " Has he uniformly held love-feasts at his quarterly meetings?" and concerning each traveling preacher, " Has he uniformly attended his appointments and met the classes?"

Upon the conference seminary the following action was had: A committee of three was appointed to meet and confer with a committee appointed by the Missouri Conference at its last session (and who were announced by the president to be in waiting), on the subject of a conference seminary, with instructions to report as soon as convenient to the conference. John Dew, John Strange, and Peter Cartwright were the committee.

The committee appointed at the last session to take into consideration the subject of a conference seminary, and report to this conference, were discharged from the performance of any further duties on that subject, they having made no report.

The joint committee of the two conferences presented the following report: "That in the opinion of the committee, the members and friends of the Methodist Episcopal Church within the bounds of the two conferences are sufficiently numerous and wealthy to establish a literary institution that would do honor to any country. We have but to enlist the hearty co-operation of the members and friends of our Church herein. Your committee doubt not for a moment the practicability of establishing a seminary of learning that shall not only vie with, but excel, any now in operation west of the Wabash River. Your committee, therefore, respectfully submit to your consideration the following preamble and resolutions:

"*Whereas* the Missouri Annual Conference at its last session did appoint a committee to confer with this conference on the subject of a seminary of learning, and did fully authorize said committee to agree upon a union between that conference and this, if in the opinion of this conference it be advisable, and to do all other matters and things on behalf of said Missouri Conference in relation to a joint seminary of learning:

"*Resolved*, Therefore, that the Illinois Conference do approve of a union, and by and with the consent of the Missouri Annual Conference, through their committee now present, do unite both conferences for the purpose of establishing a seminary of learning under the patronage of the Methodist Episcopal Church."

This was adopted, and the committee was then

instructed to locate the site for said seminary, and do all things necessary for the accomplishment of the object contemplated in said report, and report as soon as convenient to the conference.

The president informed the conference that he had received a communication from certain citizens at Mt. Carmel on the subject of the conference seminary site. It was placed in the hands of the committee.

The joint committee presented this further report:

"Your committee have had under consideration the subject of locating the contemplated seminary, and have not come to any thing definite on that subject; but your committee have agreed to report the following places as suitable sites for said location: Lebanon, in St. Clair County in this State, and Mount Salubria, one mile west of the city of St. Louis, in the State of Missouri.

"Your committee submit the following articles of confederation, as a compact between the two conferences, and recommend their adoption:

"ARTICLES

Of Confederation and Agreement between the Illinois and Missouri Annual Conferences of the Methodist Episcopal Church, for the Purpose of establishing a Joint Seminary of Learning for both Conferences, made and entered into at Edwardsville, September 23, 1829, by the Illinois Conference on its own Part, and by Alexander McAllister, Andrew Monroe, and Jesse Green, Delegates empowered to act on the Part of the Missouri Conference.

"ARTICLE 1. There shall be by the conferences aforesaid a seminary of learning located and established at ———, under the following regulations and restrictions:

"Article 2. The Illinois and Missouri Annual Conferences shall have equal claim to all the rights, privileges, and immunities belonging to, or growing out of, said seminary of learning.

"Article 3. It shall be the duty of said conferences respectively at each annual session to appoint a committee of ways and means to adopt such measures as to them may seem necessary to raise funds to carry into effect the designs of this confederation. And all moneys or other means collected for the above purpose shall be subject to the order of the board of managers or trustees, as the case may be, who may be appointed to superintend said institution.

"Article 4. Each conference shall annually elect —— trustees, who shall constitute a board, who shall have authority to receive conveyances of all real estate, and superintend said seminary, transact its business, make all necessary rules and regulations for their own government and for the government of the institution; to fill vacancies that may occur in their body during the year; appoint their own secretary and treasurer, and do all other matters and things pertaining to the management of said institution. Provided nothing be done which shall in any wise infringe the articles of this confederation.

"Article 5. Any of the foregoing articles of this confederation may be altered, amended, or rescinded upon the concurrent majority of each of these conferences agreeing thereto."

The conference then proceeded to fill by ballot the blank in the first article of the confederation, and on counting the votes it was found that Mount Salubria, Missouri, had a majority, and the blank was filled accordingly.

The next day the conference proceeded to fill the blanks in the remaining articles of confederation as contained in the report of the joint committee of Missouri and Illinois Conferences on the subject of a conference seminary, and proceeded to adopt the several articles separately. But on the question of adopting the report as a whole, after some discussion, the question was decided in the negative, and the report and articles were not adopted. The vote by which the first report of the committee was adopted was then reconsidered and the report was rejected.

The explanation of this strange action is given by Dr. Aaron Wood in a letter to the writer. It was supposed at first that but two sites would be presented for the proposed seminary, Mt. Carmel and Lebanon. The Indiana preachers desired the school to be located at Mt. Carmel, and would have co-operated heartily in its establishment and support. But the leading Illinois preachers were pledged to Lebanon as the location. And in order to secure it, and thus defeat the wishes of the Indiana preachers, they invited the aid of the Missouri Conference, who would be willing, they of course supposed, to come over the line so short a distance as to Lebanon. But to their surprise, when the commissioners from Missouri came, they presented

St. Louis as the site, or rather Mt. Salubria, as it was termed, the property now held by the Roman Catholics for their university. When the vote was taken the Indiana preachers, to show their appreciation of the ignoring of Mt. Carmel by the committee, united with the Missouri Conference, and left the friends of Lebanon in the minority. " Indiana would have united at Mt. Carmel, but the leading Illinois men were committed to Lebanon, and wanted to draw us all there, and brought over Missouri to checkmate Indiana, and lost both."[1] This of course caused great excitement among the friends of Lebanon. Peter Cartwright declared he would rather send his children to a Calvinistic school than to one in a slave State. And when the final vote was taken the Illinois men succeeded in rejecting the whole arrangement, and leaving open for future settlement the question of a conference school.

The Pottawattomie Mission was closed at this conference, as the following resolution shows:

Resolved, That, whereas the Pottawattomie Indians have disposed of their lands where the mission was located, it is inexpedient longer to continue a mission among the Pottawattomie Indians, and the same is hereby discontinued.

A committee was appointed to audit the accounts of Brother Scarritt, the missionary to them; and another committee to take into consideration the claims of Jesse Walker to certain property at the missionary station.

------

[1] Dr. A. Wood.

The former committee reported, after examining the accounts, that there was a balance in their hands of one hundred and forty-six dollars, which was ordered to be placed in the hands of the treasurer of the Illinois Missionary Society. Brother Scarritt was also instructed to furnish a list of the property at the Pottawattomie Mission to the missionary who may be appointed to the Fox River Mission, and that said missionary, together with the presiding elder of the district to which said mission shall be attached, take charge of said property and dispose of the same according to their best judgment for the use of the Missionary Society of the Methodist Episcopal Church, and report to the next session of this conference.

The committee on the claim of Jesse Walker reported him to be justly entitled to the mill, smith-tools, wagon, and remnant of hogs, if any, which he claimed, and that these articles were purchased with his own funds.

The mission to the Indians having been closed, the conference turned its attention to missions among the rapidly extending, but poor, white settlements in the northern portion of their territory, and three new missions were established, two in Illinois and one in Indiana, and a committee appointed to meet the superintendent to estimate the amount necessary to support these missions.

For the Galena Mission, embracing the mining district on and near Fever River, on the Upper Mississippi, and which was attached to the Illinois District, one hundred dollars was appropriated.

For the Fox River Mission, which was to commence at Sandy Creek settlement, on the Illinois River, and, extending up the river, to include the Vermillion and Fox River settlements, and all the settlements up said river to *Chicaugo*, on the Lake Michigan, two hundred dollars was appropriated.

And for the Logansport Mission in Indiana, including the country north and west of Crawfordsville Circuit, and north of the Vermillion Circuit, on the Wabash River, fifty dollars.

The presiding elders, in conjunction with the preachers, were requested to use their utmost exertions to organize one or more branch missionary societies in each circuit and station in this conference.

Various documents were presented to the conference from private individuals, or local preachers, the nature of which is not specified in the journal, though in some cases we can infer their character.

A document was presented from Benjamin Watt, an expelled local preacher, which was considered by the conference, and it was ordered that he be allowed a new trial before the quarterly conference of which he was a member, and the document was returned to him.

Two documents were presented to the conference, one from Alexander Colbert and another from Henry Allen, which they were allowed to withdraw.

Another paper, presented to the conference by Pierce Holley, was ordered to be returned to him.

At the last session of the body the secretary was requested to insert, at the close of the minutes transmitted to the publishers of the *Christian Advocate and Journal* and *Zion's Herald* for publication, "an account of the good feeling that has existed among the members while in session, the profitable campmeeting held during conference, and the amount of the conference collection, together with the amount of missionary funds raised on the occasion."

Numerous changes were made this year in the plan of the work. The south-western portion of the Wabash and the southern portion of the Illinois District were formed into a new district, the Kaskaskia, and the name of the Illinois District was changed to Sangamon. The Vermillion Circuit was divided, the Paris Circuit being formed from the southern part of it. The old Cash River Circuit disappears, and the Brownsville, Jonesboro, and Golconda Circuits appear in the place of it. The name of the Illinois Circuit was changed to Lebanon. The Shoal Creek Circuit was divided, the north-eastern part of it being formed into the Shelbyville Circuit. Sangamon Circuit was divided, and the northern part styled Salt Creek. A new circuit, the Spoon River, was formed west of the Illinois River, from parts of Peoria and Atlas Circuits. And, as stated above, the Pottawattomie Indian Mission disappears, and in its place appears the Fox River Mission to the white settlers.

Under the changes that were made, the work continued to prosper, not only in the older settlements, but by the formation of new societies in the newly established settlements. During this year the first society was formed in Dewitt County by

W. L. Deneen, who was traveling the Salt Creek
Circuit. The class was organized in the house of
Judge William Lowry, a mile and a half east of the
present town of Kenney, and consisted of nineteen
members. Some years afterwards the circuit preaching was removed to the house of Joseph Howard,
in which it continued for eighteen years, and until
the erection of a church.

The increase in the membership in Illinois this
year was 1,258, and the entire membership was
8,233 whites, and 131 colored.

The only appointment of JOHN A. DECKER in
Illinois was his first, the Paris Circuit. After this
he traveled two years in Indiana, and then located.
In 1840 he was readmitted in the Indiana Conference, received three appointments, one of them as
supernumerary, and was then placed on the superannuated list. He was born in West Tennessee, May
19, 1808. When but a child he moved with his
parents to Harrison County, Indiana, and at the
age of eighteen, through the instrumentality of Rev.
George Locke, was brought to the knowedge of salvation. He was licensed to preach in the Fall of
1828, and the next year united with the conference.
He " was a man of feeble constitution, but possessed
a vigorous mind. His attainments in theology, and
especially in Bible knowledge, were very respectable. As a Christian minister his deportment was
dignified and commanding, and a vein of unmixed
piety ran through his whole course of conduct. His
public ministrations were always rich in instruction,
and we doubt not but many will rise up in eternity

and call him blessed. In the Summer before he died, he suffered an attack of hemorrhage from the lungs. From this time he declined rapidly, and on the 25th of October, 1843, after commending his wife and children to Almighty God, he departed this life, triumphing in the grace of that Gospel which he had preached to others."[2]

It is probable that the Illinois Conference never received a more brilliant man than ALFRED W. ARRINGTON, who was this year assigned to the Wabash Circuit, with John Fox as his colleague. His next appointment was Lawrenceburg, Indiana, with John W. McReynolds as his senior. Here "he at once took high rank among the ministers and people of that section as a young man of no ordinary attainments in knowledge and in powers of eloquence; but no one dreamed till towards the middle of the year of the hidden powers that lurked within him. At a protracted meeting in a village near Lawrenceburg his powers as a revivalist began to develop themselves, and by his wonderful eloquence and zeal for the conversion of the people, he swept the entire neighborhood, embracing a class of men who were generally supposed to be absolutely beyond the power of the Gospel. These he swayed with the ease of a giant playing with a child."[3] In 1831 he was appointed to Vevay as junior preacher under John T. Johnson. At the close of the year he was transferred to the Missouri Conference, and in 1833 was sent to Boonslick Circuit. At the next session of conference he was ex-

---

[2] General Minutes. [3] Early Methodism in Indiana.

pelled from the Church. Rev. J. C. Smith thus describes him as he preached at a camp-meeting near Greensburg, Indiana, in 1831.

"A young man, tall and magisterial in appearance, with broad shoulders, large head, massive forehead, large gray eyes, dull and inexpressive while at rest, but rolling like balls of liquid fire when excited in public harangue, with light hair bordering on the blonde, carelessly though rather genteelly dressed, calm, sober, and decorous in behavior, stepped upon the stand filled with ministers, old and young. After a moment's pause he rose and read the opening hymn, beginning 'Father, how wide thy glories shine, how high thy wonders rise.' The reading of the hymn was done in easy, graceful style, every word and sentence properly emphasized, and the true poetic meaning and force brought out. His prayer was in keeping with the hymn, solemn, reverent, comprehensive; no rant, no false adulations of the Deity, no semblance of a devotion he did not feel, no affectation of learning, or attempt to inform God of things he knew not of before. It was *prayer*, confession, contrition, and earnest petition. The prayer ended, he soon announced his text. It related to the wisdom and power of God in creation, and his goodness in redemption. The sermon was a close, profound, masterly argument, *a priori* and *a posteriori*, to prove the existence, the power, the omnipresence, and omniscience of God, and his goodness in redemption. The whole empire of learning and thought seemed to lie at his feet. At will he gathered resources from the kingdom of matter and mind, from the ocean, from the clouds, from the firmament above and the earth beneath. He seemed as familiar with the whole planetary world as you are with your flower garden. He strayed with ease along the milky way as a familiar path often trod, and seemed at home in the remotest regions of space, where even angels stand abashed. Never was language more chaste, classic, and elegant, or argument more logical and conclusive, than those employed in that sermon. But what of the effect on the audience? That was the proper exponent of the merit of the sermon and the orator. The effect was his highest eulogium. During the delivery of the discourse there was no loud shouting, no boisterous applause, no sleeping, no walking about or whispering one with another; every eye was fixed on the speaker, and every ear and every thought was chained in rapt and mute attention. The sermon occupied one hour and three-quarters, and at its close most of the audience were standing upon their feet leaning forward, eagerly gasping for more. The young orator retired directly from the stand to the preachers' tent, and, as if utterly indifferent to praise or censure, fell into a profound sleep."

After his expulsion from the Church, he engaged in the practice of law, first in Arkansas, and afterwards in Chicago, Illinois, where he was transferred from the bar to the bench. He was an able judge, and as an eloquent and powerful pleader he had no superior. He united with the Roman Catholic Church, and died in 1867.

ANTHONY F. THOMPSON was a native of Kentucky, born September 2, 1806. In his twelfth year he was converted and united with the Church. After laboring some years as a local preacher, he was received into the conference in 1829 and appointed to Mt. Carmel. His next appointment was Brownsville. In 1831 he was sent to Corydon, Indiana, and falling into the Indiana Conference, was appointed the next year to Terre Haute Circuit. Here he labored only about three months, when he was stricken by paralysis and forced to abandon the work. He lingered until the next Spring, and died in peace May 19, 1833. "He was regarded as a more talented man than his brother, Samuel H. Thompson, and more brilliant in the pulpit."[1]

If Alfred W. Arrington was the most eloquent man ever received in the Illinois Conference, WILSON PITNER was certainly the most eccentric. He was born on Cedar Creek, Wilson County, Tennessee, in the Spring of 1806. He had six brothers and five sisters, who with his parents afterward became members of the Methodist Episcopal Church. But at the time of his conversion, which occurred when he was about sixteen, his parents were irreligious, and much opposed to the noisy religion of the Methodists, through whose instrumentality he was led to the Savior. Soon after his conversion he joined the Church; but so ignorant was he that he thought every one uniting with it had to pay quarterage, which he understood to be a quarter of a dollar; and so, when he went forward to give his

____
[1] Rev. N. P. Heath.

hand to the preacher, imagining, perhaps, that he might not be regarded as suitable for admission, he cried out with confidence, "I 've got the money!" At a Bible meeting in Belleville, in 1848, he related this of himself:

"Soon after I joined the Church I felt that I must have a Bible. I had never owned one, but I could read, and was determined to have a Bible of my own. Father had given me a little piece of ground to work for myself. I put it in cotton; and when it was gathered I took it to Nashville and sold it, and with the money I received I bought a Bible. I was so delighted I could hardly contain myself. I put it in my bosom and hurried home as fast as I could to get an opportunity to read it. But I could not resist the temptation of taking it out of my bosom and smelling of it, and it seemed to me that it smelt of the Holy Ghost."

Whilst yet a youth, one night, after he had retired, like Samuel, he heard a voice calling to him, "Wilson, Wilson!" He got up and searched the room to find out where the voice came from, but could find nothing. After a while he got courage to speak, when the voice said to him, "Go, preach my Gospel." But he felt that he could not preach. He had but the rudiments of an education. His father had threatened him severely, commanding him to desist from his prayers and songs of praise. But the Spirit of God wrought powerfully upon him, and impelled him not only to attend the meetings himself, but to hold meetings at which not a few were awakened and converted.

While thus hesitating about preaching, he felt moved to pray in his father's family, but he was afraid to ask permission. So, late one evening he retired a little distance from the house to pray, and while there wrestling with the angel of the covenant, both the parents were powerfully convinced of sin, and sent for him to come to the house and pray for them. As he received this message he was so overcome that he felt himself unworthy to *walk* to the house, but falling on the ground, he *rolled* nearly all the way. With two of his sisters, who had by this time found the Savior, he labored with the old folks till a late hour, when both were happily converted to God.

In 1829, having received license to preach, he was received on trial in the Illinois Conference and appointed to Shoal Creek Circuit as junior preacher with William Chambers. He did considerable good, but his unlettered mind, his peculiar and awkward deportment, his impulsive and erratic mode of speech, and his very singular illustrations in the pulpit, while taking finely with some, were strongly objected to by others as unbecoming in a minister of the Gospel, and the result was that at the next session of the conference he was discontinued.

He had some ludicrous adventures this year, to one or two of which it may not be amiss to refer. The following was related by himself to the writer as they were returning together from conference at Nashville in 1844, and passing very near the place where the circumstance occurred. He heard that a little town had sprung up in the Okaw timber in

which the Gospel had never been preached. Greatly
desirous of being a pioneer preacher to some, he
accordingly sent them an appointment. When he
reached the place he found the whole population
assembled in a little log school-house, and preached
to them as best he could. After the sermon he began singing (he was a good singer), and, as was
common in those days, he thought he would go
through the congregation and shake hands with the
people. It happened that the first person to whom
he offered his hand was a Connecticut dancing master who had recently come to the place and started
a dancing school, and who, by the people, was
looked on as the very pink of politeness. Now,
the dancing master had never seen any such thing
as this Western hand-shaking in meeting, and so,
when the preacher offered his hand, thinking that
it was a friendly way of taking his leave of the
congregation, he rose, and with a polite bow, took
his hand and said, "Good-bye, sir." This was almost too much for the preacher's gravity. He had
to keep on singing to avoid bursting out in laughter. The next one he approached was a raw native,
who took it for granted that the dancing master's
move was the latest fashion, and so he jumped up,
and with an awkward bow, cried, "Good-bye, sir."
By this time the preacher was almost upset, and it
was only by persisting in singing, at the top of his
voice that he kept from screaming with laughter.
But he thought it would not do to stop then, and
so he went on through the male portion of the congregation, every one, however, imitating the exam-

ple of the dancing master. As soon as he had received the "good-bye, sir," of the last one, he seized
his hat and saddle-bags, and without dismissing the
congregation, left the house, hastily mounted his
horse and rode away, convulsed with laughter, and
never had the courage to visit them again.

The following is related by his brother-in-law,
Rev. J. H. Dickens: "It was during this year he
was called on by his presiding elder, S. H. Thompson,
to exhort at a camp-meeting, held below Carlisle,
in a sassafras grove. The meeting had been a drag,
and so Pitner was put up as a kind of forlorn hope,
to exhort and move the masses, as he often did. He
pulled string after string, but there was no move.
At last he undertook to tell sinners how strong the
Lord was with whom they were trifling; as a climax
he said, ' I would n't be surprised if God Almighty
would come down in a thundergust of woodpeckers
and sweep all these sassafras bushes and sinners
down to hell together,' and just then he grasped one
of the saplings and shook it, when down fell the
top of it, for it was dead, upon the people in the
altar. The effect was fearful. The people thought
they were going down. The women screamed terribly. But in a little while the reaction came, the
excitement was felt to be any thing but religious,
and the meeting closed without a mourner. Wilson's mortification was indescribable. He felt that
he had been led into over-acting, and heartily
ashamed, he got away as soon as he could."

At the instance of his friends he concluded he
would go to school for a while and acquire an edu-

cation that he might be better fitted for the work of the ministry. He accordingly attended Illinois College at Jacksonville, with his talented cousin, Peter R. Borein; but after remaining six months, he could not be persuaded to continue longer. And when asked the reason, he replied, " It will be lost time and money, for my head is chock-full of learning, and as fast as I get a new idea in my head, it crowds out an old one." He felt, too, as he told the writer, that it was wicked for him to stay there in college, when souls were perishing all about him whom he might direct to Christ. Leaving the school then, he was employed by the presiding elder on the Athens Circuit for the remainder of the year, and in 1832 he was again received on trial in the conference, and appointed to Carrollton Circuit, with John Van Cleve as his senior. For the two following years he was alone on the Pittsfield Circuit. In 1835 he was sent to Rushville, but traveled the circuit only part of the year, being removed by his presiding elder to the Black Hawk purchase in Iowa, Dr. John P. Richmond being employed for the remainder of the year. In 1836 his appointment was Canton; 1837, Buckhart; 1838, Canton again; 1839, Vermillion; 1840, Mercer Mission; 1841, Peoria Circuit; 1842, Carthage; 1843, Randolph; 1844 and 1845, Jacksonville Circuit; 1846, Urbana; 1847, Charleston. In 1848, at the resuscitation of the Missouri Conference, he was transferred to it, and appointed to the St. Louis County Mission, in which he labored two years. In 1850 he was re-transferred to the Illinois Conference and appointed to Ewington, and the next year to Mt. Pulaski. At the close of the year he located and soon afterwards removed to California. In 1859 he was readmitted in the California Conference, traveled in succession the Colusi, Cosumnes, and Michigan Bar charges, and in 1862 again located. He afterwards removed to Washington Territory, where he closed his labors and sufferings in February, 1880.

Mr. Pitner was, probably, less influenced by artificial rules than any one who ever traveled in Illinois. In all his actions and addresses he was a perfect child of nature. He looked at things as no other man did; and whatever thought came into his mind, no matter how odd or incongruous or foreign to the occasion or subject, would be very likely to find utterance. He was preaching once to a large audience, and with much freedom, when he suddenly stopped and quaintly remarked, " Brethren, I had a good idea, but somehow it's gone. We'll sit down and sing a verse or two, and it will come back again." So he sat down, started a familiar hymn, and in a few moments sprang up, crying, " I told you it would come back, I have it now," and went on with his sermon as though nothing had happened. Of course his hearers were greatly amused, but on the whole the effect was good.

He was so constituted that he could not preach at all if there happened to be any thing very strange or novel before him. " I was present once," says Mr. Dickens, " when he preached in his brother's house. There was hanging just before him a new-fashioned pin-cushion. His eye fell upon it as he was preaching. He tried for a few moments to preach while attempting to make out what it was, when he suddenly stopped, and asked what sort of a thing it was, saying that he had never seen such a droll thing in his life. At his request it was removed, and then he proceeded with his sermon with a good degree of liberty; but it was not easy for the amused hearers to bring back their feeling to a devotional frame again."

On another occasion, while preaching at a private house, after he had commenced his sermon, he espied on the opposite side of the room a very oddly constructed spinning-wheel. For a little while he tried to divert his mind from it, but the more he tried the more confused he became, until at length he suddenly paused in his sermon, and addressing the man of the house, said, " Brother, I wish you would take that wheel away. I never saw such an ugly looking thing before. I could make a better wheel than that myself." So, amid the laughter that such a ludicrous remark would produce, the brother removed the wheel from the house, and the preacher resumed his sermon.

While preaching in a country school-house by the side of a public road on the Jacksonville Circuit, one warm Summer afternoon, he was much annoyed by the antics of a little dog just in front of the desk behind which he stood. Still preaching, he stepped from behind the desk, seized the dog by the back of his neck, deliberately walked to the open door and threw the little beast as far into the road as he could, and deliberately marched back to the desk, preaching all the time as hard as he could, as though his act was nothing out of the way. The congregation had been a little drowsy before, but that act thoroughly aroused them, and if no spiritual good was accomplished, he certainly had the wakeful attention of those present during the rest of the service.

At another time, while exhorting after a sermon preached by G. W. Robbins, in a grove, in the midst of his exhortation he happened to look up, and saw on one of the trees before him a limb with a peculiar crook in it. He suddenly stopped in his exhortation, and said, "That limb would make a first rate saddle-tree." Of course none sought religion as the effect of that exhortation.

He was a great hunter, and in some of his early charges drew no small portion of his support from his fishing and trapping. He was particularly expert in finding bee-trees and securing the honey lodged in them. Once at a camp-meeting in Fulton County, he was put up to exhort, and, if possible, arouse the people, who seemed quite indifferent to their spiritual interests. While exhorting at the top of his voice, he suddenly paused, and, pointing in a certain direction, cried out, "There went a bee!" There were no seekers of religion at that exhortation. Once, while immersing a person in one of the streams in the military tract, just as he was about to plunge him under the water, and had commenced the formula, "I baptize thee," his eye caught sight of a bee; he paused for a little while, until he had got the exact direction in which the bee was flying, and then completed the ceremony. And as soon as possible after he came from the water he started in search of the bee-tree.

In the central portion of Illinois there is a weed vulgarly called cuckle-burr, that is a great annoyance in the fields and gardens. One Sabbath afternoon, in the Summer of 1845, the writer had preached, and called on Brother Pitner to pray at the close of the sermon. It seems that there was something in it with which he was pleased, and with more than ordinary fervor he prayed, " O Lord, bless the sermon we have just heard, bless it mightily; make it the means of doing great harm to the devil's kingdom; O Lord, make it like cuckle-burrs in the devil's garden."

But despite these eccentricities, he was a deeply devoted and conscientious Christian. Perhaps no member of the conference was more faithful and regular in his private and family devotions than he; for he firmly believed that if he neglected these duties God would send some great calamity upon him. Though illiterate, in the ordinary sense of the term, for it is said that he declared he had never read but three books in his life, the Bible, the Hymn-book, and the Discipline, his close and constant study of the Scriptures had given him a wonderful command of language, and sometimes when preaching, and more frequently in exhortation, his language would not only be grammatically correct, but the most appropriate words would spring forth to express his ideas, and thoughts the

most sublime would roll from him in measured ca-
dence like the grandest blank verse, reaching the
souls of the most cultivated as well as the most
illiterate of his hearers, and stirring them to their
profoundest depths. There were times, indeed, when
he seemed to be inspired, and when the people felt
that it was not Pitner who was speaking, but God,
who was speaking through him.

At a conference in Springfield he was appointed
to speak at the missionary anniversary and take the
collection. The railroad from Naples to Springfield was then in operation, the cars being drawn by
mules. After the speaker had portrayed as best he
could the necessity of saving the world and the
grandeur of the work, he compared the missionary
machinery to a long train of cars, heavily freighted
with all the appliances of salvation. "But where,"
he asked, "is the motive power? Brethren, I tell
you it has to go. This grand train must go, and
it will go, for God Almighty himself is hitched to it."
Rough and irreverent as it was, the effect was elec-
trical; shouts were heard all over the house, and the
collection was a grand one.

Dr. Cartwright describes a camp-meeting in Fulton County, at which Pitner was present, and says
of him: "We had a very singular and remarkable
man among us, a traveling preacher in the Illinois
Conference; his name was Wilson Pitner. He was
at this camp-meeting. He was uneducated, and it
seemed impossible for him to learn; but, notwith-
standing his want of learning, and in common he
was an ordinary preacher, yet at times, as we say in

the back-woods, when he swung clear there were
very few that could excel him in the pulpit, and,
perhaps, he was one of the most eloquent and powerful exhorters that was in the land. On Monday
he came to me and desired me to let him preach at
11 o'clock, saying, 'I have faith to believe that God
will this day convert many of these rowdies and persecutors.' I consented, and he preached with great
liberty and power. Nearly the whole congregation
were powerfully moved, as he closed by calling for
every rowdy and persecutor to meet him in the altar;
for, said he, 'I have faith to believe that God will
convert every one of you that will come and kneel
at the place of prayer.' There was a general rush
for the altar, and many of our persecutors, and
those who had interrupted us in the forepart of
the meeting, came and fell on their knees and cried
aloud for mercy; and it is certainly beyond my
power to describe the scene; but more than fifty
souls were converted to God that day and night.
Our meeting continued for several days, and about
ninety professed to obtain the pardon of their sins,
most of whom joined the Church, and much good
was accomplished, although we waded through tribulation to accomplish it. Such success often attended
the Gospel labors of this brother."

"In 1841," says Mr. Beggs, "W. Pitner was
appointed to Peoria Circuit, and held a camp-meeting at Princeville. I had the privilege of attending this camp-meeting. It was increasingly prosperous till Sabbath morning, when W. Pitner was
to preach and I to exhort and call up the mourners.

The preacher began in his odd way of portraying the downward path of the sinner. His apt and un-varnished illustration of a sinner on the way to hell excited laughter all over the house. Every one seemed too merry and trifling to have any good re-sult from such a sermon, and most of us gave up all expectations of inviting up the mourners at its close. I felt that I could not exhort after that ser-mon, and told the elder so; when all of a sudden he changed to one of the most terrific descriptions of the finally impenitent, and the wailings of the damned, till it seemed as if the sound of those wail-ings reached our ears, and we could almost feel the darkness of despair brooding over the sinner, and see his tearless eyeballs rolling in their burning sockets, and his poor, unsheltered soul cry out, 'Lost, lost, lost!' All eyes seemed as if turned toward the yawning pit, and the deep sighs heaved from a thousand breasts, 'Lord, save! Lord, save the sin-ner!' And then he pointed to the Savior as the sinner's only refuge, telling how, through him, there was yet hope; that all might come and receive par-don, and that the joys of heaven were freely offered, without money and without price. I have never witnessed another such a scene. It was as if they realized that the judgment was near at hand. Some fell, and lay all night and cried for mercy; others screamed as if hell was moving from beneath to meet them at their coming. And how beautifully he cleared up the way and invited the sinners to the altar. Such as had strength came rushing and fairly tumbling along, some, with uplifted voices, crying,

'Thou son of David, have mercy on us.' In the midst of all this the preacher's mellowing tones and his invitation to come to Jesus, beggar all description. The cries for mercy, the bursting forth of praise, and the preacher's voice sounding out over all with its melting tones of pardon, produced a scene, I imagine, like that of God's ancient people when laying the foundation of the second temple, when the old men ' wept with a loud shout, so that they could not discern the noise of the shouts of joy from the voice of the weeping people.' This camp-meeting ended with glorious results, which may be seen to this day."

He was appointed to preach one Sunday night at a camp-meeting in Hancock County. There had been a good religious interest, and some souls had been converted. After supper the men and women had been out in the woods holding prayer-meetings, each on its own side of the ground. As the horn blew for service, rejoicing in God they came in from their prayer-meetings and met at the head of the main aisle. As they marched up to take their seats on either side of it, Brother Pitner, who was already in the pulpit, seized the horn, which hung on one side of it, and blew a blast loud and long, and then grasping the Bible, and holding it open toward the moving crowd, he cried out with a voice like a trumpet, "Hallelujah, the Lord God Omnipotent reigneth." The people, already powerfully excited, seemed now to be overwhelmed, some fell; when the preacher blew another blast, and again cried, "Hallelujah, the Lord God Omnipotent reigneth."

Saints shouted aloud, sinners began to cry for mercy. The preacher leaped from the pulpit and gave a brief invitation to seekers of salvation. Multitudes rushed to the altar, and multitudes were that night led to the Savior, how many eternity will reveal. Brother Pitner told the writer afterwards that while he had intended to take as a text the words he uttered, and while the Bible was open at the passage, the thought of the trumpet flashed into his mind the moment he seized it, and that as he stood there holding the open Bible before the congregation, he felt flashes of power darting out from the ends of his fingers, and his whole frame was convulsed as if from the shocks of a battery.

" His conversion," says Mr. Dickens, " was clear and powerful. His call to preach was convincing and even miraculous. His preaching, when he swung clear, as he expressed it, was masterly and often overwhelming. When energized with the Spirit, he was the most powerful and successful exhorter I ever knew, and thousands, I doubt not, will own him in heaven as their spiritual father. His preaching and exhortations were unlike any other man's. He was always original. A true Benjaminite, he always hit on the left side." The writer was his colleague in 1844 on the Jacksonville Circuit, and heard him frequently. While in his sermons he often failed, at times his exhortations were eloquent and powerful beyond description. With the simplicity and guilelessness of a child, he possessed the intellect of a giant, and had that intellect been cultivated, he must have been one of the most powerful men in the Church. He was an original thinker. While his illustrations—and his addresses abounded in them—were sometimes crude and sometimes ridiculous, they were often the most sublime that the mind could grasp, and clothed in language so appropriate, beautiful, and poetic that the most fastidious critic could find no fault in them. Of the business of the Church he had very little idea. His forte was to save souls and to build up the Church. A man of wonderful faith, at times he was yet subject to deep depression of spirit, when he thought he had not a single friend in the world. When he attempted to speak in his own strength he always failed, but when he spoke in dependence on God, and feeling that without divine help he must fail, then the Spirit seemed to speak through him as he spoke through the prophets of old, and mighty results followed.

For several years before he died he was able to preach but little. But he remained deeply pious, loving the Church, with all her ministers, members, and institutions, to the last. He was ready when the summons came, and died in full faith and hope.

Lorenzo Edwards traveled but one year in the Illinois Conference. He had been received on trial in the Missouri Conference in 1822, and appointed to the St. Francis Circuit, but at the close of the year was discontinued. After laboring this year on the Shelbyville Circuit, he was again discontinued. He settled in Scott County near Winchester, where he long labored as a local preacher.

JAMES BANKSON was the only son of pious parents, who taught him to know the Scriptures from his youth. He was born in Oglethorpe County, Georgia, January 8, 1795, and when about eight years of age, removed with his parents to Illinois. When about fourteen he embraced religion, and it is said of him that when he was converted, he sprang from the mourner's bench, and at the top of his voice shouted, " Whoop-pee, hallelujah! Jesus, Jesus!" Though his educational advantages were but limited in boyhood, he yet possessed an insatiable thirst for knowledge, and from the time of his conversion applied himself to study with such diligence that he became a respectable scholar; and before his death acquired a good knowledge of Latin, Greek, and Hebrew, besides making considerable progress in the sciences. In 1821 he commenced his itinerant life in the Missouri Conference, in which he traveled eight years, mostly on frontier circuits, until 1829, when he was transferred to the Illinois Conference, and assigned to the Apple Creek Circuit. The next year he was appointed to Spoon River. But while crossing a stream on the ice, in the Winter of 1830–1, on his way to Calvin Hobart's, his horse fell, and inflicted on him an injury from which he did not recover. In the Spring he returned to his father's house, and was never afterwards able to resume his labors. For the benefit of medical aid, he was, of choice, taken to the St. Louis Hospital, where he underwent a painful surgical operation. After lingering in pain for some weeks, he died in triumph,

September 4, 1831. Though his beginning in the ministry was very unpromising, by his diligence in study and fidelity to God, he became a very eloquent and powerful preacher. It is related by one who was present when he made his first attempt to preach, soon after taking his text, his embarrassment quite overcame him. He stopped short, sat down in the pulpit, and crossing his legs, shook as if he had an ague. There was, however, that in him that was not to be discouraged or broken down. Though he retained, in some degree, his awkwardness in gesture and manner, he yet became " a polished arrow in the Gospel quiver, a burning and shining light in the Methodist Church, and when he died he had few equals in the Illinois Conference." [5]

DAVID B. CARTER was born in Virginia in 1793. He removed to Tennessee before he was married, which occurred when he was nineteen years old. He was converted soon after his marriage, and united with the Church. At this time " he could not read a hymn intelligibly, but believing God had called him to preach the Gospel, he industriously applied himself to books, and soon learned to read very well." [6] In 1827 he moved to Illinois, and settled in Sangamon County. He was received on trial in the Illinois Conference in 1829, and appointed to Sangamon Circuit, which he traveled two years as junior preacher, the first under Smith L. Robinson, and the second with Jesse Haile as his senior. In 1831 he was appointed to

---

[5] Rev. E. M. West.   [6] Dr. Cartwright.

Spoon River, and the next year to Fort Edward
Mission. In 1833 his appointment was Quincy,
and for the two following years he again labored on
the Fort Edward Charge. In 1836 he was sent to
Rushville Circuit, and at the close of the year, his
health having failed, he was granted a superannuated relation. The next year he was placed on the
supernumerary list, and assigned in that relation to
Rushville again. But consumption having fastened
on him, he was, at the conference session of 1839,
again placed on the superannuated list, on which
he remained until he died, in great peace and triumph, October 28, 1840. Brother Carter was not
a great or brilliant preacher or a profound theologian, but he was, as his memoir states, "a thorough
reformation preacher." During his short ministerial career many were the seals to his ministry. He
was a very industrious preacher, always enlarging
his circuits by taking in new appointments. He
was much beloved in life and greatly lamented in
death. In Rushville, his last field of labor, and
where he died, he is "affectionately remembered as
a faithful minister of the Lord Jesus Christ, as an
excellent preacher, an industrious pastor, and a wise
counselor; and to his labors the Church is greatly
indebted for its permanent and efficient organization. To him must be accorded the credit of organizing what has ever been, and is to-day, the glory
and pride of our Church—the Sabbath-school."[7]

JAMES LATTA was brought up in Champaign
County, Ohio. In 1824 he removed to Illinois and

____
[7] Dr. W. Stevenson.

settled in Blooming Grove, where the present city of Bloomington is. In 1827, while the Winnebago Indians were making some trouble in the mining regions, he obtained a position in connection with the militia, and was afterwards known as *Colonel* Latta. Having served for some years as a local preacher, in 1829 he was received on trial in the Illinois Conference, and appointed to the Peoria Circuit, then including the region in which Bloomington is situated, and at the close of the year was discontinued at his own request. He was a good preacher, very effective, and, though faithfully and pointedly telling the people of their sins, he was yet very popular and greatly beloved. After he ceased traveling he removed to Indiana, and died near Crab Orchard. Dr. Samuel A. Latta, of the Ohio Conference, was his younger brother.

BENJAMIN C. STEPHENSON was converted in his sixteenth year, and was received as a traveling preacher in the Illinois Conference in 1827. For two years he traveled in Indiana, and in 1829 was appointed to the Galena Mission. His next appointment was Madison, Indiana. In 1831 he was appointed to Indianapolis, but died before starting for his new field of labor. He "was a dignified young man, of respectable talents, and promised much to the Church."[8]

---

[8] General Minutes.

CHAPTER VII.

1830.

WABASH DISTRICT—George Locke, P. E.
Vermillion—James McKean, John E. French.
Paris—William H. Smith.
Wabash—Thomas H. Files, Philip T. Cordier.
Mt. Carmel—John Miller, John Fox, Sup.

·KASKASKIA DISTRICT—Samuel H. Thompson, P. E.
Kaskaskia—John Van Cleve.
Brownsville Mission—Anthony F. Thompson.
Jonesboro Mission—Boyd Phelps.
Golconda—James P. Crawford.
McLeansboro—Amos Prentice.
Mt. Vernon—John H. Benson.
Shoal Creek—John Dew, Edward R. Ames.
Shelbyville—Miles Huffaker.
Grand Prairie Mission—Simeon Walker.

SANGAMON DISTRICT—Peter Cartwright, P. E.
Lebanon—Stith M. Otwell, Wm. L. Deneen.
Apple Creek—Wm. D. R. Trotter, Wm. H. Askins.
Jacksonville—John Sinclair.
Atlas—Spencer W. Hunter.
Spoon River—James Bankson.
Tazewill—Stephen R. Beggs.
Salt Creek—Asahel E. Phelps.
Sangamon—Jesse Haile, David B. Carter.
Galena Mission—Smith L. Robinson.
Chicago Mission—Jesse Walker.
Fort Clark Mission—Isaac Scarritt.

THE seventh session of the Illinois Conference was held at Vincennes, Indiana, beginning on Thursday, September 30th, and closing on the following

Thursday. No bishop being present, Bishop Roberts, whose work it was, having been taken sick at St. Louis, Samuel H. Thomson was elected president, and Calvin W. Ruter, secretary. Twenty-seven preachers were present at the opening service. Two sessions were held each day, from 8 A. M. to 12, and from 2 P. M. to 5.

Seventeen preachers were received on trial—John C. Smith, Spencer W. Hunter, Isaac Kimball, William Taylor, William S. Crissey, Henry S. Talbot, John Richey, James M. Massey, James P. Crawford, Josiah H. Hill, Philip T. Cordier, Simeon Walker, Edward R. Ames, Amos Prentice, William D. R. Trotter, Daniel M. Murphy, Ancil Beach.

Four were discontinued: George West, Wilson Pitner, Lorenzo Edwards, James Latta.

Four were granted a location: Thomas Davis, William Chambers, Asa D. West, Samuel Bogart.

Three were transferred from the Kentucky Conference to this: William H. Askins, Samuel Julian, and John Sinclair.

One had died—Josiah Patterson. He was the first member of the Illinois Conference, who had labored in Illinois, to be called to his reward. Two others had died, John Cord and William Cravens, but their labors had been confined to Indiana.

One local deacon was elected to elder's orders, viz.: James Conwell.

Twenty-two local preachers were elected to deacon's orders: James P. Crawford, Jesse Spradling, Harbert P. DeBuelle, Joseph Walker, Joseph Springer, Barton Randle, Robert Thomas, Levin

Green, David Bruner, Jonathan Prosser, Francis Standaford, Benjamin Jones, Thomas Evans, Hardy Cain, Jeremiah Sherwood, Solomon Cross, Vance Jones, George M. Hanson, Stephen C. Rentfro, William Echols, Simeon Walker, Abraham P. Casey.

As no bishop was present, there were, of course, no ordinations. The persons elected received certificates of the fact from the secretary of the conference, and were ordained whenever they could meet with a bishop.

A draft on the Book Concern was ordered for $300, and on the Chartered Fund for $80.

Among the miscellaneous business transacted was the following: After the reading of a communication from the book agents at New York, the following was adopted:

"*Resolved,* That the members of this conference do express their entire satisfaction with the report and address of their general book agents at New York, and that we will do all in our power to aid them in publishing and circulating our very valuable books."

The subject of Sunday-schools took up a good deal of the time of the conference. An agent of the American Sunday-school Union being in town, and desiring an interview with the conference, was granted permission to address them on the second afternoon at four o'clock. The journal states that he delivered an interesting address, and immediately after it the conference adjourned. The whole of the Monday afternoon session was spent in discussing a resolution on the subject, which was, after all, laid on the table. The next day the resolution was called up, and, after amendment, a motion was made to postpone the subject indefinitely, but before this was acted on, conference adjourned. Two days afterwards the subject was again called up, when the motion to postpone indefinitely was withdrawn, and the question on the adoption of the amended resolution was decided in the negative. It is unfortunate that the journal does not give this much discussed resolution. It would have been interesting as showing the demands of the Sunday-school Union at that early day, and the feeling of the conference in regard to it.

The case of Thomas Davis was called, and some objections being made in consequence of his not having attended to the duties of a traveling preacher during the last year, it was moved that he be deprived of his ministerial office, and, after some discussion, the motion was withdrawn, whereupon his character was passed, and his presiding elder asked and received for him a location.

A small sum of money, unappropriated by the stewards, was directed to be put in the hands of the presiding elders, to be by them appropriated to those persons whom they shall deem most needy.

A report having been sent to conference by Jesse Walker, who had been on the Fox River Mission the past year, in which was embraced the old Pottawattomie Mission, a committee was appointed to consider it, who reported as follows: "That they have examined the documents, and find that they contain a report of his missionary labors during the past year, and the amount of property belonging to the old Pottawattomie Mission, which has been sold by said Walker, together with a list of property belonging to said mission, remaining unsold. Your committee would say that they are fully satisfied with the transactions of your missionary, and report as the proceeds of the sale the sum of $303, which is now on hand and at the disposal of the conference." Peter Cartwright was appointed a committee to settle the claims against the Pottawattomie Mission, and it was ordered that the amount raised from the sale of the property of the mission now on hand be appropriated to the payment of those claims in an equal proportion to their amount as far as the money will go.

Two appeal cases were brought before the conference. Benjamin Watts, a local elder, appealed from the decision of the quarterly conference of the Lebanon Circuit, by which he was expelled from the Church; and, after an examination of the case, the conference confirmed the decision. William J. Mayo, a local elder, appealed from the decision of the quarterly conference of Paris Circuit, by which he was expelled. The case was sent back to the quarterly conference for a new trial on the ground of informality.

A committee having been appointed to take into consideration the expediency of adopting the McKendree College as the literary institution of the conference, reported in favor of it, and the following resolutions were adopted:

"1. That the conference accede to the proposals

of the managers of the McKendree College of Illinois at Lebanon, and now agree to adopt the said college as a conference seminary.

"2. That a committee of three be appointed by this conference to appoint a president whose literary and religious qualifications are such as will do credit to the institution.

"3. That each preacher of the conference be required to open subscriptions and solicit donations from the friends of literature within their respective charges, which moneys, when collected, shall be paid to the person who may be legally appointed, either by this conference or the managers, to superintend the moneyed concerns of said institution."

John Dew, Peter Cartwright, and Samuel H. Thompson were elected as the committee to nominate the president, and were instructed to act in conjunction with the managers of said institution in the matter; and also as soon as possible to address a circular to each member of the conference, giving such information as they shall deem necessary.

As soon as this action was had, fixing the conference seminary at Lebanon, the Indiana brethren began to make arrangements for a similar institution in Indiana, and a committee of five was appointed "to make inquiry respecting a suitable site where to establish an institution of learning, and also as to the amount of money that can be obtained in the vicinity of such site to aid in the erection of suitable buildings for the purpose," and report to the next session of the conference. The president appointed as the committee John Strange, Calvin

W. Ruter, James Armstrong, Edwin Ray, and Allen Wiley.

Missions were constituted as follows: Grand Prairie Mission, including all the country lying between the Little Wabash and Kaskaskia Rivers, lying on and near the State road leading from Maysville to Vandalia not included in any other circuit, except those preaching places now included in the Mt. Carmel Circuit west of the Little Wabash, and those appointments included in Shoal Creek Circuit lying east of the Kaskaskia River. To this $100 was appropriated. Brownsville Mission, embracing all the country formerly included in the Brownsville Circuit, except that portion now embraced in the Mt. Vernon and·Jonesboro Circuits. $75 was appropriated to it.

Jonesboro Circuit was transformed into a mission, and fifty dollars assigned to it.

Fort Clark Mission, to which $200 was appropriated, embracing the district of country lying on both sides of the Illinois River from Fort Clark to the mouth of Fox and Vermillion Rivers.

To the Galena Mission, which was continued the same as last year, was assigned $250.

The name of Fox River Mission was changed to Chicago Mission, and $250 was appropriated to it.

The whole amount appropriated to the work in Illinois was $925.

Some other changes were made in the plan of the work besides those indicated in the formation of these missions. A new circuit, McLeansboro, was formed from the Mt. Vernon and Mt. Carmel

Charges, embracing Hamilton County, and perhaps parts of Saline and Wayne. The north part of Apple Creek Circuit was constituted into the Jacksonville Circuit, including what are now Morgan, Scott, and Cass Counties. The Tazewell Circuit was formed from the east part of the Peoria Circuit, embracing the counties of Tazewell, McLean, and parts of Logan and De Witt.

Many excellent revivals occurred this year, in spite of the great difficulties of travel during the Winter, for this was the Winter of "the deep snow," the hardships of which are still remembered by the old settlers of the country. On the Apple Creek Circuit, at the Sappington appointment, was an extensive work of grace; and on the whole circuit there was a continuous advance. On the Tazewell Circuit, under the pastorate of S. R. Beggs, two camp-meetings were held, at which a number of souls were converted. A good revival occurred at Lebanon. One of the valuable accessions to the Church there during it was BENJAMIN HYPES, who for near half a century has been a pillar in the Church. He was born in Botetourt County, Virginia, February 10, 1805. His conversion took place in an old mill in Lebanon, on the 27th of January, 1831, and he united with the Church in the March following. He has held every office in the Church to which a layman is eligible, and was the first lay representative of the Southern Illinois Conference in the General Conference. He has been intimately connected with McKendree College as trustee from its commencement, and has given largely of his time and means for the promotion of its interests.

At a camp-meeting on the Sangamon Circuit, at Waters's camp-ground, was a gracious revival. Among the converts was Dr. GEORGE H. HARRISON, who has for many years occupied a prominent position in the community.

In the Fall of this year Dr. W. T. Crissy moved to the newly laid off town of Decatur, and settled where the fair-ground now is. The next Spring his nephew, Rev. W. S. Crissy, visited him, and while there preached the first Methodist sermon ever preached in the town, at the house of Brother Isaac Miller, just east of where the Illinois Central Railroad is now. There had been a small society a mile and a half off, which was afterwards removed to the town, and became the germ from which has sprung the flourishing Churches now existing there.

The first church in Jacksonville was built this year. It was of brick, and was the first brick church in the county. It was on East Morgan Street, a little north of the present Centenary Church.

The first church was also erected this year in Springfield. It was a frame building, put up on the site of the present First Church, on lots donated by P. P. Enos, on the corner of Monroe and Fifth Streets.

Several persons united with the Church this year who afterwards became pillars in it, and whose names deserve mention. Among them was SAMUEL SACKETT, a native of Butler County, Ohio, born

September 1, 1797. In 1829 he removed to Sangamon County, Illinois. He lived many years in Clinton, Illinois, and in 1875 moved to Linn County, Kansas, to spend his last days with his daughter. He was, during most of his religious life, an officer in the Church, having been Sunday-school superintendent, trustee, class-leader, and steward. He was a good man, spurning all conformity to the world, and seeking, through earnest prayer and diligent study of God's Word, to become an Israelite indeed, and his efforts were rewarded with a rich and happy experience. His last words were, "Christ is all my hope." [1]

In November of this year Rev. WILLIAM PETER and family removed to Illinois. He had been a traveling preacher in connection with the Tennessee and Kentucky Conferences since 1819, and had filled some of the most important circuits in Kentucky. In 1829 his name disappears from the minutes without any intimation of the cause. Dr. Redford says of him: "His zeal and devotion to the work to which he was called rendered him remarkably useful. During his ministry in Kentucky but few men were more useful than William Peter." He died in great peace, eleven days after his arrival in Illinois, leaving a widow with ten children. All of them she saw become heads of families. She died in 1880, at the age of ninety, having been for sixty years a member of the Church. She was an uncomplaining, happy Christian. "Before she died she uttered many expressions indicat-

___
[1] Rev. J. M. Payne.

ing her triumph in the last conflict, such as 'The Lord is my Shepherd,' etc." "And until consciousness was gone she never ceased to talk of God and his goodness."[2]

THOMAS KERSEY, a native of Delaware, born in 1803, moved to Winchester, Illinois, in 1830, and died September 17, 1880. He was for many years a practicing physician. After leaving the practice of medicine he engaged in business, and when misfortune came upon him, he bore his losses and troubles with the highest degree of Christian grace, and acted toward men who suffered financially by his misfortunes in a manner of the very highest degree of honor. Being a pioneer Methodist, his house was the home of the early preachers, where they found the comforts and joys of life in their hard, itinerant pilgrimages. He was a faithful class-leader during many years, and a just steward, looking after the temporal wants of the servants of God. In a class-meeting, the Sunday before he died, he said: "I am poor in this world's goods, but God will take care of me. I am the son of a King who is rich." "He was one of nature's noblemen, and a grand prince in Israel, one of the pillars of the Church whose place can never be filled."[3]

JOHN E. AYERS and wife moved this year from New Jersey to Illinois. For many years he lived in Pike County, a few miles west of Griggsville, filling many of the offices of the Church, and being universally esteemed as a consistent Christian, a useful officer, and honest man. In 1855 they moved

[2] Rev. J. W. Caldwell.   [3] Rev. W. S. Hooper.

to Moawequa, where they lived till called to their reward. Brother Ayers was for years "one of the main members of the Church there; consistent in life, and liberal in the use of his means for the benevolent as well as the local uses of the Church."[4] He died in 1879, and his widow, who, in devising liberal things, imitated his example, survived him only about two years.

In November of this year HIRAM M. TREMBLE, an exhorter, moved from Harrison County, Indiana, and settled on Robinson's Creek, in Shelby County, Illinois. He was born in Ohio, April 21, 1808. In the fall of 1832 he was licensed to preach, and delivered his first sermon in the neighborhood in which he lived. While there, and before he was authorized to preach, he kept up an itinerant prayer-meeting at four appointments surrounding Shelbyville, at which, during the Fall and Winter, seventy-six were converted. On Robinson's Creek lived an old Baptist lady, who had two sons and two daughters, all grown. Her children were all converted at the meeting. The old lady was very happy, but she would not give way to her emotions and shout. Soon she took the jerks and continued jerking until she did shout. A wicked cattle buyer named Byles, having gone to the meeting out of curiosity to see the jerks, undertaking afterwards to show another how they worked, was seized with them himself, and for awhile was unable to restrain them. He behaved himself better after that. A year or two afterwards Mr. Tremble moved to Coles County, near

---

[4] Rev. J. B. Colwell.

where Mattoon now is, where he continued to reside until his death. While there he was abundant in labors, and by his zeal and faithfulness not only won many souls to Christ, but exerted a strong influence in the community. He was among the first advocates of the anti-slavery cause in Illinois. When the war of the rebellion broke out he heartily supported the cause of his country, and in 1862 was commissioned chaplain of the Sixty-second Regiment of Illinois volunteers. He served three years, and when he retired he was presented with a certificate signed by the officers of his regiment, attesting his fidelity as chaplain and overseer of refugees, and asserting that in his discharge the army had lost a most valuable officer and an upright man and honorable gentleman. On returning to his home he resumed his labors as a preacher, and in the language of his memoir, "he was a true representative of what a local preacher ought to be, traveling and preaching whenever and wherever he could, and assisting the traveling preachers when possible. As age crept upon him, his labors did not abate; he did not become fossilized, but remained the zealous advocate of progress to the last."[5] Among his expressions as he grew older were, "I am living by the day;" "I am living by the hour;" and, finally, "I am living by the minute, yet enjoying the presence of God continually." He died while on a visit to his daughter, near Eureka Springs, March 14, 1881, but his remains were brought to Mattoon for interment. He was a man of intelligence, of good

---

[5] Rev. W. M. Poe.

mind, of great energy and force of character, devotedly attached to the Church, and as a preacher far above mediocrity, and deservedly popular.

There was a decrease in the colored membership this year of 88, but an increase in the whites of 1,296, making an aggregate increase of 1,208, and leaving Illinois with 9,529 white members, and 43 colored.

Some ministers, who afterwards became distinguished in the Church, commenced their labor in Illinois this year. Chief among them was EDWARD RAYMOND AMES. He was born at Amesville, Athens County, Ohio, May 30, 1806. In 1827, while a student at the State University at Athens, Ohio, during a great revival, in which many of the students were converted, he was brought to a saving knowledge of the Lord Jesus Christ. He soon after united with the Methodist Episcopal Church. The next year he left college and became the principal of the Lebanon Seminary, at Lebanon, Illinois, which afterwards grew into McKendree College. He was quite successful as a teacher, though some complained of him for his rigid discipline. While at Lebanon his case was brought before the society for recommendation for license to preach. He was opposed by Joseph Foulks, a located itinerant who lived there, and who did not believe that he would make a successful preacher. Several meetings were held before the recommendation was obtained. At the quarterly-meeting held at Padfield's, he received license to preach, but when his friends asked for him a recommendation to the annual conference, he was again objected to, and when the vote was taken it was a tie. It was taken again, with the same result. The conference then adjourned until afternoon. Meanwhile Emanuel Wilkerson, a colored local preacher, arrived, and on the case being called up at the afternoon session, there was a majority of one in favor of the recommendation; so that it was often said afterwards that a colored preacher made Edward R. Ames a bishop. The objections urged against him were that he was a dyspeptic, and would never be able to do the work of a Methodist preacher, and that he was too fastidious in his taste, particularly in regard to eating, to become acceptable with the people. Of his ability none entertained any doubt. Having been admitted into conference, his first appointment was the Shoal Creek Circuit, with John Dew as his senior, and Samuel H. Thompson as his presiding elder. A more judicious appointment could not have been made; and the training he received from his colleague and presiding elder told favorably upon all his after life. The next year he was sent to Vincennes, and in 1832 fell into the Indiana Conference, of which he remained a member until his election to the episcopacy, with the exception of one year, in which he was stationed in St. Louis. Rev. S. G. Patterson, who was his neighbor on the St. Louis Circuit, describes him at this time as "a man of social qualities, prepossessing in his manners, of fair attainments, sound in doctrine, a good preacher, and one who enjoyed the reputation of being a good pastor." From 1840 to 1844 he was one of the secretaries of the Missionary

Society, during which he traveled extensively, visiting all the Indian missions on the Western frontier, from Lake Superior to Arkansas, and aiding in establishing schools among them. In 1852, at the General Conference in Boston, he was elected to the office of bishop, in which he continued until his death at his residence in Baltimore, April 25, 1879. He was in circuits and stations seven years, two years agent of the Conference Preachers' Aid Society, nine years on districts, four years missionary secretary, and twenty-seven years in the episcopal office, making an itinerant career in all of forty-nine years. He was a member of the General Conference of 1840, 1844, and 1852.

"God blessed him with a powerful physical frame and a commanding person. In his earlier years he had a strong voice, with great oratorical power and pathos; and as in clarion notes he rang out the great truths of God, men were moved under his appeals; great religious revivals everywhere attended his preaching; sinners were awakened and brought to Christ, and believers were strengthened and built up in the faith and hope of the Gospel. In his later years his voice was more subdued, and its tones were soft and sympathetic, but the old fire and the old power pervaded his sermons to the last, and the preachers and the people always heard him with great delight, and were abundantly instructed and blessed under his ministry. The salient points in his character, and which fitted him for eminence and success in his office as a bishop, were quickness, clearness, and comprehensiveness of perception, enabling him to grasp almost any subject at once, and to perceive also its collateral relations and bearings; a strong, unbending will to maintain the right as he saw it, which, when sanctified to God, as it was, made him a master over men; to which may be added an intuitive perception of human character, enabling him to see through men, scarcely ever misjudging them, and scarcely ever failing to judge rightly in estimating their capacity to succeed in any given line of action; so that in his superintendency, having formed his plans, he selected his agents to execute them, and the result almost always justified the wisdom of his plans, and the sagacity of his appointments."[6]

"As a preacher," says Daniels, " Bishop Ames was capable of wonderful eloquence, which was only occasionally manifested; but sometimes with some simple narrative, some tender little story, told with all the pathos of his great nature, he would melt a congregation to tears; or in some grand statement of doctrine or duty he would stir the blood of a conference, until the 'Amens' became so loud that he would be obliged to pause for silence. There was a broad, deep vein of humor in him; his smile was sunshine; his commendation was a power and blessing to those who received it; and his rebuke had so much of the terrible in it that few ventured to incur it a second time."

He was one of the best presiding officers the Church ever had; ready and correct in his decisions, rapid in the transaction of business, and de-

---

[6] General Minutes.

cided in the repression of all disorder. Possessed of great personal dignity, he was yet affable, courteous, and accessible to all. His knowledge of human nature, and his thorough acquaintance with all the phases of the itinerant work, particularly in the the West, rendered him peculiarly successful in making appointments for the preachers, for he rarely failed to send the right man to the right place. He had no sympathy with pretension, or sham, or unfairness, or meanness of any kind; and sometimes, in his reproofs of those whom he thought guilty of such conduct, he would use language that many of the hearers would characterize as unmercifully severe. Occasionally his indignation would get the better of his judgment and make him too hasty, as well as too severe in his reproofs. An instance of this occurred at one of the sessions of the Illinois Conference at which he presided. A brother had been charged with imprudent language in connection with the subject of holiness. The case was referred to a committee, who in their report recommended that the brother be admonished by the chair. As soon as the report was read, the bishop called up the brother and administered to him a severe reproof; and as he took his seat, was about to proceed with other business, when the secretary whispered to him that the report of the committee had not been acted on by the conference. The question was taken, and, fortunately for the bishop, the report was adopted. Had it been rejected he would have been placed in a very awkward position. In one respect Bishop Ames has been greatly misjudged. Because he left no legacies to the benevolent enterprises of the Church he was charged with being penurious. The truth is, he was one of the most liberal of men in the use of his means. He exercised his own judgment in his gifts, never giving for show, or because others thought he ought to give, but because he believed that the object or person was both worthy and needy. From his own early experience of the hardships of the itinerant life he had learned to sympathize with the preachers in their sufferings and privations, and it was upon them his benefactions were chiefly bestowed. The writer has heard of cases in which gifts of ten, twenty, fifty, and a hundred dollars were made to preachers in distress. And this was his constant habit. It is safe to say that he never attended a conference where cases of need were presented without contributing largely to their relief. And it is safe, also, to say that his gifts to needy preachers, privately, largely exceeded in amount his public contributions.

He loved the Church. Many tempting opportunities were afforded him of attaining high civil office, and strong inducements were presented to him, but he promptly rejected them, esteeming the reproach of Christ greater riches than the highest honors or offices of this world. "Take him all in all, he had few equals and no superiors in the Church he loved so well."[7]

WILLIAM H. ASKINS was born in Virginia July 8, 1803. He was converted at a camp-meeting in

---

[7] General Minutes.

Clarke County, Kentucky, in 1820. "Being very soon impressed that it was his duty to preach the Gospel, he conferred not with flesh and blood, but obeyed his convictions, and being authorized by the Church, he entered upon his new life with all the zeal and fervor peculiar to his character. He gave himself up entirely to the great work assigned him, and labored to the utmost of his strength for the salvation of immortal souls."[8]

After traveling six years in the Kentucky Conference, and filling some of its most important appointments acceptably, he was transferred to the Illinois Conference, and assigned to the Apple Creek Circuit with W. D. R. Trotter. The next year he was appointed to Jacksonville Circuit, which he traveled "until February, 1832, when his afflictions compelled him to desist. About the first of April he received a stroke of paralysis, and about six weeks after, another, which deprived him of his speech, and mostly of his hearing. In this condition he continued several weeks, and died July 6th, aged twenty-nine years. He was a popular and very successful preacher, lived beloved and died lamented, but he bore his sufferings with patience, and gave evidence to the last that God was with him in the mighty deep."[9] One of his colleagues describes him as "a true Christian, and a thorough Wesleyan in all his feelings—an old-time Methodist. He had tact, self-reliance, and spiritual power. He was a fair preacher, but as an exhorter he excelled. He dared once in Kentucky to follow with an ex-

---

[8] Dr. Redford.   [9] General Minutes.

hortation one of the most powerful sermons of Bishop McKendree."[10] Jonathan Stamper says of him, "He had a remarkable mind; never forgot what he once learned, and possessed the rare faculty of bringing every thing he knew into requisition in the very best manner. But the most important secret of his success as a preacher lay in the fact that he was filled with love toward God and man. A clear, musical voice, dignified gestures, and correct, well-chosen language, all characterized his pulpit efforts. He was certainly one of the most powerful exhorters I ever heard, and, when engaged in this peculiar exercise, often grew wonderfully eloquent. Take him altogether, he was one among the foremost ministers of his age, in respect both of talent and usefulness."

PHILIP T. CORDIER, who was this year received on trial and appointed to Wabash Circuit, traveled only three years. In 1831 his appointment was Rock Island, and in 1832, Grand Prairie. At the close of this year he was located by the conference. Dr. Cartwright says of him: "He was a man of feeble talents, unstable, and did but little good. He was finally expelled."

Of JAMES P. CRAWFORD we have no account but the record of his appointments in the General Minutes. He traveled six years, four of them by alternate appointments on the Golconda Circuit, in 1831 on Jonesboro Circuit, and in 1834 on Frankfort Circuit. At the conference of 1836 he was granted a location.

---

[10] Rev. W. D. R. Trotter.

Spencer W. Hunter was born of Baptist parents in Shelby County, Kentucky, December 21, 1801. In his twenty-second year he was converted, and four years afterwards was licensed to preach. He traveled for two years under the presiding elder, and in 1830 was received on trial in the Illinois Conference and appointed to Quincy Circuit, to which he was reappointed the next year. In 1832 he was transferred to Indiana Conference, in which he traveled three years. In 1835 he was, at his own request, left without an appointment, and the next year was transferred to the Illinois Conference and again appointed to Quincy Circuit. In 1837 he was sent to Pittsfield Circuit, and reappointed to it the next year, but on his way home from conference, at Alton, he was attacked by severe disease, and, after suffering for twenty-eight days, on the 18th of October, 1838, he fell asleep in Jesus. "For some days previous to his departure his mind was troubled; but, on the day of his departure, the sun of righteousness dispelled the cloud and shone divinely clear upon his rejoicing soul. The prospect before him was glorious, and with his latest breath he shouted, ' Victory !' Brother Hunter was a good and useful minister of the Gospel. In him was blended a discriminating mind with a good delivery. The graces which ornament the man united in him with the gifts of a sound Christian minister. In the pulpit he was plain and energetic; in the social circle, a man of God; and as he visited from house to house, his agreeable manners and the holiness of his life made him both a welcome and a useful guest. He lived most beloved, and died greatly lamented."[11]

AMOS PRENTICE was born in the State of New York, September 4, 1804. When twelve years old he removed with his parents to Illinois, and in 1825 was converted and united with the Church. In 1827 he was licensed to preach, and then spent a year as teacher at the Pottawattomie Mission, to which Jesse Walker was missionary. The next year, having married, he moved to Decatur, and engaged in the mercantile business. But his wife dying, he settled his secular' business and entered the itinerancy. His first appointment was McLeansboro Circuit. The next year, 1831, he was assigned to Salt Creek, but at the close of the year, his health having failed, he was, at his own request, discontinued. He then settled in Greenfield, and went into partnership with G. W. Allen in the mercantile business. In 1833 he was again received into the itinerancy, and appointed to Shelbyville Circuit, on which he labored quite successfully for a year, having several good revivals, and commencing the first church in Shelbyville, but in consequence of failing health he was again compelled to retire from the work at the close of the year. He afterwards settled at Sullivan, laboring as a local preacher, as his strength would permit, until his death.

He was a man of a remarkably sweet spirit, modest, gentle, sympathetic, loving every one and universally beloved. His preaching was greatly

---

[11] General Minutes.

admired for its tenderness, and he was much in demand for funeral sermons and at the sick bed. He was an instrument of good to many souls. One who knew him intimately for many years, says, "I never saw him angry or heard him speak an unkind word to any one." [12] He died at the residence of his brother William, at Shelbyville, whither he had been removed for medical attendance, August 17, 1849.

One of the most valuable accessions to the conference this year was JOHN SINCLAIR. He was born in Loudoun County, Virginia, April 9, 1793. When he was six years old his parents moved into East Tennessee, where he remained until he was twenty. They then removed to Kentucky, and settled at Lexington. In 1819 he was married to Miss Lydia Short, who for near forty years shared with him the labors and privations of the itineracy, and surviving him many years, passed away in 1878. About a year after his marriage he was deeply convinced of sin, and, having united with the Church as a seeker of religion, was soon after powerfully converted at a class-meeting. He was very soon made a class-leader, leading two classes, while he himself was a member of a third. In 1824 he was licensed to preach, and soon after was received into the Kentucky Conference, in which he labored for six years, and where "he was remarkably useful, and his ministry was blessed in the conversion of hundreds." [13] But, "having for some time felt that the existence of slavery in the State of Kentucky

______

[12] Dr. W. S. Prentice.　　　[13] Dr. Redford.

was a serious thing, and dreading its consequences
upon after generations—and this was the feeling
generally of Methodist preachers at that time" [14]—
in 1830 he sought and received a transfer to the
Illinois Conference, to which his father's family had
removed in 1829, and had settled in the neighborhood of Jacksonville. His first appointment was
the Jacksonville Circuit. In 1831–2 he was on the
Sangamon Circuit, and in 1833 he was made presiding elder of the Chicago District, which then
embraced all the settlements now embraced. in the
Rock River, Central Illinois, Upper Iowa, and
Wisconsin Conferences, and some in the Illinois
Conference. The next year he was returned to the
district, which was somewhat diminished in size by
the formation of the Galena Mission District, which
included the north-western portion of the territory
he had traveled the year before. In 1835 he was
appointed to the Sangamon District. These were
years of great affliction of body, both to himself
and wife. In the Winter of 1836–7 he came near
losing his life in one of the sudden changes of
weather for which Illinois is noted. He had started
across the prairie between the Vermillion River and
Ottawa, when suddenly the wind changed to the
north. A good deal of snow had fallen that had
partially melted, and the earth was covered with
slush. Before he reached Cole's Creek he became
so cold that he got down from his horse to walk.
Soon his leggings became so clogged with ice that
he could not bear the weight, and so left them

[14] Beggs.

standing on the prairie. His horse's legs became covered with ice and his own so clogged that he could not mount his horse again to cross the creek. All he could do was to let the horse drag him through the stream, he holding to the stirrup, until at length, utterly exhausted, and almost frozen to' death, he reached a house some miles beyond, where he was cared for.

At the conference of 1838 he was placed in a supernumerary relation, and appointed to Ottawa. The next year he was sent to Ottawa District, and, in 1840, falling into the newly-formed Rock River Conference, he was returned to it, and also for the two following years. In 1843 he was appointed to Rock River District, and "elected delegate to the General Conference, which held its session in the city of New York, May, 1844. From New York he returned home sick, and at the session of the annual conference in the Fall he was, at his own request, given a superannuated relation, which he sustained until 1847, when he was made effective and appointed to Rock River District, where he was continued for four years. In 1851 he was appointed to Chicago District, and remained on it four years. In 1855–6 he was pastor at Evanston, and in 1857 he consented to take a superannuated relation, and made his home in Evanston, where he resided at the time on his death,"[15] in 1861. Mr. Sinclair was a decided Methodist, making no compromise in regard to any of the doctrines or usages of the Church. Says Mr. Beggs: " In the Summer

---

[15] General Minutes.

of 1834 I accompanied John Sinclair, presiding elder, to his quarterly-meeting at Galena. Barton Randle and J. T. Mitchell were laboring on that circuit. After a profitable and pleasant meeting, we started for a camp-meeting that was to be held near Princeton. The meeting was somewhat advanced, and there was a prospect of a good work. Two Congregational ministers came to the camp-grounds, and proposed to join us in our efforts. There was to be no doctrine preached, and at the close of the meeting the converts were to join whom they pleased. To this our presiding elder strongly objected. He said he was a Methodist, and he must preach their doctrines, and that there could be no union on such terms. We had an unusually successful meeting, the fruits of which, I trust, will be seen in eternity."

" Brother Sinclair was a faithful, good Christian, who lived with good conscience toward God and in fellowship with his brethren; a man of a sweet, amiable disposition, and while he was true and honest himself, he was kind and forgiving toward others. As a husband, he was tender and affectionate; as a neighbor, he was generous and obliging. In his own house he was given to hospitality. As a preacher, he was plain, simple, and good, a preacher of the true Methodist type. Few men were ever more beloved than he was. His friends were many and lasting, because he pleased all men for their good and to edification. He was always cheerful and happy, a firm believer in divine revelation, and a happy partaker of the grace of salvation; he trusted

God at all times. He did not fear death, enjoying a clear title to a glorious inheritance. Death he called a 'falling,' 'departing,' 'going away.' A few days before his death, and when in his usual health, he said to his wife: 'When I go away, dress me as if I was going to meeting.' She replied, 'I will, if it be your wish.' 'I wish it,' he said. 'Do n't,' said he, 'put on mourning; it seems to me that it is very improper to mourn for a minister who has gone to so good a place as heaven.' This was his dying request. He died suddenly, but he was ready. For years he had been ready."[16]

SIMEON WALKER was born in Jackson County, Georgia, April 13, 1802. In 1809 his parents moved to the then Territory of Illinois, but the Indians being troublesome, they removed to Kentucky the next year, where his father died, and his mother, with the children, returned to Illinois in 1813. In 1819 he was powerfully converted at a camp-meeting at Shiloh, and from that hour till his death he was a faithful laborer for the cause of Christ. He often said of himself, "I was converted a preacher." The next year he was licensed to exhort, and six years afterwards to preach. He was received into the conference in 1830, and appointed to Grand Prairie Mission, a new work to embrace the settlements between the Little Wabash and the Okaw. He traveled this charge two years, and reported at the expiration of his term 303 members and twenty-eight preaching places. In 1832 he was sent to Mt. Vernon Circuit, on which he had great revivals of religion,

<hr>

[16] General Minutes.

and reported an increase of nearly 300 members. His next appointment was Carlyle. Here his health failed, and with his means all spent, and a family of six children, he felt that he must retire from the regular work for a season, and at the session of conference of 1834 he was granted a location. In this relation he continued for twenty-two years, laboring constantly, however, for the cause of Christ, manifesting the same zeal that had influenced him from the beginning, and really performing as much ministerial labor as many of the itinerants. In 1856 he was readmitted in the Southern Illinois Conference, and was sent to McLeansboro; in 1857 and 1858 he traveled Mt. Vernon Circuit; in 1859 and 1860, Carlyle; in 1861, Pocahontas, and in 1862, Tamaroa. In 1863 he entered the army as chaplain of the Fifteenth Illinois Cavalry, and remained in that position until his health utterly failed. In 1864 and 1865 he was on the supernumerary list, and in 1866 he was granted a superannuated relation, in which he remained until his death at the residence of his son at Carbondale, February 22, 1880. " His opportunities for early education were quite limited. But he had an unquenchable thirst for knowledge, and was a diligent student, often bending over his books by a dim light till the hours of midnight. He thus obtained a fair English education. For sixty years, mingling study and work together, he lived and labored with the one desire to save souls and bless the world, ever preaching as much by example as by precept. It was ever his rule to make daily a strict personal examination into his standing with God. He died, as he lived, in the triumph of a living faith."[17]

WILLIAM DAVID RICE TROTTER was born in Glasgow, Kentucky, March 17, 1807. His father, dying when he was in his fourth year, he was raised in the family of Judge Underwood, of Bowling Green, Kentucky. In the year 1825, at the age of eighteen, he entered the United Sates Navy as a midshipman. At the end of two years he returned home on account of sickness, and thinking that the work did not agree with him, he resigned his position. When he recovered his health, he entered the office of his brother-in-law, Judge Underwood, as a student of law. He was pushing his studies with energy and success, and would soon have been admitted to the bar, but for an event which altered his plans, and molded his after life. Attending a camp-meeting held in the neighborhood of Bowling Green, he was converted and joined the Methodist Church. This event changed the direction of his thoughts, and he commenced preparation for the ministry."[18] In 1830 he came to Illinois, and was that year received into the conference, and assigned to Apple Creek Circuit. In 1831 he was appointed to Lebanon with John Dew as his senior, and in 1832 to Blue River Mission. A camp-meeting was held here in August, 1833, at which Bishop Soule was present. He was on his way to the Missouri Conference at Salem, in Arkansas, and stopping at the residence of Peter Cartwright, accompanied him to his quarterly meeting. Mr. C. thus describes the

[17] Rev. C. E. Cline.   [18] Dr. F. W. Phillips.

trip: "After we crossed the Illinois River, we had a hilly country to pass through to get to the quarterly-meeting, almost without roads. So steep were some of the hills, and so deep the hollows and ravines, that we had to loose the horses from the bishop's carriage, and let it down by hand; then hitch on and drive up the hills. After much labor to man and beast, we got safe to the quarterly-meeting. The bishop stayed with us over the Sabbath, and preached two excellent sermons, which had a good effect on the congregations; and the curiosity of many was gratified, for if circumstances had not transpired to bring him to our camp quarterly-meeting, they would have lived and died without ever seeng a Methodist bishop."

Mr. Trotter's next appointment was the Henderson River Mission. Whilst on this charge he crossed the Mississippi, and preached the first sermon in Burlington, Iowa. Dr. Cartwright thinks this to have been the first Methodist sermon ever preached in the State, but this is probably a mistake, as Barton Randle had preached at Dubuque just before this. "Burlington, as it is now called, was built on the Bottom, at the mouth of a creek emptying into the Mississippi River, and the character of its inhabitants may be inferred from this incident. A man crossed over from this side the river, and told the people they had better quit their carousing and gambling, for a preacher named Trotter was coming over and was going to bring the Sabbath with him."[19]

---

[19] Dr. Phillips.

In 1834 he was teacher in Pleasant Plains Academy; in 1835 he was sent to Rushville Station, and in 1836 to Sangamon Circuit. In 1837 and 1838 he was on the superannuated list, spending the first of these years in teaching on Spring Creek, in Sangamon County, and the second year in the Ebenezer Manual Labor School. In 1839 he was placed on the effective list and appointed to Jacksonville Station, and in 1840 and 1841 to Winchester Circuit. In 1841 he was appointed to the Bloomington District, on which he labored two years. In 1844 he was placed on the Springfield District, on which he remained three years. In 1847 he was appointed agent for the Conference Female Academy at Jacksonville. In 1848 he was assigned to the Jacksonville District, from which he was removed to the Griggsville District, on which he labored but a single year. In 1852 he was placed upon the superannuated list, in view of his connection with the publication of the *Central Christian Advocate* at St. Louis, of which he was the first editor and publisher. As an editor he fully met the public expectation, and his personal management of the business was satisfactory; but such was the financial condition of the country and so great the difficulty of securing a sufficient circulation to the paper, that Brother Trotter, who had assumed the whole pecuniary responsibility of it, became so greatly embarrassed financially that he never fully recovered from it. Efforts were made by him and his friends to induce the General Conference, after taking charge of the paper, to relieve him, but they failed, and he had to bear the loss alone. In 1854 he was appointed professor in Illinois Conference Female College, and the next year was financial agent for it. In 1856 and 1857 he was on the superannuated list, endeavoring, by engaging in business, to recover from the losses he had suffered while in charge of the paper, but with small success. In 1858 he was on Exeter Circuit, in 1859 on Jacksonville Circuit, and in 1860 at Concord. In 1861 he was appointed to Paris District, on which he remained four years. In 1865 and 1866 he was on the Quincy District, on which he continued two years. In 1867 he was stationed at Alexander, in 1868 at Havana, and in 1869 and 1870 at Carrollton. In 1871 he was placed on the superannuated list, on which he remained until his death, at his residence in Jacksonville, July 25, 1880.

" Few pleasanter men than Brother Trotter are to be found in social life. Ever cheerful, he brought the very sunshine into your house when he visited you. A reader all his days, possessed of a retentive mind, his fund of information, acquired by study and observation, being always at command, he was a conversationalist who both instructed and interested. As a preacher he was possessed of more than ordinary ability. His sermons were methodical in their arrangement, and might often have been taken as models by younger ministers. His *manner* of preaching required more time than this swift moving age is willing to give to a minister, but when he had pursued one line of thought after another to legitimate conclusions, the summing up was

often with wonderful effect upon the audience."[20]
One who heard him frequently says, "His sermons
were logical and clear, though sometimes two hours
and a half long.   In the beginning of his sermons
he was very deliberate and slow of speech, but when
he became warmed up with his theme he was often
exceedingly eloquent."

One of the most efficient and useful of those who
commenced their labors in Illinois this year was
JOHN VAN CLEVE, who had united with the conference two years before, during which he had labored in Indiana.   He was born in Shrewsbury,
New Jersey, May 28, 1804.   His parents moved to
Scipio, New York, in 1808, and from thence to
Ohio in 1815.   He was religiously inclined from
childhood.   While an apprentice in Cincinnati, in
his eighteenth year, he became an earnest seeker of
salvation.   He was converted August 12, 1822, and
a few days afterwards united with the old Stone
Church in Cincinnati.   From this time forth he
never wavered in his religious integrity; his piety
was constant and fervent.   In February, 1825, he
was licensed to exhort, and in September following
to preach.   As remarked before, he was received
on trial in the Illinois Conference in 1828 and appointed to Bloomington Circuit, Indiana, and the
next year to Salem.   All the rest of his appointments, save one, were in Illinois.   In 1830 he was
sent to Kaskaskia, and then in succession to Apple
Creek, Carrollton, Jacksonville Circuit, and Lebanon.

In 1835 he was appointed to Mt. Vernon Dis-

____

[20] Dr. Phillips.

trict, and for the three following years. He was then two years in Rushville Station, and two years at Mt. Carmel. In 1842 he was sent to Hillsboro. In 1843 and 1844 he was presiding elder of Mt. Vernon District, and for the three following years on Mt. Carmel District. Then for two years he was in Quincy Station, and the two following on Griggsville Circuit. In 1851 he was transferred to Missouri Conference and stationed at Ebenezer, St. Louis, and at the end of the year was transferred to the Southern Illinois Conference, just organized, and stationed at Belleville, where he remained two years. During the next four years he was on the Lebanon District; and the following four on the Alton District. In 1862 he was appointed to Jerseyville, and returned the following year. Then for three years he was stationed at Centralia, and in 1867 at Cairo. The next year he was sent to Edwardsville, the two following to Bunker Hill, then to Olney and to Flora two years each. In 1875 he received his last appointment, Carlyle, in which he labored only about a month, when he was called from labor to rest. He was elected delegate to the General Conference four times, and at the time of his death he was a member of the General Missionary Committee. It was while attending the session of this committee in New York that he was stricken down by disease, and died there in St. Luke's Hospital, to which he had been taken for medical treatment. McKendree College honored itself and him by conferring on him the degree of Doctor of Divinity.

"Brother Van Cleve was emphatically a self-made man. By the providence of God he was dependent upon his own efforts in his boyhood. His early education was limited, but by dint of persistent effort he overcame obstacles and attained to scholarship. He possessed a vigorous intellect, a well disciplined mind, and a generous, noble heart. He was a methodical, clear, strong, earnest preacher, sometimes eloquent. Thirty years ago, to meet a demand of the times, he often preached controversial sermons. In this department of pulpit effort he had no superior in this country. He was strong in his convictions and positive in his statements, yet he always treated with respect those who differed with him. He was thoroughly in sympathy with all the work of the Church, and enthusiastic in his devotion to the cause of education."[21]

Brother Van Cleve was a man of strong common sense, eminently practical, and free from all pretension. He was an excellent presiding elder, a good business man, well acquainted with Methodist law, and strongly attached to Methodist usages. As a preacher he was able, dignified, clear, and forcible, never wearying his hearers, and always leaving upon their minds a clear and distinct impression of his subject. His sermons were always timely and appropriate to the occasion. He was a good administrator of discipline, attending faithfully to all the details of a Methodist pastor's duty, and always leaving his charge in good order for his successor. In his intercourse with society he was ever

---

[21] General Minutes.

the genial, Christian gentleman. In short, as his memoir says, he was "a devoted husband, a kind father, a genial companion, an earnest Christian, a friend of humanity, and an able minister of the Lord Jesus."

BOYD PHELPS was received on trial in the Illinois Conference in 1829, and appointed to Carlisle, Indiana. His only appointment in Illinois was the Jonesboro Mission, to which he was sent this year. In 1831 he was sent to Lafayette, and continued to labor in the Indiana Conference until 1838, when he located. In 1851 he was readmitted in the Wisconsin Conference, in which he labored until 1856, when he was transferred to the Minnesota Conference, and located in 1857. Two years afterwards he was readmitted, and labored in the effective ranks until 1880, when he was placed on the superannuated list.

STITH MEAD OTWELL was a native of Georgia, born in Jackson County, August 2, 1805. He moved with his parents to Illinois in 1811. He was religiously brought up, and when only twelve years old gave his heart to the Savior. In 1826 he was licensed to preach, and immediately received on trial in the Illinois Conference. His first four appointments were in Indiana. This year he was on the Lebanon Circuit, and the two following years on the Macoupin Mission. In 1833, his health having failed, he was granted a superannuated relation, in which he remained three years. In 1836 he was appointed agent for McKendree College. The next year he was again placed on the superannuated list, in which he continued until his death, March 26, 1843. For several years he faithfully discharged the duties of treasurer of the Conference Missionary Society. "He suffered much in the work of the ministry, yet he never murmured, and rarely spoke of his afflictions. Having embraced religion when very young, and having maintained an irreproachable standing in the Church of his choice, all through life his mind had become deeply imbued with the spirit of piety, and it shone out with increasing luster in all his various relations. He was thirty-eight years of age when he died, having lived twenty-six years in honorable standing in the Church and seventeen in the ministry. He was gentlemanly and dignified in his deportment, and a man of industrious, economical, and business habits. Being very amiable and affable, and a consistent Christian, he was as extensively beloved as he was known. He was a good citizen, and, therefore, had the confidence and esteem of the general community. He was an obedient son, an affectionate husband, and a good parent. On his dying bed we find him engaged in teaching his little daughter Harriet her daily lesson. In one word, 'those who knew him best, loved him most.'

"He was a good preacher. His style was correct and chaste, simple and strong. His gestures were good, and in his preaching generally there was a pathos and solemnity, an emphasis in the intonations of his voice, and the manner of his delivery, that failed not to secure the attention and affect the heart. His preaching was practical, doctrinal, and

sometimes polemical. Indeed, he was faithful in
endeavoring to fulfill his ordination vow, to edify
the Church, and to drive away error in doctrine,
and evil in practice from her borders. He was a
good pastor, and hence attended to as many of the
interests of the Church as he possibly could. He
was very active in the missionary, Sunday-school,
and temperance causes, and he was a good nurse for
the young converts, the babes in Christ."[22] One
who knew him well says of him : "He was a handsome man, slender, but dignified, and would command respect in any company. He had a great
deal of personal magnetism. He was an intelligent
gentleman, and a good preacher, persuasive in manner, but faithful in declaring the whole counsel of
God."[23] "He was one of nature's noblemen, a very
devout Christian. After he ceased traveling he
settled at Carlinville and engaged in the dry-goods
trade. He was a sweet-spirited, pure-minded man,
very useful in his local capacity, and very skillful
in handling the Word."[24] In his last illness he was
abundantly sustained by the grace of God. When
dying, he exhorted his companion to trust in the
Lord, saying, "He will take care of you. I feel
Jesus in my soul. I have peace, *peace*, through our
Lord Jesus Christ."

STEPHEN R. BEGGS was born in Rockingham
County, Virginia, March 30, 1801. When he was
four years old his parents moved to Kentucky, and
two years afterwards to Clark County, Indiana,
about seventeen miles above Louisville. As he grew

[22] General Minutes. [23] Dr. J. Logan. [24] Rev. N. P. Heath.

up he became noted for his physical power, and was looked on as the strongest man in Clark County. He had but slight opportunities for education in his youth, but by diligent study in after years he became a respectable English scholar. He enjoyed from a child the advantages of religious instruction, and was early taught to read the Bible. He says: "I formed the habit of prayer very young, and continued it regularly till my conversion." In his nineteenth year he attended a camp-meeting, and then he was soundly converted to God, as were about two hundred others, seven of whom afterwards became preachers. He was soon appointed class leader, then licensed to exhort, and soon afterwards to preach. He had intended to go to school for two years before entering the itinerant field, but his pastor, James Armstrong, told him he could better receive his education and graduate at Brush College, as most of the preachers had done, and so he consented to join the conference at once. He was received in the Illinois Conference in 1822, and appointed to Mt. Sterling Circuit, Indiana. The year was one of severe labor, some sickness, but great spiritual prosperity to the preachers, and increase to the Church. At a camp-meeting among the hills of Patoka he sought and found the blessing of entire sanctification. "God's will," says he, "became my will, and I learned to live in him continually. All my soul was love, and for weeks I could continually sing:

"'Not a cloud doth arise to darken my skies,
Or hide for a moment my Lord from my eyes.'"

There were numerous Church trials and difficulties during the year, but an increase of ninety in the membership. The next year, 1823, he was sent to Lamoine Circuit, Missouri, five hundred miles from his former charge. This, too, was a successful year. He attended the conference at Padfield's in 1824, at which the Illinois Conference was formed, but he was continued in the Missouri division, and sent to Falling River Circuit. At the close of the year, at his request, he was transferred to the Illinois Conference, and appointed to Rushville, Indiana. This was a very successful year, many sinners being converted, and many believers brought to the enjoyment of full salvation. In 1826 his appointment was Vincennes, and the next year, Wayne, Indiana. Here he met with great success, as described by W. C. Smith in his *Indiana Miscellany*, His next appointment was Crawfordsville, and in 1829 he was sent to Logansport, remaining on it, however, but one quarter, and being then removed by the presiding elder to Bloomington Circuit. From the conference of 1830 he was sent to his first charge in Illinois, the Tazewell Circuit. Here he had a prosperous year, and at its close was married to a Miss Heath, who for many years shared with him the toils and privations of the itinerancy. During this Summer, in company with Jesse Walker, he visited Chicago, and after spending a few days there a class of ten members was formed, constituting the first organization of Methodism in what is now the metropolis of the North-west. The next year, 1831, he was sent to Chicago as a mission station. At first, his labors were attended with some success, and additions were made to the membership. But the Black Hawk war breaking out, and the cholera being brought to the place by the troops of General Scott, caused most of the people to leave the place, and as no good could be accomplished, Mr. Beggs himself also left. In 1832 he was appointed to Des Plaines Mission, to which he was returned the next year. In 1834 and 1835 he spent two successful years on Bureau Mission, the membership being more than doubled during the second year. In 1836 he was appointed to Joliet. He says of it: " It was a glorious year to me. We had several conversions with strong evidence of their being born into the kingdom, and especially at our camp-meeting did the work of grace thrive." He built this year the first church in Joliet, having it completed in time for the last quarterly meeting. His next appointment was Forked Creek Circuit. " This year," says he, " was a great spiritual feast to my poor soul." In 1838 he was again sent to Joliet, and in 1839 to Peoria. Here he was very coldly received, the people having made arrangements to secure another preacher. But despite their indifference, by the help of those " without," he succeeded in building the first Methodist church in the town, and having it ready for the last quarterly meeting, where the Lord graciously revived his work, many joining on probation. In 1840 he was sent to Peoria Circuit; in 1841, to Canton, and the next year to Knoxville. In 1843 he was transferred to the Rock River Conference and assigned to

Joliet. His subsequent appointments in that conference have been: 1844, Milford; 1845, Sycamore; 1846, Washington; 1847, Napiersville; 1848 to 1850, superannuated; 1851, Flagg Creek; 1852, Pawpaw; 1853, Little Rock; 1854, superannuated; 1855, Channahon. In 1856 he was again placed on the superannuated list, on which he has remained to the present time. His residence is Plainfield, Illinois. He is now, 1883, eighty-two years old, tall, erect, with white flowing beard and hair, and not looking more than sixty-five. In 1868 he published " Pages from the Early History of the West and North-west, embracing reminiscences and incidents of settlement and growth, and sketches of the material and religious progress of the States of Ohio, Indiana, Illinois, and Missouri, with especial references to the history of Methodism." The work, though destitute of proper arrangement, and sometimes in error in its dates, contains, nevertheless, a very valuable collection of facts; and the writer is glad to acknowledge the great use he has made of it in the preparation of this work. Rev. W. S. Crissey thus describes him in his prime: " He was fully six feet high, straight as an arrow, a little full in the chest, of good health, and strong constitution. He was industrious, faithful, and quite successful when young; but as society changed, his services were less in demand. In his manner of preaching, he strikingly resembled John Strange. He bought the school section at Walker's Grove, near Plainfield, and settled on it, not moving to his appointments afterwards."

CHAPTER VIII.

1831.

CRAWFORDSVILLE DISTRICT—James Armstrong, P. E.
Eugene—A. L. Risley.
Paris—Jesse Haile.

WABASH DISTRICT—George Locke, P. E.
Mt. Carmel—James McKean, John Fox.
Wabash—Thomas H. Files, James M. Massey.
Shawneetown—Charles Slocumb.

KASKASKIA DISTRICT—Samuel H. Thompson, P. E.
Kaskaskia—William L. Deneen.
Brownsville Mission—John E. French.
Jonesboro—James T. Crawford.
Golconda—William Evans.
McLeansboro—William McHenry.
Mt. Vernon—James Walker.
Shoal Creek—John H. Benson.
Shelbyville—Barton Randle.
Grand Prairie Mission—Simeon Walker.

SANGAMON DISTRICT—Peter Cartwright, P. E.
Lebanon—John Dew, W. D. R. Trotter.
Apple Creek—John Van Cleve, Levi Springer.
Jacksonville—William H. Askins, John T. Mitchell.
Atlas—Spencer W. Hunter.
Spoon River—David B. Carter.
Tazewell—William S. Crissey.
Salt Creek—Amos Prentice.
Sangamon—John Sinclair, Asahel E. Phelps.
Macoupin Mission—Stith M. Otwell.

MISSION DISTRICT—Jesse Walker, Superintendent.
— *Deplain*—Jesse Walker, Missionary.
Chicago—Stephen R. Beggs.
Fort Clark--William Royal.
Galena—Smith L. Robinson.
— *Rock Island*—Philip T. Cordier.

THE session of 1831 was held at Indianapolis. It was presided over by Bishop Roberts, and Calvin W. Ruter was elected secretary. The session commenced on Tuesday, October 4th, and closed on the afternoon of the following Monday. Twenty-one members were present at the first roll call.

Eleven were received on trial, viz.: George W. Beswick, Nathan Fairchild, William M. Daily, James T. Robe, Cornelius Swank, William McHenry, James Walker, John T. Mitchell, William Royal, Levi Springer, Barton Randle.

Joseph Oglesby, Thomas Davis, Hackaliah Vredenburg, and Charles Slocumb were admitted.

Two had died, Edwin Ray and James Bankson.

Four received a location: Hardin A. Tarkington, Aaron Wood, Isaac Scarritt, and Geo. Randle.

The following local deacons were elected to elder's orders: Gamaliel Taylor, Isaac G. Lewis, Samuel Hull, Thomas C. Collins, and Jeremiah Dodson.

And the following local preachers to deacon's orders: Thomas T. Spillman, Stephen Liddle, John Hughes, John Cook, Hull Tower, Nathan Fairchild, William Clark, Henry Barnwell, John Cartwright, Daniel Harcoat, William Taylor, James Walker.

Drafts were ordered on the Chartered Fund for $80, and on the Book Concern for $800, and $200 in addition, which was left undrawn last year.

At this session the following delegates were elected to the General Conference of 1832; John Strange, Allen Wiley, George Locke, James Armstrong, Samuel H. Thompson, John Dew, William Shanks, Peter Cartwright, and Calvin W. Ruter.

Four alternates were elected: Thomas S. Hitt, James Scott, Joseph Oglesby, Jesse Haile.

Of the delegates elected, John Strange, John Dew, and Peter Cartwright failed to attend the session of General Conference, which was held in Philadelphia, and only one of the alternates, Thomas S. Hitt, was present; so that, although the conference was entitled to nine representatives, it had only seven.

The usual collection for defraying the expenses of the delegates was ordered to be taken in every charge, and in case any of the delegates should fail to attend, they were instructed to give timely notice to the secretary of the conference, who was to notify the alternates in the order of their election.

When the name of James Bankson, deceased, was called, and an account was given of his last illness, Brother McAllister, of the Missouri Conference, who was present, was requested to bear the grateful acknowledgements of this conference to the brethren and friends in St. Louis for their kindness to him in his illness, and W. L. Deneen was appointed to receive any money which any of the preachers might have on hand for Brother Bankson.

A resolution was offered that the preachers who had been employed by presiding elders should be considered as claimants on the conference funds. The resolution was not adopted, but the stewards were afterwards instructed to consider Joseph Oglesby, Nathan Fairchild, Leven Green, and Barton Randle, who had served as supplies, as legal claimants in proportion to their labors rendered as traveling preachers during the year.

Sunday-school matters again occupied much of the time and attention of the conference.

A communication from Rev. Samuel Sneed was read, in which he requested the privilege of addressing the conference on the subject of Christian education as connected with the Sunday-school, he being superintending agent of the American Sunday-school Union in Indiana. His request was granted, and Brother McAllister was requested to respond to Mr. Sneed, if necessary, and to give a general view of the claims of the Methodist Sunday-school Union. After the addresses, a vote of thanks was given to Brother McAllister for the course he took with the American Sunday-school agent for saying what he did, and for saying no more than he did. The following was offered:

"*Resolved*, That in the opinion of this conference it is inexpedient for any of our traveling preachers to accept an agency in the American Sunday-school Union."

It was moved to amend by adding "without the consent of his presiding elder and the consent of the quarterly conference of which he is a member."

The amendment was defeated, and the original motion was adopted by rising vote, only one voting against it.

The conference then resolved that every member would use his best efforts to organize and promote the interest of Methodist Sunday-schools, and all other benevolent institutions of the Church as far as practicable. It was also

"*Resolved*, That as a matter of expediency this conference have a special agent to promote the interest of the benevolent institutions of the Church, namely, the Sunday-school, the Tract, the Missionary, and Bible Societies; and that he receive twenty per cent on all the money collected by him for Sunday-school purposes to defray his traveling expenses and to pay his salary, provided that he do not receive more than his allowance as a traveling preacher."

A committee of five was appointed to examine the probable missionary ground within the bounds of the conference. Their report was "considered in its various fields" by the conference, and then adopted in full, and appropriations were afterwards made to them as follows: Logansport, $100; Fort Wayne, $75; Iroquois, $200; South Bend, $75; Grand Prairie, $100; Jonesboro, $100; Brownsville, $50; Macoupin, $100; Desplaines, $250; Chicago, $200; Fort Clark, $100; Galena, $250; Rock Island, $75—Total, $1,675. The report was approved by the bishop and then adopted by the conference.

A communication was received from the Marion County Temperance Society, inviting the conference to meet with them. The invitation was at first declined on account of the pressure of business, but the conference expressed their best wishes and hearty resolve to co-operate in the advancement of the temperance cause; but afterwards resolved to meet with them on Monday night "at the lighting of the candle." But before that time conference had adjourned.

Peter Cartwright reported that he had made some payments to those who had demands on the Pottawattomie Mission, and he was continued as a committee to liquidate the claims against it, and instructed to proceed in the settlements as he should deem most conducive to the ends of justice.

An unfortunate difficulty occurred at this session, that resulted in the retirement from the conference of one of its most useful members. Peter Cartwright stated to the conference that in consequence of Brother Isaac Scarritt, who was last year appointed to the Fort Clark Mission, having failed, in part, of discharging the duties assigned him, he had withheld one of the drafts in favor of said Scarritt, amounting to $50. The draft was presented to the conference and ordered to be destroyed. Brother Scarritt had asked and received a location.

Feeling aggrieved at the action of Mr. Cartwright and the conference, Mr. Scarritt was granted the privilege of appearing before it at its next session. After making his statements, the conference

"*Resolved,* That in withholding from Brother Scarritt his draft for his last installment as a missionary on the Fort Clark Mission, no impeachment of his moral character was intended; and from all such imputation this conference fully exonerate him."

The result of the affair, however, was that Mr. Scarritt, who had as a traveling preacher been quite successful, remained in a local relation until 1860, when he was readmitted in the Rock River Conference and placed on the superannuated list.

An expression of opinion having been asked by the delegates elected to the General Conference in regard to the division of the conference, the members, by rising vote, expressed a desire for a division, two only voting against it.

The following preamble and resolution were adopted:

"*Whereas* the General Conference has become so large as to be burdensome to the brethren where it sits, to be slow in its proceedings, and expensive to the Church to defray the traveling expenses of the delegates, and, also, to draw from the work many that would be otherwise employed in their respective fields of labor;

"*Resolved*, That this conference recommend to the next General Conference an alteration of that part of our Discipline that requires one delegate for every seven members of our annual conferences, so as to lessen the number of delegates."

Bishop Roberts informed the conference that the stewards of the last session, at which no bishop was present, in making the dividends, had appropriated a larger amount to the superintendents than they claimed, and stated that he was prepared to return the overplus. The conference requested the superintendents to retain the surplus amounts that had been appropriated to them.

John Strange was elected conference vice-president of the Missionary Society of the Methodist Episcopal Church.

Henry Buell complained of some grievances, and the conference ordered that he be tried by a committee of traveling preachers, as the Discipline directs, and that the presiding elder, who may be appointed in charge of the district in the bounds of which the charges originated, proceed to try him as soon as convenient. And the proceedings of George Locke in the case were, on motion, approved.

The usual resolution of thanks was then passed, the appointments were read, and the last session at which the preachers of Illinois and Indiana met together was closed.

A few changes were made in the arrangement of the work this year. Two appointments that had previously been in the Wabash District were placed in the Crawfordsville District, Vermillion and Paris, and the name of the former was changed to Eugene. The Shawneetown Circuit was cut off from the Wabash. The east part of the Apple Creek Circuit, and the newly-settled country between the Lebanon, Sangamon, and Shoal Creek Circuits, was formed into the Macoupin Mission and connected with the Sangamon District. And the Galena, Chicago, and Fort Clark Missions were taken from the Sangamon District and, with two new missions, the Des

Plaines and Rock Island, formed into a Mission District, with the indefatigable Jesse Walker as missionary presiding elder.

During this year Methodism was organized in Macoupin County. Sermons had been preached in the south part of the county at an early day by local preachers, but no society had been formed. The county had been organized two years before, in spite of the opposition of Peter Cartwright, who was then in the legislature, who declared that "God had set apart this region as a reservation for geese and ducks." S. M. Otwell preached the first sermon in the county seat, Carlinville, in the Fall of the year in an old log tavern. His audience consisted of four women and as many children. The men were attending a horse-race outside. Mr. Otwell soon after gathered a class of nine members there; and not long after James Cane, a local preacher, organized a class in his own house in Palmyra, in the north-west part of the county.

The first Methodist society was organized this year in Vandalia. There had been preaching in the place ever since 1818, but no class was formed. But now a class of seven members was gathered, consisting of Dr. N. M. McCurdy and wife, Moses and Susan Phelps, and John Delaplaine, wife, and daughter. A church was commenced by them in 1835, but was not completed until 1837.

Among the numerous camp-meetings held this year, we have an account of the first one ever held in Randolph Grove, in McLean County. Peter Cartwright, James Latta, and others preached at it.

Among other things, Cartwright, who despised Eastern missionaries and correspondents, said: "They represent this country as a vast waste, and the people as very ignorant; but if I were going to shoot a fool, I should not take aim at a Western man, but would go down by the seashore and cock my fusee at the imps who live on oysters." Mr. Latta preached at popular vices, and was particularly severe on horse-racing. He said: "There is a class of people who can't go to hell fast enough on foot, so they get on their poor, mean ponies, and go to the horse-race. Even professors of religion are not guiltless in this respect, but go under the pretext that they want to see such a man or such a man; but they know in their own hearts that they want to see the horse-race."

The first church was erected this year in Belleville under circumstances somewhat peculiar. During a quarterly-meeting, which was held in a hall, Brother McAllister, who was then on the St. Louis District, having come over to attend it, the congregations were so large that they had to adjourn to the woods. During the Sunday service a heavy rain fell, and the congregation got very wet. The next day, Mrs. Blackwell, one of the first members of the class, wrote to her brother in Maryland, asking him to raise money to aid them in building a church. He sent them fifty dollars, and the society then went on until enough was raised to put up a respectable frame building, which was used until the erection of the present one in 1849.

Among the persons who settled in Illinois this

year, and were or became Methodists, was JAMES PLASTERS, who was born in Loudoun County, Virginia, in 1791. He served as a soldier during the war of 1812, and participated in the defense of Fort McHenry. He settled near Livingston, Clark County, and remained there until 1858, when he removed to Marshall. He was converted at a Cumberland Presbyterian camp-meeting, in 1832, and united with that Church. But when he came to examine its creed, he found that with the doctrine of unconditional final perseverance he could not agree, and so he took a letter and united with the Methodist Episcopal Church, of which he remained a worthy member until his death, October 25, 1882. One of his daughters became the wife of Rev. C. D. James, of the Illinois Conference.

The increase in the membership this year was smaller than for several years before. The entire membership in Illinois was 10,257 whites and 61 colored, an increase of 746 over the year before.

Among those who labored in Illinois this year for the first time was JAMES M. MASSEY, who was born in Tennessee, while his parents were moving from South Carolina to Illinois in the year 1809. In his eighteenth year he was converted at a camp-meeting in White County. After serving as class-leader and exhorter, he was licensed to preach in 1830, and the same year united with the Illinois Conference. His first appointment was Petersburg, Indiana. During the rest of his itinerant life he labored in Illinois. The following were his appointments: 1831, Wabash; 1832, Mt. Carmel; 1833,

Eugene; 1834, Shelbyville; 1835, Vandalia; 1836, Okaw; 1837, Mt. Vernon; 1838, Mt. Carmel Station; 1839 and 1840, Nashville; 1841, Mt. Vernon; 1842, Mt. Carmel Circuit; 1843, Fairfield; 1844 and 1845, Shawneetown; 1846, Lebanon; 1847 and 1848, Carlyle; 1849, Highland. In 1850 he was on the superannuated list, but the next year he was sent to Equality. In 1852 he fell into the Southern Illinois Conference, and was appointed in succession to Xenia, Chester, and Salem. In 1855 he was again superannuated. But in 1856 he was again effective, and was sent to Mt. Erie, in 1857 to Xenia, and in 1858 to New Middleton. Here he ceased his labors and sufferings March 14, 1859. "Brother Massey was a faithful man, emphatically a Methodist preacher, a man of one work. He loved and defended the doctrines and discipline of the Methodist Episcopal Church. He was at all times ready to resist the innovations upon any of our long tried rules and usages. His preaching was clear, his manner strong, and his appeals sometimes irresistible. It is said by some that he had no poor sermon. He suffered much during the last two years of life with rheumatic pains, but he suffered as seeing him that is invisible. His last sickness was accompanied with the impression that his work was done. He spoke of death as a matter with which he was familiarly conversant. His physician came into the room when he was about dying, and he said to him, "Doctor, the waters of Jordan are coming upon me fast;" and added, "O tell my brethren in the ministry that the religion I have preached to others is sufficient to sustain me in death; it is indeed the power of God unto salvation."[1] One of his colleagues says of him that he "was an admirable declaimer. He had a voice like a bugle, and lungs that never got sore or hoarse. He was a great revivalist and a splendid recruiting officer for Christ. He always had revivals in his charges, and large ingatherings; sometimes too large, necessitating a good deal of pruning by his successor. He was a very pleasant man, quite companionable, and showing all good fidelity. He was not an original thinker or investigator, but relied almost wholly on the opinions of others. He was an indefatigable worker and very zealous. He made it a rule never to neglect an appointment when it was possible for him to get there. His frequent journeyings through storm and exposure brought on rheumatism, from which he suffered severely for many years, and which finally carried him off."[2]

The itinerant career of WILLIAM McHENRY was a short one. He traveled but two years. In 1831 he was appointed to McLeansboro, in 1832 to Fairfield, and at the next session of conference he was discontinued at his own request.

JAMES WALKER was a native of Georgia. He was received as a traveling preacher this year, and sent to Mt. Vernon Circuit. During the next two years he was on Brownsville Mission; in 1834, on Wabash Circuit, and at the next session of conference he was elected to elder's orders, and granted a location at his own request. He was readmitted

____

[1] General Minutes.   [2] Rev. E. Joy.

the next year and appointed to Fairfield Circuit, but at the session of 1837 he again located. He never afterwards united with the conference, but for about thirty years labored quite extensively as a local preacher, and occasionally filled appointments under the presiding elder until his death. He was a good Christian man, enjoying the confidence of all, and a respectable and useful preacher.

Of BARTON RANDLE nothing but good can be said. He was born in Scriven County, Georgia, November 7, 1796. In his sixteenth year he was converted in Madison County, Illinois. In 1831, after he had traveled part of a year under the presiding elder on the Spoon River Circuit, he united with the Illinois Conference and was appointed to the Shelbyville Circuit. This charge then embraced the counties of Shelby, Moultrie, the larger portion of Coles, and parts of Fayette and Cumberland. He had a successful year, closing with a camp-meeting at Wabash Point, at which much good was done. His next appointment was the Henderson River Mission. This was a new charge, embracing the scattered settlements in Henderson, Warren, and adjoining counties. Mr. Cartwright, who was presiding elder of the district, states, that at one of his quarterly meetings on the charge this year there were present the six members of the Church and eight who were not members, and these comprised the whole settlement, save one family, who were so much opposed to the Methodists that they would not attend the meeting. "At another quarterly meeting in this mission, on Sunday, we had twenty-seven for our congregation, and yet the scattered population were all, or nearly all, there for many miles round, and when we administered the sacrament on Sabbath we had just seven communicants, preachers and all. Barton Randle, the missionary, though a man of feeble health and strength, was yet faithful in hunting up the lost sheep in this new and laborious field of labor. He suffered many privations and hardships, but he endured all as seeing Him who is invisible, and I have thought that he was among the very best missionaries I was ever acquainted with. He did great good in this new and rising country, and laid firmly the foundation of future good, which the increasing and now densely populated country has realized. No doubt, many, in the great day of retribution, will rise up and call Brother Randle blessed, and he will hail many of his spiritual children in heaven from this field of labor."[3] The next appointment to which Mr. Randle was sent in 1833 was also a mission-field—Galena and Dubuque. While on this charge he preached the first Protestant sermon ever preached in the State of Iowa. His colleague was John T. Mitchell, who had filled the Galena mission the year before. "On account of the difficulty of crossing the river (the Mississippi) at that time, the work on the mission was practically divided, Mitchell remaining at Galena, and Barton Randle taking the new work at Dubuque. To that place, accompanied by his colleague, he proceeded on Saturday, November 6, 1833, and there, in the tavern

---

[3] Dr. Cartwright.

of Jesse M. Harrison, on the present site of the Julian House, on the same evening, he preached the first Methodist sermon of which we have any account as preached on Iowa soil. The next day his co-missionary Mitchell preached the second sermon at the same place. The next May a society was organized, consisting of twelve members; and during the Summer a hewed log meeting-house, twenty by twenty-six in the clear, was built, and a two days' meeting held in it."[4] Mr. Randle's next appointment was Alton Station. But his health having failed, at the end of the year he was placed on the superannuated list. During his second year, however, his health being partially restored, he was employed by the presiding elder to assist G. G. Worthington on the Carlinville Circuit. In 1837 he was sent to Carrollton Circuit, and in 1838 to Vandalia and Hillsboro, a double station. During the two following years he was on Vandalia District, and from 1841 to 1843 on the Mt. Carmel District. In 1844, having been injured by a shock received from a stroke of lightning, from which he never fully recovered, he was placed on the superannuated list, on which he remained five years. Having somewhat recovered, he was in 1849 again sent to the Shelbyville Circuit, then much smaller than when he had traveled it before. But the work was still too much for him, and at the session of conference of 1850 he was again granted a superannuated relation, in which he continued till his death, January 2, 1882. One who recollects him

---

[4] Rev. E. H. Waring.

on his first circuit, says of him, " He was a strong preacher and a fine theologian. He was particularly strong on baptism and the divinity of Christ. He was a good scholar and a hard student." " The last twenty years of his life were spent at the house of his sister, Mrs. M. P. Ripley, at Staunton, Illinois. For six months before his death he was entirely deprived of sight and confined to his bed. All his faculties, except the spiritual, seemed to fail; but he never lost his interest in Christ, and was always patient, cheerful, and happy in the midst of his sufferings. Often when his pastor would inquire after his welfare, his answer would be, 'As happy as a king.' "[5]

LEVI SPRINGER removed from Indiana to Illinois in the Fall of 1823. He traveled with his wife on horseback. They slept two nights on the open prairie, with no protection save their blanket, while the wolves were howling around them. They settled in what is now Cass County, a short distance from Virginia. Mr. Springer united with the conference this year, and was appointed to Apple Creek Circuit. In 1832 he was sent to Salt Creek; in 1833, to Fort Edward Mission, and in 1834 to Carlinville. The next two years he was on Pecan Mission, and in 1837 on Athens Circuit. At the end of the year he located. He was a strong preacher, sometimes rather lengthy. As a local preacher he labored quite extensively and usefully. He loved the Church, and was highly esteemed on the circuit on which he lived.

[5] Rev. W. Van Cleve.

The following sketch of JOHN T. MITCHELL is mostly condensed from the excellent memoir of him in the General Minutes. He was born August 20, 1810, near the village of Salem, Botetourt County, Virginia. In 1817 his father moved to Illinois and settled near Belleville. In the Fall of 1829, John, then a lad of nineteen years, attended what was denominated in those times a conference camp-meeting, " when he was awakened to a sense of his lost condition as a sinner, and formed a resolution to devote his life to the service of God. He accordingly united with the Church as a probationer, but did not then obtain an evidence of his conversion. At a camp-meeting, however, held later in the same season, near Carlyle, he obtained the forgiveness of sins and the witness of the spirit that he was a child of God. The next Spring he was appointed assistant superintendent of a Sunday-school, and while engaged in that work became convinced that God had called him to the work of the ministry. He accordingly received license to preach, and in April, 1831, delivered his first sermon in the town of Hillsboro." That Fall he was received into the Illinois Conference, and appointed to Jacksonville Circuit with William H. Askins as his senior. The next year, 1832, he was sent to Galena Mission, and in 1833 to Galena and Dubuque, with Barton Randle as his chief. In 1834 and 1835 he was at Chicago. Mr. Beggs declares of his labors at that time, " To the zeal and efficiency of John T. Mitchell, Chicago Methodism is greatly indebted. He gave to the Church a thorough organization, and laid the foundations of her future usefulness and stability." In 1836 he was appointed to Jacksonville, and reappointed the next year. During his pastorate here he sought and found the blessing of entire sanctification. Becoming deeply anxious to promote the doctrine and experience of Christian purity, he organized a "select society" in accordance with the plan of Mr. Wesley. In his journal he thus records his experience: "My soul this evening was drawn out in prayer that the blessing might be given now. I confessed my unfaithfulness, I pleaded the merits of Christ, the infinite love of God, his delight in making his children like himself, his promise to cleanse from all unrighteousness, and, glory to God, his Spirit broke into my heart, the darkness fled away, the glory of God was revealed in the face of Jesus Christ, my sin was all destroyed, the love of God filled and overflowed my heart, and all my soul was love." His after life was a constant heart-struggle to maintain this high and rare experience. It was the theme of very much of his preaching. No congregation to whom he ever ministered can forget his frequent and powerful appeals to the Church to arise and put on her beautiful garments. In 1838 and 1839 he was stationed in Springfield, and at the close of his term was transferred to the Rock River Conference and appointed presiding elder of the Chicago District, on which he remained two years. In 1842 and 1843 he was sent to Mt. Morris District, and was at the same time appointed financial agent of the Rock River Seminary at Mt. Morris. By the General Conference of 1844 he was elected assistant agent of the Western Book Concern, and for four years he performed the delicate and responsible duties of this post with marked ability. In 1848 he was transferred to the Ohio Conference, and stationed at Ninth Street, now Trinity, Cincinnati, where he labored with zeal and success for two years. In 1850 he was stationed at Wesley Chapel, in Cincinnati, and remained two years. In 1852 he fell into the Cincinnati Conference, and was sent to Urbana, where as pastor, presiding elder, and one year as supernumerary, he lived and labored for seven years. In 1859 he was reappointed to Wesley Chapel, where he remained two years. In 1861 he was stationed at Park Chapel, and the next year was appointed to the Cincinnati District, on which he labored until his death. He was a delegate to the General Conference in 1840 from Illinois Conference, in 1844 from Rock River, and in 1860 from Cincinnati. He was for many years secretary of the different conferences to which he belonged. From the beginning of his ministry he was a close student. Not only did he apply himslf to the study of theology, but he found time and means likewise to gain considerable knowledge of philosophy, mathematics, general literature, and the Latin and Greek languages. As a minister of the Gospel he had a high and growing position to the close of his life. He possessed a combination of social, intellectual, and moral qualities which are rarely found in one individual. A heart overflowing with love for a perishing world, an understanding clear and discriminating, an imagination remarkably chaste, a social manner, serious, affectionate, yet very winning and gentle, all combined to make him a minister of extraordinary influence and usefulness. No one who attended his ministry ever doubted that the love of Christ constrained him. His style was exceedingly neat, simple, and dignified, and yet very impressive. At times when his soul kindled with the themes of the Gospel, he would speak with a tongue of fire, and stir every heart by the power of his earnest and eloquent utterances. In the use of language he seemed to seize by intuition the words best adapted to convey to the understanding of his hearers the clear and forcible conceptions of his own mind. He was greatly skilled in the use of pure English undefiled. His sentences were often striking aphorisms, brief, comprehensive, suggestive. As a speaker he was in many respects a model. A graceful dignity of mien, a fervid, affectionate style, and a directness and pungency of appeal to the hearts of sinners, comprised to make his ministrations a great blessing wherever they were enjoyed. Few of his brethren in the ministry have excelled him as a doctrinal, and at the same time practical, preacher.

In his religious belief he was steadfast and unmovable. He embraced with his whole soul the theology of Wesley, and never wavered in the conviction that it was more nearly a transcript of the teachings of Christ than any other system of doctrines held among men. There was no appearance of fickleness or indecision in his religious life. He did not grow weary of opinions because they were old; nor did he ever manifest the slightest inclination to embrace new views of Church polity or doctrine from a mere morbid desire for novelties. No cunning of men or wind of doctrine could turn him aside from the deliberate convictions of his mind. His personal experience was so inwoven with the grand, fundamental doctrines of the cross, that he could not be otherwise than firmly rooted and grounded in the faith delivered to the saints. He loved the Church of his fathers with a great and overmastering affection. He was exceedingly zealous of her honor, and seemed to court life and strength only for her service. A more thoroughly tried and true watchman has rarely fallen from the walls of our Zion. And yet he was in no sense a bigoted sectarian. Enthusiastically devoted as he was to Methodism, no narrow and exclusive spirit characterized his private or public life. He was, on the contrary, a truly Catholic spirited Christian.

As an executive officer of the Church, charged with the administration of discipline, he was proverbially firm. Very few men are endowed in this world with more practical wisdom than he possessed. On all questions of grave moment that arose in the conference, no man's opinions had more weight. His brethren will never forget, I am sure, how often the clear, brief statements of the secretary have unraveled the most perplexing difficulties. His cool judgment and evenly balanced mind always comprehended the practicability as well as the desirableness of a thing. As a counselor in the Church his place can not easily be supplied.

In private life he was an example to his brethren. There was a simple, unaffected courtesy in
his manner, a genuine politeness in all his deportment towards others, a fascinating charm in his
fireside and social intercourse with society, a hearty
and open-handed hospitality in entertaining friends
that won the hearts of all, and made him a welcome
guest wherever he was known.

In March, 1863, he was seized with hemorrhage
of the lungs. After suffering for some time in Cincinnati, having somewhat improved, he resolved to
visit a sister in Minnesota. But before he reached
her residence, Red Wing, he died on a steamer on
the Mississippi, on the 30th of. May. While in full
view of death before he left Cincinnati, he said to
one: "I am going home to rest. The port is in
sight. My peace flows as a river. I have a desire
to depart and be with Christ." To another he declared: "I am unspeakably happy. I am waiting
in weakness and pain, but not impatient, for God
to call me home. I am a sinner saved by grace."
To another: "I am very weak, but very happy.
My Savior is ever near me. I have no fear—but
peace, perfect peace. I am waiting for my change
to come."

WILLIAM STODDART CRISSEY was born in Salisbury, Connecticut, April 21, 1811. In 1815, his
parents, who were Presbyterians, moved to Cincinnati, and died there three years afterwards. William then went to live with his uncle, who was a
druggist and physician in Cincinnati. When he
was ten years old he was converted and united with

the Methodist Episcopal Church at the Old Stone
Church, afterwards Wesley Chapel. A large number of boys were converted at the same time, and
formed into a class, with Samuel Huston as leader.
In 1823 he removed with his uncle to Louisville,
Kentucky, and two years afterwards to Bloomington, Indiana. While there he received license to
exhort from James Armstrong, and, in 1829, having removed to Paris, Illinois, he was licensed to
preach. The next year he was received into conference, and sent to Paoli Circuit, Indiana. In
1831 he was appointed to Tazewell Circuit. This
was the year of the Black Hawk War, and the circuit being on the frontiers, there was, of course,
great excitement among the people. But despite
this, the year was a prosperous one; two good camp-
meetings were held, at both of which there were
gracious revivals, and some increase in the membership was reported at the close of the year. In
1832 he was sent to Jacksonville Circuit. The
charge included what are now Morgan, Cass, and
Scott Counties. For the first half of the year Mr.
Crissey was alone, but in the Spring C. B. U. Mc-
Cabe, a local preacher, who had just come from the
lead regions of Missouri, was employed to assist
him. During this year the Asiatic cholera made its
first appearance in the country. There were about
one hundred deaths in Morgan County and nearly
sixty in Jacksonville. And yet, despite the panic
created by the disease, there was a general advance
at most of the appointments, and a slight increase
in the membership. Mr. Crissey's next appointment

was Mt. Carmel Circuit. In 1834 he was sent to Eugene, and in 1835 to Danville. The latter charge had been included in the former, which was divided at the conference of 1835. Mr. Crissey's residence was at Danville during both years. During his first year he commenced the building of a church at Danville, and completed it the next year. It was, for those days, a great undertaking, and the whole country for twenty miles around was canvassed for means to build it. At the last quarterly-meeting a camp-meeting was held, a few miles from Danville, at which there were about one hundred and twenty conversions and accessions to the Church, and about twenty-five professed to be entirely sanctified. His next appointment was Milwaukee, and in 1837 he was sent to Joliet, where he remained two years.

These were very successful years. Many souls were won to Christ, and general advancement was made. A church that had been begun before at Plainfield was completed, and another at Joliet. In the Winter of 1838 Mr. Crissey formed the first class at Lockport. Mr. Beggs, who was his colleague on this charge, says of him: "He was a good preacher, a faithful pastor, and possessed a good business tact. He was an indefatigable laborer, attending to all matters both small and great." So faithful was he in attending to all his disciplinary duties that, it is said, while on this circuit he read at *all* the appointments Mr. Wesley's sermons on Dress and Evil Speaking, and the General Rules. At the conference of 1839 he was granted a superannuated relation, which he sustained until 1842, when he was appointed to Decatur Circuit. This was a very prosperous year. Between sixty and seventy were added to the Church in Decatur, and on the entire charge there was an increase in the membership of one hundred and twenty-five. His next appointment was Springfield Station. Here, though there was a decrease in the membership, was a good revival of religion and a number of souls clearly converted. At the close of the year he was again placed on the superannuated list, on which he continued until 1848, when he was appointed to Rushville. He had notified his presiding elder that it would be impossible for him to fill an appointment, and yet in spite of this he was appointed. He did not go to the charge, and at the next conference he was granted a location. Mr. Crissey, as stated above by Mr. Beggs, was a good preacher, somewhat given to metaphysical discussion, but acceptable and popular. He was scrupulous in observing all the requirements of the Discipline, fasting every Friday, visiting among the people, and regularly meeting the classes. In this duty he was particular in inquiring of the members in regard to their attention to family and secret prayer, and their abstinence from intoxicating drinks. He was a faithful administrator of discipline; and while blessed with many gracious revivals of religion, his forte seemed to be the purification and building up of the Church. He is now (1883) enjoying a vigorous and honored old age in Decatur.

No better man ever belonged to the Illinois Conference than WILLIAM ROYAL, who was this year received on trial and appointed to Fort Clark. The next year he was sent to Bloomington, in 1833–4 to Ottawa, and the next year to Fox River Mission. In 1836, his appointment was Des Plaines; 1837, Waterloo; 1838, Waynesville; 1839, Winchester; 1840–41, Pulaski; 1842, Monmouth; 1843, Richland; and 1844, Greenville. In 1845 he was transferred to the Rock River Conference and appointed to Peoria Circuit. In 1846–7 he was on Little Rock Circuit, and in 1848 at Newark. The next year he was on the superannuated list, but in 1850 he was appointed to Livingston Circuit. At the close of the year he was again superannuated, and continued in that relation until 1860, when he was transferred to the Oregon Conference and appointed to Portland Mission. In 1861 he was sent to East Tualatin. In 1862 he was appointed conference tract agent, a position to which he was annually reappointed until 1868, when he was again placed on the superannuated list, in which he continued until his death, in 1871. Brother Royal was a deeply devoted Christian. It was his habit to pray in his family after each meal. He was a very kind-hearted man, loving his neighbor as himself. As a preacher he was very moderate, but he could talk about religion; and his deep personal piety and the interest he took in the welfare of others rendered him acceptable to the people. He was an excellent pastor, and a very prudent and careful man. He afforded one of the best examples of the success of a preacher of very moderate abilities, but possessed of an eye single to the glory of God, ever known. The one talent used, in such a character, becomes more than the ten talents wasted in men who live to themselves. He made the glory of God the great aim of his life, and, as a natural result, God blessed his labors wonderfully, and made him an instrument of good to multitudes of souls. In 1859 he removed with his children to Oregon. A considerable company was formed and he was appointed commander and chaplain. Every Saturday, at noon, they pitched their tents, and did not leave until Monday morning, he preaching to them on the Sabbath. This course was kept up until they reached the edge of the desert. Then the rest of the company concluded that it would not be prudent or safe for them to make any further stoppage until they were safely through the dangerous desert and Indian country, and so they pushed on, leaving him and his family, for Brother Royal had made up his mind that, whatever might be the danger, he would trust in God and honor his day. The result was that, while the other party lost about twenty head of cattle, stolen by the Indians, and suffered severely from storms, Brother Royal and his family got through pleasantly and safely, and overtook the others before they reached their destination. He was mighty in prayer. At a quarterly-meeting on the Ottawa Circuit, at which John Sinclair, Stephen R. Beggs, and William Royal were present, a brother who had recently come to the country remarked, " that if he only had Brother Beggs to preach, Brother Sinclair to exhort, for he was mighty therein, and Brother Royal to pray, he wanted no more."[6]

IT is designed that this volume shall be followed by others on " Later Methodism in Illinois." As stated at the beginning of the work, a large amount of material has been collected by the author, and he is daily adding to his stores. He hopes, if life and health are spared, to send out a second volume in 1884.

[6] Rev. S. R. Beggs.

INDEX.

	PAGE.
Ames, E. R.,	348
Amos, Abraham,	74
Apple Creek Circuit,	257
Armstrong, James,	214
Arrington, A. W.,	312
Askins, W. H.,	353
Atlas Circuit,	244
Axley, James,	87
Ayers, John E.,	345
Baker, Jacob,	284
Bankson, James,	331
Bascy, Joseph,	179
Bassett, Samuel,	215
Beauchamp, William,	158
Beggs, S. R.,	373
Belleville Methodism,	234, 387
Benson, John H.,	297
Bigbay Circuit,	107
Blackman, Learner,	79
Blackwell, William,	248
Blaisdell, John,	188
Bogart, Samuel,	276
Brownsville Circuit,	228
Buell, Henry,	288
Camp-meetings,	50, 51, 52, 53
	61, 70, 111, 131, 144, 155
	167, 171, 191, 192, 248, 265
	301, 386
Carmi Circuit,	228
Carter, David B.,	332
Cartwright, Peter,	99, 218
Casad, A. W.,	189
Casey, Zadoc,	147
Cash River Circuit,	76, 212
Chambers, William,	242
Chicago Methodism,	57
Chicago Mission,	341
Church in Illinois, First,	46
" " " Second,	56

	PAGE.
Clarke, John,	30
Class in Illinois, First,	29
Clingan, John,	66
Colbert, George A.,	86
Cole, Philip,	239
Cooper, John,	169
Cooper, S. C.,	270
Cordier, P. T.,	355
Corrie family,	171
Crawford, J. P.,	355
Crissey, W. S.,	400
Curtis, Joseph,	162
Davidson, George,	83
Davis, Thomas,	154
Decatur Methodism,	343
Decker, John A.,	311
Delap, Robert,	180
Delegates to Gen'l Conf.,	264
	380
Deneen, W. L.,	294
Desplaines Mission,	385
Dew, John,	194
Dewitt County Methodism	310
Dixon, James,	97
Dixon, Joseph,	168
Dow, Lorenzo,	164
Echols, William,	272
Edwards, Lorenzo,	330
Essay, Preliminary,	13
Eugene Circuit,	385
Evans, William,	252
Farmer, Eli P.,	250
Files, Thomas H.,	252
Fisher, Orceneth,	196
Fort Clark Mission,	341
Foulks, Joseph,	240
Fox, John,	267
Fox River Mission,	309

	PAGE.
Fraley, Daniel,	76
French, John E.,	299
GAINES, RICHARD,	249
Galena Mission,	282
Galena Methodism,	195
Garrett, Lewis,	39
Gilham, James,	32
Gilham, John D.,	163
Glanville, John,	182
Golconda Circuit,	310
Goodner, David,	99
Goshen Society,	37
Grand Prairie Mission,	341
Green, Jesse,	198
Green, Leven,	232
HADLEY, JAMES,	237
Haile, Jesse,	138
Harbison, John C.,	106
Hargrave, Richard,	209, 252
Harris, John,	143
Harrison, Reuben,	184
Harrison, Thomas,	37
Hart, Miles,	267
Hellums, Thomas,	152
Heresy, Case of,	262
Hobart, Calvin,	210
Hogan, John,	271
Holliday, Charles,	234
Hopewell Methodism,	184
House, Isaac S.,	255
Huffaker, Miles,	290
Hull, Samuel,	185
Hunter, S. W.,	356
Hussey, Nathan,	163
Hypes, Benjamin,	342
ILLINOIS CIRCUIT,	212
" Conf. Session, 1st,	205
" " " 2d,	228
" " " 3d,	246
" " " 4th,	257
" " " 5th,	278
" " " 6th,	300
" " " 7th,	335
" " " 8th,	379
" Mission,	38
" First settlers in,	27

	PAGE.
Illinois Territory,	28
" State,	151
Iowa Methodism,	392
JACKSONVILLE CIRCUIT,	342
" Methodism,	178, 343
Johnson, James E.,	217
Johnson, John T.,	276
Jonesboro Circuit,	310
Jones, W. R.,	143
KASKASKIA CIRCUIT,	183, 212
Kerns, John,	272
Kersey, Thomas,	345
Kirkman, Thomas,	78
Kirkpatrick, John,	38
LANDIS, ISAAC,	249
Lapham, Alonzo,	191
Latta, James,	333
Lawrenceville Methodism,	265
Leach, F. B.,	194
Lebanon Circuit,	310
" Methodism,	234
Lillard, Joseph,	29
Locke, George,	284
Logan, Dr. John,	248
Lowry, James,	166
Lurton, Jacob,	172
McALLISTER, ALEXANDER,	172
McHenry, Daniel,	127
McHenry, William,	
McKean, James,	295
McKendree, William,	46
McKendree College,	339
McLean County Methodism,	191
McLeansboro Circuit,	341
McReynolds, J. W.,	238
McReynolds, William,	192
Macoupin Methodism,	386
" Mission,	385
Massac Circuit,	95
Massey, James M.,	388
Matheny, C. R.,	45
Mavity, William,	289
Maxey, Bennett,	163

	PAGE.
Mayo, Jonathan,	190
Medford, William,	217
Meth. Prot. Church,	282, 283
Miller, John,	200
Missionary Society, First,	164
Mississippi Circuit,	183, 212
Mitchell, John T.,	395
Mitchell, Samuel,	146
Moore, Enoch,	64
Moore, Francis,	175
Moore, John,	96
Moore, William,	215
Mt. Carmel founded,	157
" " Circuit,	157, 211
Mt. Vernon Circuit,	183, 212
New Design,	37
Noland, James,	105
Ogle, Joseph,	29
Oglesby, Joseph,	41
Okaw Circuit,	107
Otwell, S. M.,	371
Padon, William,	179
Palestine Methodism,	265
Paris Circuit,	310
" Methodism,	191
Parker, Samuel,	71
Patterson, Josiah,	102
Pekin Methodism,	265
Peoria Circuit,	228
" Methodism,	213
" settled,	27
Peter, William,	344
Phelps, A. E.,	290
Phelps, Boyd,	371
Piggott, I. N.,	188
Pinckard, N.,	162
Pitner, Wilson,	315
Plasters, James,	388
Porter, James,	102
Pottawattomie Mission,	229
246, 261, 280, 307, 338, 383	
Pownal, Joseph,	148
Prentice, Amos,	357
Randle, Barton,	391
Randle, Josias,	82
Randle, Parham,	172, 181
Randle, Thomas,	216
Rice, Thomas,	180
Rigg, Hosea,	32
Risley, A. L.,	288
Robinson, Smith L.,	272
Rock Island Mission,	386
Royal, William,	404
Ruddle, Cornelius,	188
Sackett, Samuel,	343
St. Louis Methodism,	59, 120
St. Mary's Circuit,	104
Salt Creek Circuit,	310
Sangamon Circuit,	167, 212
Scarritt, Isaac,	273, 383
Scarritt, Nathan,	169
Scott, James,	181
Scott, William,	33
Scripps, John,	110, 118
Schuyler County Methodism,	211
See, William,	243
Seminary, Conference,	260, 280
	302
Sharon Methodism,	179
Sharp, David,	165
Shawneetown Circuit,	385
Shelbyville Circuit,	310
Shiloh Methodism,	37
Shoal Creek Circuit,	151, 212
Simms, James,	176
Sinclair, John,	358
Slocumb, Charles,	154
Smith, John,	98
Smith, William H.,	186
Spoon River Circuit,	310
Springer, Levi,	394
Springfield Methodism,	179
	343
Stephenson, B. C.,	334
Sterrett, William,	149
Stewart, John,	175
S. S. Union, American,	337, 381
Tarkington, H. A.,	299
Tarkington, Joseph,	254
Tazewell Circuit,	342
Thompson, A. F.,	315

	PAGE.		PAGE.
Thompson, S. H.,	131	Walker, James,	390
Townsend, William,	188	Walker, Jesse,	48, 110
Tremble, H. M.	346	Walker, Simeon,	362
Trotter, W. D. R.,	364	Ward, James,	66
		Watt, Benjamin,	309
Union Grove Methodism,	77	Webster, E. T.,	217
		West, Asa D.,	239
Van Cleve, John,	368	Whiteside, Jacob,	110, 142
Vermillion Circuit,	190, 211	Wilhelm, Richard,	148
Vredenburg, H.,	173	Williams, Abel L.,	266
		Wood, Aaron,	269
Wabash Circuit,	107, 211	Wrather, Baker,	86
" " Little,	95		
Walke, Ivy,	101	Young, Benjamin,	34

www.ingramcontent.com/pod-product-compliance
Lightning Source LLC
Chambersburg PA
CBHW020237110726
47898CB00004B/1300